D0482871

Matthew Collin has written about popular culture, travel, music, technology and drugs for the *Observer, Guardian, Daily Telegraph, Time Out, Wired* and *The Face*, amongst others. He is deputy editor at *The Big Issue* and senior contributing editor to *i-D*. John Godfrey, who collaborated on the original planning, research and drafting of this book, was deputy editor at *The Face* and is now series producer of Channel 4's *Eurotrash*. They are both former editors of *i-D* and previously worked together on the book *A Decade of Ideas*.

This is the updated second edition of *Altered State*.

Altered State

The Story of Ecstasy Culture and Acid House

matthew collin
with contributions by john godfrey

Library of Congress Catalog Card Number: 96–70952

A complete catalogue record for this book can
be obtained from the British Library on request

The right of Matthew Collin and John Godfrey to be
identified as the authors of this work has been
asserted by them in accordance with the Copyright,
Designs and Patents Act 1988

Copyright © 1997 Matthew Collin and John Godfrey

First published in 1997 by Serpent's Tail,
4 Blackstock Mews, London N4
website: www.serpentstail.com

First published in this edition 1998

Phototypeset in 11pt Bembo by Intype London Ltd
Printed in Britain by Mackays of Chatham plc

10 9 8 7 6 5 4 3 2 1

contents

For Stephanie,
for our families,
and for all the friends who lived it with us.

prologue

a night in the eighties

manchester, 1988

We were handed the capsules at about ten o'clock. I cupped the little gelatin bullet in my palm and took a surreptitious look: it had an opaque white casing, just over a centimetre in length, slightly sticky with the heat and the perspiration of my fingers. It was just a capsule; its appearance offered no clues as to what its contents might bring. Well, *here goes* . . . I popped it into my mouth and crunched it between my teeth, feeling the gelatin splinter like cracked plastic and the white powder ooze out. Bitter, not like the queasy taste of Paracetamol, but a sharper chemical tang which spread unpleasantly over the tongue and teeth. I washed it down with a mouthful of Coke, which didn't quite rinse away the repulsive aftertaste, and we sat down at a table on the balcony overlooking the dancefloor.

Ten minutes and counting. We were both slightly edgy, trying to make small talk, lapsing into fretful silence, both wondering what would happen next. Neither of us knew much – if anything – about this stuff, what it would do, what its after-effects were, whether it could harm us in any way. Where would it take us? Were there demons in this other world? Would we come back unharmed? Would we still be the same people when we returned? None of these thoughts took real shape, they just flitted darkly around the corners of our consciousness.

Twenty-five minutes. Another sip of Coke. Rather have a

beer – not Red Stripe, they only sell Breaker here – but we'd been told that this stuff didn't really mix with alcohol. Sip the Coke. Sip, sip. Wait. Sip. Wait . . . was that something? A twinge? The lights seemed to shimmer strangely, just for a millisecond, a flutter in the belly, a tiny glow. I searched my metabolism for signs of weirdness. No?

Forty minutes. Almost imperceptibly, everything shifted, like an elevator accelerating upwards. An overwhelmingly powerful charge surged through my body, rising through the veins and the arteries and the bones and the teeth, pushing me down into the plastic chair. Sit back . . . *fuuuuck* . . . sit back and hold on, let it carry me . . . My mind began to reassure my body: *ride it, ride it, go with it. You'll be all right, it's good, it's good, ride it.*

Then it eased slightly, and I felt a desperate urge to talk – to voice the babble of feelings that were welling up inside me. We exchanged a few, brief words, hardly a conversation, but it seemed infused with an intensity of meaning it never had before – like no conversation we'd ever had before. I understood his faults, his hopes, his dreams, his pain and joy, what he had been through, what we had been through together, what we had all been through, and I knew he felt the same. Now, in this moment, it was all resolved . . . it was going to be all right. Everything was going to be all right.

Then that wave crashed over me again and I was dumb-struck . . . Oh . . . the feeling . . . *sooooo* strong . . . I couldn't speak but my emotions raged more intensely than they ever had before. *Need to be touched* . . . my skin felt clammy but sensitised beyond belief. "Are you all right?" Paralysed, I found it difficult to nod yes. "It's OK," he held my arm. "It's OK." The light caress felt glorious. We clenched hands. Sensuous. Great. "I'm alright." I tried to sip. Couldn't. Not possible. The rush seemed to last for hours but it must have been only a few seconds.

Suddenly the music that had been pounding out of the speakers suspended above the dancefloor flashed right into focus, searing into the consciousness. It felt like the sound, each gorgeous slash of the riff, was slicing through every single cell in my body, transmuting its physiology. The drums seemed to sparkle in midair, reverberating as if in a cathedral, and the bass . . . *it was as though I'd never heard it before*. It resonated through to the core, pulsing from both inside and outside simultaneously. The tune separated out into its constituent parts, a lattice of textures, each ringing with angelic clarity, each sliding right into me, locking, holding, releasing . . .

The pressure in my head lifted dramatically and I felt warm all over; stroking my arm gently I realised I'd broken into a sweat without even moving. The world had opened up all around, the blank warehouse somehow changed into a wonderland designed just for us, glistening with a mystic iridescence that I couldn't see earlier. New world. New sound. New life. Everything felt so right. A huge, glowing, magical YES.

The friend who'd given us the capsules came back to our table. It was like seeing him again for the first time after a long absence; we'd all changed, but the elapsed time – could it be that it was only an hour? – made us realise how much we loved him and missed him. "Are you all right?" he asked, gauging the response from our smiles. "The music's great, isn't it? You've got to stand up, you've got to move, we've got to go and dance. Otherwise you'll just sit here all night." We stood up unsteadily, and as we negotiated the stairs down to the dancefloor, we began to slide into the contours of the rhythm, becoming immersed in it, the bass curling round the spine which felt like it had been loosened of its inhibiting rigidity, like it had slipped the bounds of all that was holding it – us – back, and could just flow, loose, warm, *alive* . . . And in a second we were amongst the throng, synched right into the matrix of bodies and sound; transported, transformed, together. *All right*, the feeling resonated through us as the drums thrashed upwards towards climax, *let's go* . . .

london, 1997

Let's go . . . A brilliant flash of light, different and unique for everyone, but equally, massively significant. When Ecstasy was first combined with house music sometime during the 1980s, the resulting reaction triggered off the most vibrant and diverse youth movement Britain had ever seen. Ecstasy culture – the combination of dance music (in all its many and various forms) and drugs – was the driving phenomenon in British youth culture for almost a decade. It sent out shock waves that continue to reverberate culturally and politically, affecting music, fashion, the law, government policy and countless other areas of public and private life. The fundamental reason why it became so widespread and pervasive, reaching into every town and village and spreading far beyond the borders of the country, is simple and prosaic: it was the best entertainment format on the market, a deployment of technologies – musical, chemical and computer – to deliver altered states of consciousness; experiences that have changed the way we think, the way we feel, the way we act, the way we live.

There is constant friction between two competing ideologies within any culture: the élitist versus the populist, the avant-garde against the mass. Although each of its phases was marked by such conflicts, Ecstasy culture's prevailing ethos was inclusive. It had an open-access formula: rather than a defined ideology, it was a series of possibilities that people could use to define their own identity, possibilities that could be adapted to each individual's background, social status and belief system. It was endlessly malleable, pragmatic to new meaning. The recurring story within Ecstasy culture was of people coming into the scene, being inspired by the revelatory flash of the primal Ecstasy experience, then becoming involved and altering the direction of the scene itself by applying their own personal frame of reference to their experience. Clubbers, entrepreneurs, travellers, hippies, criminals and musicians all contributed new discourses to the scene by adapting it to suit their own desires and necessities – hence its relentless dynamism, its perpetual self-reinvention and, for a youth culture, its unprecedented longevity. The fact that the Ecstasy experience itself is so intensely personal – the impact of sounds and chemicals on the body and brain, the joy of dancing, the intoxication of release – further enabled people to define it on their own terms. It was a culture with options in place of rules.

At its heart was a concerted attempt to suspend normal transmission, if only for one night. A mission to reappropriate consciousness, to invent, however briefly, a kind of utopia – what anarchist philosopher Hakim Bey describes as a "temporary autonomous zone". Such zones, says Bey, are "successful raids on consensus reality, breakthroughs into more intense and more abundant life", fleeting moments where fantasies are made real and freedom of expression rules before external reality intervenes. "Let us admit," Bey demands, "that we have attended parties where for one brief night a republic of gratified desires was attained. Shall we not confess that the politics of that night have more reality and force for us than those of, say, the entire US Government?"[1]

The idea that Ecstasy culture had no politics because it had no manifesto or slogans, it wasn't *saying something* or actively opposing the social order, misunderstands its nature. The very lack of dogma was a comment on contemporary society itself, yet at the same time its constantly changing manifestations – ravers fighting police to gain access to a warehouse party, criminals shooting each other in feuds over the dance-drug trade, teenage girls baring flesh in baby-doll dresses, black-market entrepreneurs selling records from the backs of vans – served to dramatise the times. Ecstasy culture offered a forum to which people could bring narratives about class, race, sex, economics or morality. Again, its definition was subject to individual interpretation: it could be about the simple bliss of dancing; it could be about environmental awareness; it could be about race relations and class conflict; it could be about the social repercussions of the drug economy; it could be about changing gender relations; it could be about reasserting lost notions of community – all stories that say something about life in the nineties. And in the few instances when it adopted an overtly political edge – to break away from regulation and challenge licensing laws or the vested interests that control the leisure industries – vigorous efforts were made to contain it.

None of this has happened in a vacuum. The development of Ecstasy culture was shaped by time, place, and very specific economic and social conditions. It was born out of the tail end of the Thatcher years, when the psychic map of Britain was decisively redrawn, when old rules lost their meaning, old certainties evaporated and new ones had yet to take their place. The changes in society since Margaret Thatcher ascended to power in 1979 permanently altered the collective consciousness of the country as, over four terms of Conservative rule, the restructuring of economic relations led to a shift in social relations. The Thatcher dream was about breaking free from the past, casting off restraints, entering a paradise of untrammelled entrepreneurial and consumer opportunity; the idea that anything was possible if you had the will to conquer and a good credit card. Yet while libertarian capitalist doctrine elevated consumer materialism to a creed, Thatcherite assaults on collectivism, pursued through a whole range of policies, intentionally created a society that was fragmented and individualised. Its economic libertarianism was tempered with a grim authoritarian edge, its contradictions and harsh side-effects mercilessly policed. It simultaneously advocated and curtailed freedom.

The ethics that Thatcher instilled were intended to empower the individual, but at the same time they actively encouraged a sweeping insecurity through mass joblessness, low pay, the spread of casual work and self-employment, putting more power in the hands of employers and more money in the pockets of the rich as the income of the lower classes diminished. As post-war dreams of full, lifetime employment and universal social welfare began to fade, Britain became harder and more unequal. A striking chasm emerged between the power of the individual as consumer and the individual's lack of power in the employment market. The Thatcher years planted the seed of entrepreneurialism, yet fostered materialist dreams that many would never be able to fulfil.

Ecstasy culture provided an outlet for, even amplified, these entrepreneurial impulses; it enabled people to get involved, to *do something*, whether it be making a record or selling a bag of pills. From top to bottom, it was about participation rather than observation. Youth cultures are necessarily infused with the prevailing ideologies of their times, whether espousing or reacting against them, or both simultaneously. Ecstasy culture seemed to ghost the Thatcher narrative – echoing its ethos of choice and market freedom, yet expressing desires for a collective experience that Thatcher rejected and consumerism could not provide. Thatcherite Conservatism offered a blueprint for achievement with a Victorian morality built in; Ecstasy culture ran with the blueprint but inverted the morality, firing a vibrant black economy not only in illegal drugs but cash-in-hand deals for all manner of ancillary services, from DJ careers to home-produced records, creating an unprecedented number of cultural artefacts.

The dance-drug scene, as it did with technology, reappropriated libertarian capitalism and put it to uses for which it wasn't intended. Its entrepreneurialism recognised no legal boundaries. The simple act of passing one Ecstasy pill to a friend is a criminal act, and hence the exponential increase in drug use from the late eighties onwards, encouraged and endorsed by the arrival of Ecstasy, predetermined that the mainstream of youth culture became intimately bound up with law-breaking. As drug use became normalised, criminality was democratised. What Irvine Welsh calls the "chemical generation" was also a generation of outlaws.

One way to chart the evolution of Ecstasy culture is through its premier art, the music: a constantly changing sonic narrative conjuring a magic that is beyond language. Another is through its pharmacology. The idea of "set and setting" was adopted by Timothy Leary in the 1960s as the key to programming a successful LSD trip. "Set" refers to the personality of the user, their social background, educational history, emotional state, motivations; "setting" is the actual environment in which the drug experience occurs. Change the set or the setting and you get a different outcome: people may take the same substance, yet because of differences in set or setting they will divine different meaning or inspiration from it – factors of class, race, age and location creating a wealth of responses and outcomes.

The typical cycle of Ecstasy use can also be mapped culturally. The first rush begins the honeymoon period – the beatific, loved-up, evangelical phase. Within a year or so, that early excitement begins to fade and many experience diminishing returns. A few accelerate into excess, abuse sometimes leading to the emergence of physical or psychological problems. The third stage is the comedown: disillusionment, reduced use, and attempts to readjust to the fact that the initial high is gone for ever. Finally comes the re-entry to the post-Ecstasy world, a time of reassessment and the regaining of equilibrium. The myriad manifestations of the culture often reflect this pharmacological narrative, each scene experiencing its own individual honeymoon, excess, comedown and re-entry phases.

The story of Ecstasy culture is itself a remix – a collage of facts, opinions and experiences. Differing outlooks and vested interests combine to deny the possibility of a history that everyone can agree as truth; some things are forgotten, others are exaggerated; stories are embellished, even invented, and the past is polished to suit the necessities of the present. Behind one narrative are hundreds of thousands of unwritten ones, and who is to say that any one of them is not equally important? Ecstasy culture, after all, centres around an individual perception of events. Its history could be reworked in any number of ways, cutting in an anecdote here, dropping out a character there, altering the emphasis or switching the perspective around. It wouldn't be any less valid. It would just be another mix. The story could begin at any number of time–space co-ordinates, any point in history. Ecstasy culture was no freak storm that burst miraculously from the ether; instead, it was part of an evolving narrative of the development and refinement of the technologies of pleasure that crossed continents and cultures before ultimately converging to establish a series of pirate utopias, altered states of Great Britain – not just rites of passage bridging the eighties and the nineties, but phenomena that continue to shape our world-view as we move towards the millennium.

This is the story of how we reached the peak of human experience – and what happened afterwards.

the technologies of pleasure

"Where once there was frustration, alienation and cynicism, there are new characteristics among us. We are full of love for each other and are showing it; we are full of anger at what has been done to us. And as we recall all the self-censorship and repression for so many years, a reservoir of tears pours out of our eyes. And we are euphoric, high, with the initial flourish of a movement . . ." Carl Wittman, *A Gay Manifesto*, 1969

New York City at the turn of the seventies. The end of the civil rights era, the last days of the hippies. At 1.20 a.m., one hot summer night in June 1969, the New York Police Department raided a gay bar called the Stonewall Inn on Christopher Street in Greenwich Village. Police harassment of gay bars was common practice, but this time something snapped, an uprush of righteous anger sparking off a full-scale riot which lasted for several nights. Stonewall, the "Boston Tea Party of the gay movement", heralded a rising mood of militancy and public openness, the golden age of pre-AIDS euphoria. "The Stonewall riots were a watershed for gay people," remembers historian Ian Young, "and when the dam broke, a lot of idealism, anger and longing burst out of their social restraints . . ."[1] Before Stonewall, homosexuality had been considered a medical condition, a pathological state, an aberration; isolated and invisible. Now from this outpouring of repressed energy came not only the new politics of the gay liberation movement, but a new community and culture.

The heady mood was endorsed by the opening of Salvation on West 43rd Street in the Hell's Kitchen district. Salvation, one of the first flamboyantly out gay dance clubs in the city, was constructed as a temple to decadence and limitless hedonism. In his portrait of the era, *Disco*, author Albert Goldman compared its decor to a Witches' Sabbath, with a huge painted Devil flanked by a host of angels, genitals exposed and locked in sexual communion; drinks were sold from chalices and pews arranged around the walls, while the DJ, Francis Grasso, would preach from an altar above the dancefloor. Grasso helped pioneer the technique of seamlessly mixing one record into another; he would layer the orgasmic moans from Led Zeppelin's *Whole Lotta Love* over a heavy percussion break, cutting the bass and treble frequencies in and out to heighten the energy level, segueing from soul to rock then on into hypnotic African drums and chants. "Francis was like an energy mirror," wrote Goldman, "catching the vibes off the floor and shooting them back again recharged by the powerful sounds of his big horns." Salvation's dancers would load up on amphetamine pills or euphoria-inducing Quaaludes, and the men's room became an orgy of rutting males hyped by the libidinous mood. The new militancy was evident, too; when the cops came to shut the club, hundreds would chant "fuck you!" in unison. By the time this "cathedral of Sodom and Gomorrah" closed in April 1972 after a final police and fire department raid, it had influenced not only the soundtrack of nightlife, but its very shape and form.[2]

The seminal after-hours nightclub of the early seventies wasn't actually a club at all: The Loft was just that, an old factory loft at the bottom of Broadway in which young designer David Mancuso lived. Every Saturday night from 1970 onwards, the long-haired, bearded Mancuso would decorate his home like a children's birthday party, fill it with brightly coloured balloons and throw it open to a predominantly gay, black and Puerto

Rican throng who would dance, sweat and romp until well into Sunday. He would lay on a buffet of fruit, nuts and juice, no alcohol, and play music he loved – songs of passion and lust laden with state-of the-art studio effects, a bridge between psychedelia and the disco era – through a hand-tooled sound system.

Black and gay clubs have consistently served as breeding grounds for new developments in popular culture, laboratories where music, drugs and sex are interbred to create stylistic innovations that slowly filter through to straight, white society. Mancuso was a zealot with very specific beliefs about how music should be presented. "He was searching for a new disco sound, a new mix," suggested Albert Goldman. "He wanted to trip people out, to lay them under a spell. Many people regarded him as a magician."[3] If you were a "Loft baby" you felt part of a secret society of initiates (attendance was strictly by invitation), a privileged sect who were somehow describing new contours of human experience. David Morales, later to become one of New York's most famous DJs, would come down from Brooklyn carrying a spare set of clothes to change into and stay till six o'clock on Sunday afternoon; he remembers dancers on acid slipping into ecstatic reverie under Mancuso's spell, limbs and brain synched into the matrix of percussion and melody.

Up to this time the dominant club sound was lushly orchestrated disco from Philadelphia, the "City of Brotherly Love". MFSB's *Love is the Message* was its inspirational height, a careening wash of strings locked to an elastic bassline and a manifesto of joy and hope: it became the anthem of black America and a nationwide number one hit in 1974. The Philadelphia International label was the Motown of the early seventies, its in-house session players fashioning a string of gems for MFSB, the Three Degrees, the O'Jays and countless others; a dance factory founded on the sweat of virtuoso musicians playing drums, bass, guitar and strings. Philadelphia's excellence in sumptuous orchestration was continued by Salsoul – but this New York label would also spark another step forward. In 1975, a DJ called Tom Moulton began producing promotional copies of songs for his fellow DJs. Instead of small, tinny-sounding seven-inch discs, he had them pressed onto album-sized 12-inch vinyl, allowing him not only superior sound reproduction but the potential to stretch the song into more abstract form.

The 12-inch single, the first new record format in almost thirty years, was revolutionary not only because it sounded so physically devastating over huge speakers, but it gave dance music a new dynamic: both length and depth. Remixers could extend the breakdown – the few bars where the instruments dropped out leaving just bass and drums to carry the pulse – into a mesmeric tribal drum ritual, like the African drums and Latin percussion records that had fired The Loft and Salvation. The first commercially available 12-inch was Walter Gibbons's remix of *Ten Percent* by Double Exposure on Salsoul: transformed from a three-minute single into a nine-minute epic, it was aimed direct at the club underground of New York City. Salsoul's themes seemed to speak intimately to a gay community: passionate, abandoned, sensual, charged with sweat, sex and the ecstasy of release.

From 1975 onwards, a series of records began to emerge that used computers to revolutionise the form: Donna Summer's *I Feel Love*, the opulent sleaze of Cerrone, Patrick Cowley's wide-screen productions for Sylvester, and the stark minimalism of a Düsseldorf quartet, Kraftwerk. Many of these records were linked to European electronic traditions, but Kraftwerk's impact was arguably the greatest: on their 1977 *Trans Europe Express* and 1978 *Man-Machine* albums they styled themselves as robot clones, glamorous androids, *Showroom Dummies* in identical suits tapping out motorik rhythms on computer keyboards. "I don't think they even knew how big they were among the black masses back in '77 when they came out with *Trans Europe Express*," hip hop innovator Afrika Bambaataa explained. "I thought that was one of the best and weirdest records I ever heard in my life . . . It was funky."[4] Kraftwerk had come from the fringes of Germany's classical avant-garde, yet their vision of a synthesis between man and machine tore through black American dance music; Bambaataa and the Soul Sonic Force, alongside producer Arthur Baker, reworked *Trans Europe Express*, adding rapped lyrics and sparking a whole new genre, electronics-based rap: electro.

Computers seemed infused with possibility, and had come just in time. The disco boom which spread across America with the release of the film *Saturday Night Fever* in 1978 had brought an underground phenomenon to the mass market, caricaturing it and ironing out its depth and complexities in the process of commodification, shedding its black and gay context. The story that *Saturday Night Fever* was based upon, *Another Saturday Night* by Nik Cohn, was a portrait of working-class youth who poured all their frustrated dreams into a frantic outburst of weekend lunacy. The film itself helped turn disco into a multi-million dollar business but also made it seem cheap and trashy, a mere fad.

Evolving technology would change the very nature of disco. Black music has always been at the cutting edge of new invention, from the early electric guitars of the Chicago bluesmen to the primitive sound effects employed in Motown's Detroit studio and the space-age big bands of Parliament and Funkadelic, and now, just as it seemed that disco had boomed and bust, the emphasis shifted. The record labels that exemplified the new electronic dance were Prelude and West End: both employed the finest remixers of the moment to lace the grooves with subtle synthetic textures which echoed the deep space of Jamaican dub reggae. Rock critics regarded disco as frivolous, inauthentic and throwaway – "Disco sucks!" was their battle cry at the height of late seventies dance mania – yet here were disco mixers traversing the frontiers of the possible, *auteurs* who attempted to heighten consciousness using sound, virtuosos whose instrument was the recording studio itself: François Kevorkian, Shep Pettibone and, most importantly of all, Brooklyn-born DJ Larry Levan.

The Paradise Garage, where Levan played every weekend from

1976 to its closing in 1987, was a former truck garage in SoHo. It had an awesome system, the best in the world, custom designed by Levan and the city's premier sound engineer, Richard Long. "As you climb its steeply angled ramp to the second floor, which is illuminated only by rows of sinister little red eyes," wrote Albert Goldman in 1978, "you feel like a character in a Kafka novel. From overhead comes the heavy pounding of the disco beat like a fearful migraine. When you reach the 'bar', a huge bare parking area, you are astonished to see immense pornographic murals of Greek and Trojan warriors locked in sadomasochistic combat running from floor to ceiling. On the floor of the main dancing room are the most frenzied dancers on the disco scene: the black and Puerto Rican gays, stripped down to singlets and denim shorts, swing their bodies with wild abandon, while from their hip pockets flow foot-long sweat rags that fly like horses' tails."[5]

Levan, born Lawrence Philpot in 1954, was a graduate of David Mancuso's Loft, and perhaps the finest ever conjurer of the psycho-active power of dance music to create a fleeting vision of spiritual utopia. "Larry Levan used music as a unique storytelling vehicle that transported his audience on a collective journey," explained the Garage's backer Mel Cheren and François Kevorkian, "reaching to the roots of their emotions and releasing unparalleled waves of excitement and energy."[6] Although "garage" music, which took its name from the Paradise Garage, has come to mean uptempo house music with a gospel vocal, Levan had an incredibly eclectic taste, playing anything that captured the devotional, life-affirming feeling he was after: disco, soul, gospel, rock, reggae, European electro-pop, even German *kosmische* synthesiser epics like Manuel Göttsching's *E2: E4* – all sixty minutes of it. "He would experiment with records that most people wouldn't go near," says Cheren. "He really was an engineering genius as far as sound was concerned – they even have speakers that were named after him. He was brilliant. He wasn't an easy person but most artists aren't. He was very self-destructive – but there were a lot of DJs at that time that were very self-destructive."

Levan was a scientist who mixed as if he was trying to work the drugs that were percolating through the dancers' brains – trying to *play* their body chemistry – creating a homology between sonic texture and the chemically elevated cortex. "Larry invented new levels of bass and treble that worked on various parts of your body," believed fellow New York DJ Richard Vasquez.[7] As pure mood enhancement, his mixes of Gwen Guthrie's swooning *Seventh Heaven* or Taana Gardner's drugged-out, metallic *Heartbeat* were without peer, staking out new frontiers for disco in the early eighties. "The way people party now, the drugs that are in the street, everything has got to be wild and crazy and electronic," Levan once remarked.[8] At the Garage, the drugs that raised the spirit were Ecstasy, mescalin, cocaine and LSD; although drug-taking was far less open than it would become in British clubs, an astounding pharmacoepia of substances was being consumed in the name of pleasure on the gay scene of the time – pleasures that Levan freely and copiously enjoyed, despite a lifelong heart condition. The club buzzed with energies of all kinds: sexual, spiritual, musical, chemical.

The final night of the Garage on September 26th, 1987, marked the end of the disco era, the last gathering of a clan who to this day insist that the sense of communal transcendence that Levan engendered has never been recaptured. Keith Haring, whose iconic graffiti art covered the building's walls, came back from Japan just to be there. "Under the spell of Levan's narcotic mix, people seemed to transcend human limits," journalist Frank Owen wrote. "Men crawled around on their hands and knees howling like dogs, while others gyrated and leapt as if they could fly. After a 24-hour marathon, an exhausted crowd gathered in front of Levan's DJ booth and pleaded, 'Larry, please don't go.' "[9]

After the Garage closed, Levan's notoriously prodigious capacity for drugs, particularly heroin and cocaine, reached critical levels. He spent his rent money on pharmaceuticals and his mood swings became extreme. "When Larry knew the Garage was going to close, he freaked. He went on a self-destructive binge," recalled DJ David DePino.[10] He blew gigs, screwed up his studio work, and his health deteriorated. On November 8th, 1992, he died of heart failure. He was thirty-eight.

chicago and detroit

The almost devotional intensity of the atmosphere in the black gay clubs of New York created an ideological template that has been employed, knowingly or not, in dance cultures ever since. It was a euphoria born of necessity: as black people, they were excluded from the economic and social benefits of mainstream America; as homosexuals, they were excluded from its moral universe; as black homosexuals, they were even prevented from expressing their identity within their own communities. This contributed to a powerful, pent-up frustration which found its release in the clubs, the only place where they could truly be themselves and play out their desires without fear or inhibition. The explosion of energy, therefore, was enormous; the bonding too. The rhetoric of unity and togetherness which echoed down through club cultures to come was forged in these clubs, under pressure from an oppressive world; compounded by drugs, which not only banished them further from American consensus reality, but contributed to an exalted mental state: the club became church, bedroom and family. You can hear it in the music: disco and house both mix the secular, the invocations of orgy and sexual abandon, with the spiritual, the wistful utopian yearning for a "better day" when "we will all be free". The black gay dancers were doubly repressed. All they had left was each other, delicious sin and blind hope for salvation.

Larry Levan had started his career at the Continental Baths, the most famous of the many gay "bath-house" complexes in the city which were closed by New York's health department as AIDS took hold, where Bette Midler also got her break (accompanied on piano by a young Barry Manilow). The Continental Baths was a palace of sex, complete with dancefloor, sauna, showers and apartments where men would sweat out the physicality expressed in the music.

The venue's second DJ was a South Bronx-born gentle giant and Loft baby called Frankie Knuckles (his real name, not an alias). Knuckles had worked with Levan before, as assistant to another pioneering mixer, Nicky Siano, at the Gallery, where the duo's role was to ensure the vibe was high. "Part of our job description was spiking the punch," he says. "We'd be given tabs of acid and we'd spike the punch with them."[11] In 1977, the twenty-two year old was invited to emigrate west to Chicago to join a new club, the Warehouse: the space that would give house music its name.

"It was predominantly black, predominantly gay," Knuckles remembers. "Very soulful, very spiritual. For most of the people that went there it was church for them. It only happened one day a week: Saturday night, Sunday morning, Sunday afternoon. In the early days between '77 and '81 the parties were very intense – they were always intense – but the feeling that was going on, I think, was very pure."

At first Knuckles was spinning the classic gay disco anthems of Philadelphia International and Salsoul. But as the disco wave crashed onto the shore and then receded, and musicians started using electronics to create a new dance paradigm, he began to mess with the raw material of sound itself: taking records apart, re-editing them on reel-to-reel tape, extending certain parts, slicing out others, rearranging the flow to give his dancefloor extra boost. This had already been done back in New York, but in Chicago it was shockingly new. Soon Knuckles had the biggest reputation and best crowd in town. He began adding pre-programmed rhythms from a primitive beatbox to the mixes; in 1984, having left the Warehouse to set up another club, the

Powerplant, he purchased a Roland TR-909 drum computer from a hyperactive youth from Detroit called Derrick May. During the week he would play around with the box, laying down beat patterns which he would run live on Saturday night, weaving the harsh, distinctive 909 clatter in and out of records, using it to segue between tracks or to crank up the bass kick at a crucial point in the song.

Knuckles was not working in a vacuum. Chicago had its own superb dance mix show on WBMX radio. The Hot Mix 5 DJ quintet – Farley "Jackmaster" Funk, Ralphi Rosario, Kenny "Jammin" Jason, Mickey "Mixin" Oliver and Scott "Smokin" Seals – were turntable virtuosos who excelled at rapid-fire cut-and-dice collages. Soon they too were using drum machines, as was Knuckles's new rival over at the Music Box club; his nemesis, Ron Hardy.

Hardy, who died from an AIDS-related disease in 1992 after a long heroin addiction, was an alchemist who conjured with pure, clear energy. He had been perfecting his art in the city's clubs since 1974. "I'd never been to a party where the DJ had such a control over the people, where they would dance and scream, at some points cry and, depending on how high they were, pass out from pure excitement," says Cedric Neal, a Music Box regular. "The way Ron Hardy played records, you could tell how he was feeling. The sequence he played them, how long he played them. You could tell if he was depressed because him and his loverman had had a fight. You could know if he was up and happy or if he was just high, out of his mind because of the drugs. Frankie Knuckles was more refined in his spinning, more orderly. Ron Hardy was more raw. He just had an energy over the people that made them the moment: people were living for the moment. That's all that mattered, in that time and space, was the moment."

"Ron Hardy was the greatest DJ who ever lived," says Marshall Jefferson, another Music Box regular, a post office worker who was soon to become an inspirational producer. "Everybody hated him, he was mean and nasty, a drug addict, he had a huge ego. But oh man, he was great." Sometimes Hardy would let the beats batter and crunch for ten long minutes, jacking the crowds ever upwards, before dropping into the song proper. This was no longer disco, it was something else. The kids at the Warehouse had called Frankie Knuckles's luscious soul blend "house music"; now the phrase was being applied to this abrasive new sound: house.

The Music Box, a no-alcohol "juice bar" which pumped until noon, was both psychedelic and ecstatic. There was an underlying symbiosis between drugs and music that helped transform sound into magic, disco into house. "There was a juice bar because it was illegal to serve liquor in underground clubs," says Cedric Neal. "There was a lot of PCP [phencyclidine, or Angel Dust], happy sticks [joints dipped in PCP] and a lot of acid. Ecstasy was really big among the gays."

What exactly constituted "the first house track" is still subject to heated debate: every Chicago musician tells a different story. Some say it was Jesse Saunders and Vince Lawrence's *On and On Trax*, or Jamie Principal tunes like *Waiting on My Angel* and *Your Love*, which Frankie Knuckles was playing from tape years before their release. Undoubtedly, however, before long not only Knuckles, Hardy and the Hot Mix 5 boys but also the dancers whom they inspired – Adonis, Chip E, Marshall Jefferson – were translating the new sound first onto tapes, which they would bring to the Music Box or the Powerplant for Hardy or Knuckles to play, then onto vinyl, putting out roughly pressed, crackling 12-inches on Chicago's two main independent labels, Trax and DJ International.

Over a decade afterwards, it's difficult to remember just how radical these early house recordings sounded at the time. Fast, hard, raw, exciting, charged with adrenalin, relentless percussion and stark, insistent bass patterns, they seemed a violent break with the string sections and soaring choruses of disco; although of course they were a continuation of that tradition. "House music wasn't nothing but disco, and proof of that is to listen to all the early house records," says Farley Keith Williams, alias Farley "Funkin" Keith, alias Farley "Jackmaster" Funk. "All we did was steal people's music, like my first EP, *Funkin' with the Drums*, that was just MFSB [the key Philadelphia International group], we pulled a bassline from them and then added something else to it. House music ain't nothing but a harder kick drum than disco, that's it."[12]

When technology developed by corporate multinationals reaches street level it is redefined and reinterpreted. "The street finds its own uses for things," science fiction writer William Gibson once suggested. Using drum computers marketed by Roland of Japan in the early eighties which by this time were obsolete, discontinued and available cheaply on the secondhand market, Chicago's young hustlers wrenched out possibilities that the manufacturers had never envisioned. The 808, 909 and 727 models were treasure troves of synthetic percussion, their sizzle and boom locking into the mood of the clubs. Over a big sound system, they reverberated through flesh and bone. This was do-it-yourself music; anyone could join in, you didn't need a diva's vocal cords or a Salsoul orchestra; you could just fire up your box and go. New technology had thrown open the creative process to all.

One night Ron Hardy played a tune that was strange even by his own standards. Then he played it again. And again. And again. Everyone wanted to know what it was; this crazy buzzing noise that churned and writhed and twisted like a mainframe malfunction. The tape had been put together by Marshall Jefferson and his young protégé Nathaniel Jones, alias DJ Pierre. During a jam session, the pair were messing about and getting drunk, and Pierre was fiddling with the frequency control on the Roland TB-303 Bass Line, a machine originally designed as a practice aid for guitarists. The sound that Pierre teased out of the box seemed to emanate from another dimension, and they quickly captured it on tape.

The result, *Acid Trax* by Phuture, would make the 303 a revered icon of dance culture and create house music's first sub-genre: acid house. The origins of the term itself are again subject to conflicting stories. Some say it came from rumours that they were putting LSD in the water at the Music Box to make the dancers even crazier; Trax Records boss Larry Sherman commented that it sounded like the acid rock he remembered from Vietnam. Marshall Jefferson insists that the record itself just sounded so weird that it was like a simulated trip: "It was a mood, it didn't mean drugs." Whatever, the phrase felt right and it stuck.

Across the state border in Detroit, Michigan, another nexus of activity was developing that would have an equally powerful effect on the club culture of the coming decade. Juan Atkins and Richard Davis, a Vietnam veteran who called himself 3070, were making records as Cybotron. They were an electro group but without the rapped lyrics, heavily influenced by *Trans Europe Express*, with roots in both the black American funk tradition and post-punk European music.

Atkins was an evangelist who introduced his two young friends, Derrick May and Kevin Saunderson, to electronic music: Yellow Magic Orchestra, Devo, the Human League, Gary Numan, and of course Kraftwerk. In return, May and Saunderson, both committed clubbers, switched Atkins on to what was bubbling at the Music Box over in Chicago: the cathartic velocity of Ron Hardy's new electric disco.

After Cybotron split, all three launched solo projects. Atkins (under the name Model 500), Saunderson (as Reese) and May (as Rhythim is Rhythim) shared a vision one step on from Cybotron's portentous dystopian imagery. Their outlook was shaped by playing video games, by watching Ridley Scott's android fantasy *Blade Runner*, and by the idea of a new computer world replacing industrial society as framed in both Kraftwerk's records and futurologist Alvin Toffler's book *The Third Wave*.

The result was a music that sounded, May once commented, "like George Clinton and Kraftwerk stuck in an elevator".

To some extent it was a product of their environment: Juan Atkins' *Night Drive Thru Babylon* was a soundtrack to a cruise through the desperate, decaying streets of inner-city Detroit, an economically devastated landscape which had never really recovered from the riots of 1967. Through their music, the trio escaped from Detroit into an altered state in the same way as, black cultural theorist Paul Gilroy suggested, Parliament and Funkadelic had before them: "The dream of life beyond the reach of racism acquired an other-worldly, utopian quality and then manifested itself in a flash, high-tech form deliberately remote from the realities of the ghetto lifeworld. If the repressive and destructive forces unleashed by a 'maggot brained' and infanticidal America were rapidly acquiring a global character, the answer to them was presented as flight, not back to the African motherland, for that too was tainted by Americanism, but into space."[13]

While the Chicago house musicians were jacking up a new form of disco fervour, the Detroit cell was attempting to translate the electric dreams of European pop into visionary sci-fi. There was no Music Box or Powerplant or WBMX in Detroit so they had to live in the imagination. In their heads, they were cybernauts traversing the infosphere, breeding electrophonic life forms for a new era: what Alvin Toffler called "techno rebels", the frontiersmen of the society of the future. Twenty years earlier, the Motor City had spawned Motown's feel-good, up-time soul; now the auto factories were laying men off and Atkins, May and Saunderson reflected the changing social dynamic. "Berry Gordy built the Motown sound on the same principles as the conveyor belt system at Ford's," explained Atkins. "Today their plants don't work that way – they use robots and computers to make the cars. I'm probably more interested in Ford's robots than Berry Gordy's music."[14]

All three used what primitive analogue equipment they could

lay their hands on – reappropriating industrial detritus – to create sparse, kinetic funk with drums like thunderbolts, yet mournful and deeply romantic, as if the machines were whispering a lament about what it was like to be young and black in post-industrial America. They called it techno.

california, texas and washington

Out of New York, Chicago and Detroit had come sounds that would change the world of popular music: garage, house, techno, three interlinked strands with similar premises – the use of technology to heighten perception and pleasure, and the release from mundane, workaday existence into fantastic vistas of drama, vitality and joy. Elsewhere in America, others were attempting to release similar energies, but in a totally different field. Instead of sound, they worked with chemistry.

At the end of the sixties, as the hippies crashed and burned, it felt as though the psychedelic mission had failed. The acid instigators, Timothy Leary and Ken Kesey, had been hunted down and imprisoned, as had the legendary acid chemist, Augustus Owsley Stanley III. The acid rock icons, Hendrix, Joplin and Morrison, were dead. Richard Nixon was in the White House. The Vietnam War continued. "Hippie" had been commodified and sold back to young people in the forms of albums, clothes, posters . . . Amerika had not fallen. The tailend of the period in California was marked by a severe comedown fuelled by bad drugs and despair. But if this was an end, it was also the beginning of a more realistic and pragmatic mind-expansion movement, one that would concentrate on low-key lobbying rather than wild, headline-grabbing manifestos, on underground laboratories producing small amounts of bespoke substances for adepts rather than nationwide drug distribution networks, on keeping private rather than going public. This clandestine movement would come to be known as the "neuroconsciousness frontier", and the focus of its hopes would be a legal drug with the chemical name 3, 4-methylenedioxymethamphetamine – MDMA.

MDMA was first synthesised in 1912 by the Merck pharmaceutical company of Darmstadt, Germany, and patented two years later, another product of a fertile German chemical industry which had previously given the world morphine and cocaine. It was intended as an intermediate chemical for the preparation of other pharmaceuticals, not as an appetite suppressant, as contemporary myth insists. With the intervention of World War One, MDMA was shelved and forgotten for decades until it turned up again, first in a Polish journal after World War Two, then in the US Army's Edgewood Chemical Warfare Service in Maryland, one of the many drugs that were tested by the military for potential use during the Cold War. Experimental Agent 1475 was given to guinea pigs, rats, mice, monkeys and dogs to assay its toxicity. Some of the drugs tested by the military rapidly appeared on the streets – most notably LSD – but MDMA wasn't heard of again until the middle sixties, when it was resynthesised, first by drug researcher Gordon Alles, then by a Californian chemist called Alexander Shulgin.

Born in 1925, Shulgin, the son of Russian émigrés, served in the US Navy during World War Two and studied chemistry at university before deciding on a career as a psychopharmacologist. In 1960, he sampled mescalin for the first time, and discovered a vivid, miraculous world that would define the course of his future trajectory. "It was a day that will remain blazingly clear in my memory, and one which unquestionably confirmed the entire direction of my life," he wrote afterwards. "I understood that our entire universe is contained in the mind and the spirit. We may not choose to find access to it, we may even deny its existence, but it is indeed there inside us, and there are chemicals that can catalyse its availability."[15]

Shulgin took a job with Dole Chemical Company, and began to tool about with the molecules of substances which resembled mescalin, measuring their effects not on animals but on his own body. By 1966, although he was prodigiously productive, cooking up a whole stream of new compounds, his relationship with Dole had soured: the substances he was interested in, psychedelic drugs, were neither marketable nor respectable, particularly considering the climate of the times, with America gearing up for a nationwide moral panic over LSD. He gave in his notice and established his own laboratory at home in Lafayette, California, in an outbuilding down his garden path, an alchemist's lair from where he would generate a relentless flow of new mind-altering drugs for the next 30 years, hundreds of which are detailed in his autobiography cum pharmacological cornucopia, *PIHKAL* ("Phenethylamines I Have Known and Loved"), and its follow-up, *TIHKAL* ("Tryptamines I Have Known and Loved").

Shulgin believed that pharmacological exploration could yield more efficacious tools to prise open the doors of perception. This scientist of the unconscious saw no benefit in testing his "materials", as he called them, on rats and mice. How would that give any indication of the labyrinthine workings of the human mind? Instead, he drew around him a circle of adepts, including his wife Ann, who would exhaustively work through all the new substances coming out of his backyard lab. These communal drug sessions were highly civilised affairs, a very bourgeois nirvana: a handful of friends would gather at one of their homes, each bringing food, drink and sleeping bags for an overnight stay. The trippers might wander in the leafy garden, browse through art books, or listen to some classical music on a cassette player; if the mood took them, couples could retire to a bedroom and make love. Afterwards they would submit reports detailing the drug's effects.

In time, the bearded, smiling, courteous, sandal-wearing "Sasha" would become the beloved figurehead of the eighties' psychedelic generation, although his natural modesty and cautiousness would never allow him to revel in this role. How was Shulgin permitted to, continue such research? After all, he was manufacturing and taking endless numbers of psychoactive substances which were or would soon be illegal, without any preliminary animal testing. Yet he had a Drug Enforcement Administration license to possess and analyse any drug he chose to; a result of his usefulness as an expert witness and consultant to the DEA and his membership of the Bohemian Club, a bastion of Republicanism in San Francisco. A DEA lab technician officiated at his wedding, and in 1973 he even received a citation from a government drugs agency for "significant personal efforts to help eliminate drug abuse". In later years, this situation would become even more peculiar. The DEA, having picked up a new substance on the streets, would often bring it to Shulgin for analysis — and it would sometimes prove to be one of the "materials" he had invented in his back yard.

This freedom would not last, however. In 1994, DEA officers knocked on the Shulgins' door with a warrant to search the premises. Soon afterwards, they returned in force with the Sheriff's Department plus decontamination, narcotics and fire trucks: it was a raid. Ann Shulgin believes that prominent people at DEA headquarters in Washington DC were "extremely agitated and annoyed" about the dissemination of his knowledge through *PIHKAL* and determined to silence him (although some of the officers raiding the house asked him to sign copies of the book). Shulgin was stripped of his license and fined $25,000 — although this didn't end his pharmacological quest.

Shulgin had first synthesised MDMA at Dole in 1965, but did not actually try it until 1967. Although he was a veteran with LSD, mescalin and countless other psychedelic experiences, he was astounded by the sensation. "I found it unlike anything I had taken before," he reported. "It was not a psychedelic in the visual or interpretive sense, but the lightness and warmth of a psychedelic was present and quite remarkable."[16]

MDMA affects the chemistry of the brain in ways that are not yet fully understood, although current wisdom suggests it works on the neurotransmitters — chemicals in the brain like serotonin or dopamine – that affect pleasure. It is related to both the psychedelic mescalin and the amphetamines (as well as plants like nutmeg), and has been called a "psychedelic amphetamine", yet it neither induces hallucinatory visions nor encourages the same soul-searching and potentially scary mental manifestations as LSD. To stress the difference it has been called an "empathogen" (empathy-generating).[17] Empathy is the sensation of experiencing someone else's feelings as your own, and this was the effect that Shulgin (and the psychotherapists who followed his lead) celebrated first and foremost. MDMA seemed to help people to open up and really talk, to enable honesty without fear or conditioning intervening. It induced a powerful impression that everything was all right with the world. Yet what no one really hit on at first was that it also had an incredible effect on the body, seeming to free up the spine and limbs. When combined with rhythmic music it hooked the mind into the textures of the percussion and the outline of the melody. Certain sounds appealed intensely to the drug effect. No one has really studied how MDMA's chemistry works when people are dancing rather than sitting calmly with their therapist listening to a Mozart CD. It could be that the neurochemical reaction is completely different; empirical evidence would certainly suggest that it is.

In 1977, Shulgin introduced an elderly psychologist friend to MDMA. Leo Zoff was tiring of his practice and readying to retire, but he too was smitten by the drug, and, re-energised, began travelling the country, introducing it to other psychologists and psychiatrists and tutoring them in its therapeutic potential. It was estimated that this Johnny Appleseed of MDMA turned on around 4,000 of his fellow professionals, who in turn passed the knowledge onwards.

The therapeutic community distributed in the region of half a million doses of the drug in a decade. They would give their patients MDMA in the course of psychotherapy sessions to break down mental barriers and enhance communication and intimacy. The patients might be suffering from post-traumatic conditions, phobias, neurotic disorders, drug addiction, terminal illness or marital difficulties – a large proportion felt that the drug sessions helped them, eased their ailments or improved their self-esteem. These were progressive therapists, not workaday quacks, with a grounding in the evolving philosophies that descended from the sixties, the kind of people interested in holistics, "human potential", EST and ecology – the gamut of ideas lumped together under the reductive, catch-all tag "New Age". Many of them believed that MDMA could go one step further, too: make healthy people feel even better, happier, more positive about their lives. As Shulgin noted: "There was something akin to snake-oil – in the sense of an apparent cure for anything that ails you – about this elixir called MDMA."[18]

There was a general agreement amongst everyone using MDMA that it should be kept under wraps, and no scientific papers on the impact of the drug on humans were published until as late as 1978. In the early sixties, author Aldous Huxley had disagreed with Harvard professor Timothy Leary as to the potential uses of a new chemical sacrament, LSD. Huxley favoured a cautious, low-key approach: quietly enable the "brightest and the best" to become enlightened, progress slowly and get the establishment on your side, don't attract the wrath of law enforcement or prurient media. In contrast, Leary believed that everyone should have the opportunity to tune in and turn on: LSD for all! Right now! It was Leary's methodology that prevailed, with the results that Huxley feared; LSD became a common street drug, used not for intellectual contemplation or scientific study but for pure kicks, and within a few years it was criminalised and academic researchers were barred from investigating its potential. This couldn't be allowed to happen again – MDMA was far too precious a treasure to lose. Perhaps, just perhaps, this time common sense would prevail.

"The neuroconsciousness frontier, circa 1983, reminded me a lot of the psychedelic movement, circa 1962," wrote LSD historian Jay Stevens. "There was the same quality of excitement, the same mix of therapeutic and metaphysical interests, the same cautious optimism."[19] Timothy Leary, who married his wife Barbara immediately after sharing his first MDMA experience with her in 1978, presciently tagged MDMA "the drug of the eighties", although he too urged that the lessons of LSD should be learned and the drug should be kept quiet. "Let's face it, we're talking about an élitist experience," he wrote. "XTC is a drug that is known, by word of mouth, by sophisticated people who sincerely want to attain a high level of self-understanding and empathy. We're talking about dedicated searchers who are entitled, who've earned a bit of XTC. This is why the general public hasn't heard of it. No one wants a sixties situation to develop where sleazy characters hang around college dorms peddling pills they falsely call XTC to lazy thrill-seekers."[20]

But MDMA, like all killer applications of technology, has its own unstoppable dynamic. It couldn't remain secret for much longer. The adepts were enthused: they were telling their friends, and their friends were telling their friends, and the whole damn thing was snowballing. MDA – methylenedioxyamphetamine, a close relation of MDMA – had similar if less pleasant characteristics to MDMA, and had been documented within the hippie enclaves of California as early as 1967 and subsequently spread into the gay club scene of the seventies. It even had street nicknames: the "love drug", the "Mellow Drug of America". In 1970 MDA had been declared illegal and placed in Schedule 1 of the Controlled Substances Act. By the late seventies there was also a small recreational market in MDMA.

The therapists had called it "Adam" – gentle and sweet, with subtle religious undertones – but now the drug dealers conjured up a seductive new brand name: Ecstasy. "The man who first named it 'Ecstasy' told me that he chose the name 'because it would sell better than calling it "Empathy". "Empathy" would be more appropriate, but how many people know what it means?' " wrote researcher Bruce Eisner.[21] People who distribute drugs play a key role in determining how they are used; their beliefs are perpetuated through their distribution networks. The "Boston Group", the first mass manufacturers of MDMA in the early eighties, were of the élitist, therapeutic school; like the earliest manufacturers of LSD in the sixties, they did it out of sheer belief in the drug's utopian potential. MDMA would come supplied with "flight manuals", instructions on how best to enjoy your trip, what to drink, what vitamins to take and how to negotiate the comedown, showing concerns for health and physical safety that would, significantly, be lost as the drug became a consumer product. The flight manuals were written in mellowed-out California-speak: MDMA, declared one such, "is a tool for reaching out and touching others in soul and spirit. If responsibly used, strong bonds of unity and love can be forged that strengthen everyone involved. Celebrate in life, choose to evolve, create peace."[22] Central to the flight guides' concerns was establishing the correct set and setting: programming the trip for optimum outcome. Ensuring a safe, stable environment appeared to pose little problem for these privileged psychic voyagers – yet within a few years their therapeutic cocoon would be punctured.

In 1983, one member of the Boston Group recognised the potential for making bigger profits out of this *legal* drug that everybody seemed to want. With the backing of friends in Texas, a handful of former cocaine dealers who believed that MDMA's spiritual overtones made it something they could be proud of selling, he launched his own cartel. The new "Texas Group" promoted Ecstasy aggressively; they made it available in gay bars and clubs in the Southern state, brought in credit card charging systems, set up telephone hotlines, and printed up advertising handbills for "Ecstasy parties" claiming it was a "fun drug" and "good to dance to". The therapeutic fraternity was outraged: MDMA wasn't some Saturday night party favour for disco dancers, it was a serious accessory to psychological study! The Texas Group had become an organised drug-dealing gang rather than simply altruistic facilitators. They should seriously examine their set and setting, suggested one therapeutically inclined supplier: "Our perception of them was that they were just primarily capitalists and that it's too bad that they didn't take the drug more and a little longer before they embarked on their project . . . If they hadn't been on the scene we probably could have sold it for another ten years."[23]

Texas was only one of many places that Ecstasy was being used as a dance drug – the gay black scenes of New York and Chicago being perhaps more important scenarios – but it was where the drug was most widespread and its use best documented in contemporary media, perhaps because it was being taken by clean-cut, white college kids and affluent professionals. A photograph taken in a Dallas club for the August 1985 issue of *Life* magazine is most telling: a girl clutches her head, dancing through a wave of euphoria; hitched up around her torso is a T-shirt with the bold letters: "XTC". It could easily be a snapshot from a British acid house club at the height of 1988.[24] MDMA was shedding its chemical name and its therapeutic construct, and taking on new purpose: the pursuit of sheer pleasure.

How much Ecstasy was the Texas Group manufacturing? Estimates range from tens of thousands to millions of doses, tableted up and sold in little brown bottles labelled "Sassyfras", with lists of false ingredients to fool law enforcers that it was a health food product. Of course, an exuberant new drug scene couldn't pass unnoticed. What began with a few small, inaccurate articles by local reporters soon ballooned into a torrent of newsprint from papers and magazines all over the country: breathless, and initially positive, investigations of what they labelled "the yuppie psychedelic". Soon the Drug Enforcement Administration started to take action, recommending in July 1984 that MDMA be placed in Schedule 1 of the Controlled Substances Act. This, they thought, was simply a routine banning of another recreationally abused drug; nothing out of the ordinary in a country where the President, Ronald Reagan, had sanctified the "War on Drugs" as a crusade to exorcise the demons of otherness from the American body politic. What happened next took the DEA completely by surprise. A collective of psychologists, researchers and lawyers drafted a letter demanding that the proposed criminalisation should be subject to a hearing: its healing potential should not be lost to the therapeutic community as LSD had been. MDMA was the first drug to have its own law firm. In the context of the prevailing mood under Reagan, the idea that mind-altering drugs could actually be *beneficial* was shocking.

One committed young evangelist, Rick Doblin, took on the role of media mouthpiece for the drug, fearlessly praising its benefits – even recreational ones, a stance that many of his co-campaigners felt uneasy about. He wrote to a number of government agencies, including Nancy Reagan's National Feder-ation of Parents for Drug Free Youth, detailing the benefits of MDMA and proposing to the United Nations a project entitled "Shaping a Global Spirituality While Living in the Nuclear Age". MDMA, he believed, could genuinely make the world a better place – the same claim that had been made for LSD in the sixties. "The religious experience, the sense that people get that they are part of the same community which is very diverse but includes everybody, that insight about humanity has incredible political consequences because it will lead you to try to understand people rather than consider them the enemy," he says. "People will be more willing to settle disputes and more willing to pay attention to environmental issues." If LSD had been some sort of Gaian psychic regulator for the nuclear age, perhaps MDMA had come to assist in averting ecological crisis and materialist self-destruction? Doblin's dream was to become a psychedelic thera-pist to the American government, to "steady their hand on the button".[25]

Such subtleties were naturally lost on people who made a career out of the slogan "just say no", and now had a new drug to vilify. As the Texas Group stepped up production in advance of impending criminalisation, the avalanche of media coverage continued, now tinged by scare stories which recalled the moral panic around the banning of LSD in 1966. Ecstasy causes brain

damage or Parkinson's Disease, it was suggested, drains the spinal
fluid, makes even respected professionals who take it go insane.
The most charming Ecstasy myth of all describes a ceasefire in
no man's land during World War One, when British and German
soldiers laid down their guns, came out of the trenches and had
a friendly game of football together – of course, they had all
taken the newly invented MDMA beforehand. This unlikely tale,
however, was not one of the many repeated again and again in
papers all over the States during the early months of 1985.
Some psychologists joined the case for the prosecution, insisting
MDMA was an untested, potentially dangerous street drug which
should be banned until it could be evaluated properly.

Predictably, the DEA came down against MDMA, announcing
an emergency ban to take effect on July 1st, 1985. "All of the
evidence the DEA has received shows that MDMA abuse has
become a nationwide problem and that it poses a serious health
threat," a spokesman declared, claiming that the drug probably
destroyed nerve terminals in the brain.[26] He also promised that
legitimate research would be allowed to continue – although the
criminalisation meant that it would be nigh on impossible for
counsellors to run sessions with patients, and human research
effectively ceased.

In the weeks leading up to July 1st, the Texas Group switched
its Ecstasy factory into overdrive, reportedly turning out 2 million
tablets as people stockpiled supplies. In the months after criminalisation, a few of them retired with their millions, while others
carried on selling MDMA illegally or attempted to circumvent
the law by marketing a derivative called Eve (MDEA).
However, the consumers considered it inferior – more of a
stimulant than a tactile enhancer – and it, too, was soon banned
by a government Act prohibiting new variants of illegal drugs.
Although hearings continued for a year over the emergency
scheduling of MDMA, the battle was lost: the DEA rejected a
recommendation from a judge for less harsh strictures that would
enable continuing medical use. In doing so, the American

government pushed Ecstasy underground. The only people who would dare manufacture it were those with no fear of the law, the only people who would take it were those with no care for the law: drug dealers and hedonists who would use it in ways that the therapists never intended.

The people using Ecstasy by now included the whole gamut of quasi-mystical fringe groups working through the fall-out of the hippie era: New Age teachers running encounter groups and, most importantly for the wider distribution of the drug, followers of perennially beatific, white-bearded Bhagwan Shree Rajneesh, the most controversial Indian guru since the 1960s. Rajneesh, who died in 1990, wasn't above accruing material as well as spiritual wealth; he didn't believe in self-denial or asceticism. At his ranch in Oregon, he collected an enormous fleet of Rolls-Royces, and wealthy disciples were encouraged to make huge donations. He established a network of cells across America and around the world – nearly 600 at the movement's height – plus a centre in Poona, India. This was religion as big business, worth multiple millions; Rajneesh had business enterprises all over the world – nightclubs, casinos and publishing houses. Although the ranch had a strict no-drugs rule, some of Bhagwan's followers, among them former therapists, also used MDMA, as part of their therapies or amongst themselves – and to boost finances. In his book *Bhagwan – The God That Failed*, Hugh Milne, an early disciple and former bodyguard of Rajneesh, suggests that "the euphoric mood-altering drug Ecstasy was discreetly slipped into rich sannyasins' drinks just before fund-raising interviews".[27]

The fact that the Bhagwan movement was entrepreneurially minded and outward-looking, rather than insular and isolated, meant that the people who gravitated around it would not only popularise Ecstasy, but set in place distribution systems that would result in its dissemination beyond the United States. In the mid-eighties, Arno Adelaars reports in his Dutch book on the drug, "the Dutch followers of Bhagwan were taking so much Ecstasy [legal in the Netherlands until 1988] that several supply lines were necessary to meet the demand".[28] Before long, large-scale criminal manufacturers would establish production lines in Holland, Germany, Belgium, Spain, and ultimately in the breakaway states of the former Soviet Union. MDMA was coming to Europe.

new york

By the time it was declared illegal, Ecstasy was already deeply embedded in the gay club culture of New York. This would become another important conduit for its entry into Europe, primarily via European musicians working or holidaying in the city. If they had any interest in nightlife they would inevitably end up at Studio 54 or the Paradise Garage, clubs that were unlike anything that could be experienced anywhere else in the world. The Paradise Garage had a devastating impact on a whole range of British DJs, the most extreme example being Justin Berkmann who, for years after the Garage closed, strived to build a facsimile of the venue in London; his efforts resulted in the opening of the Ministry of Sound in 1991.

In 1981, Marc Almond and Dave Ball travelled to New York to record their first album as Soft Cell with producer Mike Thorne. Soft Cell were one of the many synthesiser bands spawned by the British "New Romantic" or "Futurist" pop cult at the turn of the eighties. Almond's influences came from listening to Kraftwerk and Giorgio Moroder records in Leeds's Warehouse club; like contemporaries Depeche Mode and the Human League, Almond and Ball believed that synthesisers offered novel opportunities for pop. Their recordings were typified by a camp sensibility, ironic wit and feel for the bizarre. They had already had a hit in Britain: the minimalist, pre-techno pulse of *Tainted Love*, an electronic cover version of a Northern Soul classic that had become the best-selling single of that year.

Both had considerable experience in the pleasures of the night, but New York turned them on to something unique and wonderful, thanks to a Brooklyn dealer they knew as Cindy Ecstasy, who supplied them with white capsules of MDMA at the wholesale price of $6 a hit.

Almond speaks of the experience in terms that anyone who has taken Ecstasy before or afterwards will understand. "I said: 'What is it going to be like?' She said: 'It's going to be like euphoria, a great kind of rush, it's going to be the best drug you've done in your life.' I'd tried everything else but I'd never heard of this. And it was . . . it was kind of fantastic. The first night we did it, we were listening to The Cure's album *Faith*, and a track called *All Cats are Grey*, which I'll always associate with the first time I took E because I remember thinking that it was the best record I've ever heard in my entire life. Every time I hear that record, I'm there, I can feel that feeling. I remember when it first hit me for the first time, the euphoria of the first Ecstasy I ever took, and I had to go outside and I sat on the step of her apartment building, and she came down and talked me through it. I just told her my life story and I fell totally in love with her, and we felt totally inseparable after that. It was incredible. We then went out, to Studio 54 I think, dancing – and every record I heard I wanted to buy, because it was fantastic and the best record I'd ever heard."

Soft Cell's debut album, *Non Stop Erotic Cabaret*, would be the first British Ecstasy record. "It became a whole album that was done all around Ecstasy and done on Ecstasy – when we listened to the mixes of the album we took Ecstasy to listen to them. It sounded absolutely fantastic, and the producer Mike was bemused why we'd have these bright, wide shining eyes."

They followed up the album with a collection of remixes – *Non Stop Ecstatic Dancing*. One track, *Memorabilia*, was a disco sequence reverberating with disorientating echo; Cindy Ecstasy was invited to add a louche, breathy rap defining her interpretation of hedonism. The video pictured Almond and Ball fooling about over a fast-cut Super-8 New York cityscape, with Cindy in the foreground delivering her lines deadpan: "We can take a pill and shut our eyes and let our love materialise; I don't mean love on a chocolate box, I mean love that really rocks; because they call me the baby, the good-time lady; just look at me and it's easy to see why they call me Cindy Ecstasy."[29] It was a glorious in-joke, and its implications went almost completely unnoticed in their home country. "Nobody knew what we were talking about at all and we got away with it completely," says Ball. "When we got back to London, nobody had ever heard of it."

The drug undoubtedly influenced the way Soft Cell's creative processes developed, insists Almond. "The albums I did around that time probably wouldn't have been the same without Ecstasy. The first three Soft Cell albums – *Non Stop Erotic Cabaret*, *Non Stop Ecstatic Dancing* and *The Art of Falling Apart* – were all really albums that were just done around Ecstasy and the whole E feeling. I made deep friendships with people around that time, friendships that I have to say didn't last. With all that group of us who first took Ecstasy, it all turned a bit sour in the end. Everybody fell out, it was too much too soon – friendships and bonds we had during that time all accelerated and happened too quickly, and then it became routine and everybody became pissed off with each other, and there was nothing really there to cement the friendship.

"Eventually it became kind of bad in a way, because there was a period in my life when I couldn't go out and have a good time without Ecstasy, I couldn't enjoy myself. Sexually I think it can spoil you as well. Because the Ecstasy has changed over the years and because of your tolerance, you can never get back what you first had on it. So therefore it kind of spoils you, because if you have a sexual experience on Ecstasy, you can never duplicate that, that's it: that's the peak that you can go."

Re-entry from peak experiences is notoriously difficult; how can the extremes of pleasure be reconciled with mundane reality? How can you integrate something that is so life-shatteringly sublime with everyday existence, without feeling cheated, terminally disappointed? Almond would not be the only person to ask himself this question over the coming decade.

Four years later, George O'Dowd, alias Boy George, then at the peak of his success with Culture Club, would have a very similar encounter with Ecstasy. In his deliciously candid autobiography *Take it Like a Man*, he describes how taking it for the first time in a New York club seemed the perfect remedy for his stormy love life and increasing isolation in the cocoon of pop stardom: "After half an hour the drug hit me like a sensuous tidal wave. I turned into a tactile temptress and wanted to stroke the whole world. It gave me untold confidence . . . The next morning I woke feeling liberated, like I'd opened Pandora's pillbox and found the meaning of life. I wanted to buy a whole bag of E."[30]

This was the first time he had taken drugs and, unlike the American MDMA therapists who considered Ecstasy entirely benign, O'Dowd fervently believed that it formed a perfect introduction to other drugs; not because it is addictive in itself and not only because it undermines the will to refuse, but that it provides such a positive experience of drug use that it makes the demonic propaganda about other drugs seem unbelievable. For O'Dowd, Ecstasy provided a gateway into the drug world.

"We all went down to the Paradise Garage, a sweatbox for the disco-demented down in the West Village. It opened at midnight and carried on thumping until noon . . . We made friends with the DJ Larry Levan and hung out with him in the booth overlooking the dance-floor. I took my first line of coke in that dark disco cocoon. I felt hypocritical as I put the rolled-up dollar bill to my nose. There were four lines in front of me, I aimed for the skinniest one and snorted up half of it. I was encouraged, 'Go on, finish it.' I handed him back the note. 'No, it's okay.' My eyes were watery, my mouth was dry, I could feel the chemicals slithering down my throat. That toot kept me buzzing for hours. Rabbit, rabbit, rabbit. I didn't need to take any more, though plenty was offered.

"I'd always been very wary of drugs, of being out of control, but I also had a secret yearning to know what I was missing. My initiation to drugs was so casual, especially after all the years of pontificating against them. I dropped my first E among friends in a relaxed atmosphere, not in some dingy basement with a bunch of sordid dealers, although I was to meet quite a few of those in the months to come. Coke was a natural progression from E. One led to another like stepping–stones across a murky stream."[31]

london

"CALLING CARD OF A DEADLY SALESMAN . . . South Wales is at the frontline of the battle to beat the threat of deadly so-called 'designer drugs' from the United States. Only a handful of seizures of the perversely named Ecstasy have been made in Britain. 'We have got to stamp this out,' said Detective Inspector John Wake of the South Wales Drug Squad. 'Nobody knows the full extent of the damage this can do. We believe it can lead to death.' One club-goer told the South Wales Echo how calling cards and pamphlets were handed out to youngsters in one city centre club. 'We have seen drug pushers before but nobody quite like this. He was wearing a dark pin-striped suit as he walked around handing out his leaflets. He was aged about 45 to 50 and had receding hair. He said he didn't have the drug on him but wanted us to read the leaflets. He would come back later if anyone wanted any.' The 22-page booklet contains articles from United States magazines on the use of Ecstasy, guides to its abuse and 'hippy-like' verbiage. One nonsense quote reads: 'You are in a pure space of non-thinking . . . this is the Nirvana that all the Masters and Saints talk about.' " South Wales Echo, January 18th, 1986

Ecstasy was made illegal in Britain in 1977, long before criminal–

isation in the States. During the seventies a clandestine laboratory in the Midlands had been raided where a chemist was discovered in the process of preparing a hallucinogenic amphetamine that wasn't controlled by law. He was also in possession of formulae for other, similar drugs. To stay one step ahead, the government introduced an amendment to the 1971 Misuse of Drugs Act, making MDMA and its derivatives Class A drugs, with possession punishable by up to seven years in jail, and supply by sentences up to life imprisonment.

MDA had been around in London's gay clubs and exclusive Soho niteries since the seventies, although the plastic bags of powder were a pleasure strictly for the starlets and glitterati who grouped around New Romantic venues like Club For Heroes, The Wag and the Camden Palace. It was just one of many substances that were being taken whenever they became available in addition to the traditional diet of alcohol and amphetamines. When people started returning from trips to New York in the early eighties talking about this new wonder drug, Ecstasy, everything changed: everyone wanted to try it. The first trickle of supplies were couriered over from New York in bubble-packed envelopes, or brought back Sellotaped to travellers' bodies. People would wait eagerly for the couriers' return; at £25, Ecstasy was a scarce and sought-after delicacy. The arrival of a dealer – actually more of an enthusiast with a few pills in a Tic-Tac canister than a serious, profit-oriented entrepreneur – would excite frenzied jockeying for position. He might only have fifty capsules; who would be the lucky recipients? "You had to get in there first and get your supply before everybody else," recalls Marc Almond. "It created real jealousy as well, people got really bitter and twisted over it, when someone else got hold of it and they couldn't. It's like you had some special secret."

The people that were using Ecstasy recreationally during the period from 1982 to 1986 were the Soho élite: club runners and club "faces"; music journalists; designers, models and people connected with the fashion business, and international pop stars like Boy George, Marc Almond and George Michael, who commented: "For a while I took Ecstasy when it was not very available over here. I took it simply because it made me feel that everything was wonderful."[32] One leading dealer was a fashion designer who imported it to finance his shoe business; another was a prominent photographer for the fashion monthlies. It was not, despite people's experiences of the Paradise Garage, primarily a dance drug, more of a private party for the initiated where anything went. There were little gatherings at west London homes where people would take Ecstasy and end up in the bath or in bed together, or lolling on settees, talking and stroking cushions, or rolling around on the floor waving their legs in the air. Very playful, and not at all serious. "We tend to stay at people's houses, make our own adventures," said one leading pop journalist at the time. "A lot of childish dramatics really, like re-enactments of *The Sound of Music*, impersonations of the Piccadilly line . . ."[33]

There was also another nucleus of activity centred around Hampstead: these users were in the therapeutic rather than hedonist tradition, and like their American counterparts they called the drug "Adam". Peter Nasmyth, the journalist who wrote the first article on Ecstasy in Britain for *The Face* in 1985, had become acquainted with the radical psychiatrist RD Laing, who believed that MDMA had enormous potential as an adjunct to psychotherapy. Laing provided Nasmyth's entrée to this closed world of middle-class intellectual voyagers. "They were post-New Agers, oddball types, poet beatniks who would take it because they were doing acid in the sixties and seventies. Everyone was saying this was the next step on from acid. Then there was the drop-out aristocracy group in Hampstead, they were all doing it. And they wanted to keep it secret. I had a lot of people say to me, 'Don't write about it because it's *our* little world, we don't want *them* to spoil it' – *them* being people who make the drug laws. Even though it was illegal, they felt that by publicising it in any way it would draw a lot of police attention and their sources would dry up and life would become difficult. They were really quite enjoying their nice little private Ecstasy parties.

"Most of the people I interviewed were involved in some kind of group or therapy or organisation, and they were all proselytising it. Again they were very often sixties or seventies people who were looking for the new sacrament and were very keen to believe that Ecstasy was it."

Nasmyth had to work hard to pull the feature together. Alexander Shulgin refused to be interviewed, feeling at the time that his words would be misconstrued by journalists. He didn't want to set himself up as the "new Leary" and jeopardise his research. "There was a movement to try and keep it concealed. I'd been told that one person was *the* person to talk about it but that he wouldn't talk to me because I was the enemy, the evil press who would twist everything he said, destroy it and get the police in. I got to know some of his friends quite well and finally I got this phone call at about 11 o'clock at night and this friend said: 'Go to him now, he's waiting.' So I cycled over. He gave me some tea and I suddenly realised that he'd put some in the tea. They believed that this drug was so powerful and wonderful that it would lift me from this mundane journalistic plane up to this other spiritual level."

In 1985, the same year as the first British seizures of the drug were made, the first Ecstasy parties took place in London, although the drug was still in short supply. Taboo was more of an anything-goes club than an Ecstasy club, although MDMA was more prevalent there than anywhere else, and the club was eventually shut down after a magazine report linking it to Ecstasy and marijuana use. It was hosted by two disco celebrities, Leigh Bowery and Trojan, both now dead, and populated by a freaky fashion crowd who took dressing up and going out to almost comical costumed extremes. "Probably about a third of the crowd at Taboo took E," says *Time Out* magazine club correspondent Dave Swindells, one of the few journalists to document the evolving scene. "I remember everybody writhing on the floor, Leigh Bowery spinning people round on his shoulders and people cheering."

The other was the Hug Club; named for the empathetic qualities of MDMA and promoted with a flyer decorated with a picture of a teddy bear wearing a T-shirt bearing the word "Worthington" (rather than Paddington); Worthington E used to be a popular brand of beer. People queued up to buy their Ecstasy capsules, which had been flown in specially from New York; one each and no more, there weren't enough to go around. One pop starlet even turned up early in an attempt to reserve capsules for her band. "At the time, you could only get fifty or sixty, so you'd have to pick the people you'd give it to," recalls a Hug Club dealer. "You wouldn't sell to people you didn't know, even if they offered you twice as much, it was so special and you wanted the people you knew to take it with you." There was still an enduring vestige of altruism in the distribution network, although most of the hippie trappings had been excised: "I saw people being friendly to each other who I'd always wanted to be friendly to each other but they hadn't been. We used to sometimes stand and say to each other: 'Don't you feel great because this is what we've done?' We'd see all these people laughing and having a good time and I'd go: 'It's fucking great.'"

But London was years behind New York; while Larry Levan was turning drug music into a high art, no one in London had quite worked out how chemistry and sound could create a synergistic whole which would not only pleasure, but inspire. The London Ecstasy circle was in many ways a stagnant, self-satisfied élite that had no reason to push the boundaries of the possible – they had all they wanted right now and were happy with it, thank you very much, whereas the set and setting of New York's black gay culture was catalysed by repression. It would require a similar explosion of repressed energy to set the new technologies of pleasure in motion. But where would it come from?

2

summer of love

"History is hard to know, because of all the hired bullshit, but even without being sure of 'history' it seems entirely reasonable to think that every now and then the energy of a whole generation comes to a head in a long fine flash, for reasons that nobody really understands at the time – and which never explain, in retrospect, what really happened."
Hunter S Thompson, *Fear and Loathing in Las Vegas*

Ibiza is an island whose character and economic structure is built on the heat of summer and the magic of the night. When the holiday season begins in May, the island awakens from peaceful slumber and opens its arrivals channel to a torrent of half a million hedonists, sun-worshippers and pleasure-seekers. Until the 1960s, it was a poor stump of rock poking out of the Mediterranean, an obscure rural community in the Balearic Isles, barely connected to mainland Spain, with a population of only 37,000. Few people visited, even fewer stayed, bar a handful of wealthy socialites and a small enclave of artists. Accommodation was cheap, the beaches were deserted, the transport system was rudimentary, and this sleepy outcrop of red-brown dirt, pure white houses and vivid greenery maintained an almost feudal existence, its economy underpinned by the trade in salt.

By the middle of the sixties, however, things had started to change; Spain's fascist premier General Franco began to encourage the tourist trade to Ibiza as a means of bringing foreign currency to his impoverished country. When the international airport was completed in 1967, the numbers of tourists rose exponentially, reaching 500,000 a year by the early seventies, making tourism the Ibicencos' primary source of income. Hundreds of new hotels were constructed and the island's landscape altered beyond repair. The once picturesque Ibizencan fishing village of Sant Antoni de Portmany became San Antonio, a Babylon of jerry-built tourist *urbanizaciones*, greasy cafés, souvenir shops and rowdy fun pubs with names like Wigan Pier set up to target the British market, which constituted half of the holidaymakers.[1]

Ibiza also attracted another type of visitor: beatniks, hippies and backpackers, who liked the island for its warm and peaceful isolation, and the *laissez-faire* tolerance of the Ibicencos. By 1965 it was an essential destination on a bohemian itinerary that also included Goa and Kathmandu. The *peluts* ("hairies") established their own infrastructure of communes, parties in ramshackle *fincas* (farms) and supply lines for drugs. This beatific state was short-lived: at the end of the sixties, the paramilitary police of the Guardia Civil moved in from Spain and attempted to evict the hippies, although it was the commercialisation of the island rather than any police crackdown that ultimately drove them away.

Yet despite this, the island was a liberal idyll compared to the authoritarian regime in force on the mainland. It became a magnet for gays and bohemians who saw it as a refuge from Franco's fascist conformity, and for the international leisure class that holidayed in remote villas way up in the hills and enjoyed the nocturnal decadence in Ibiza Town: politicians, aristocrats, actors and pop stars. Religious cults, including the disciples of Bhagwan Shree Rajneesh, also established bases here. Despite the encroaching banality of tourist exploitation, the island retained a golden aura tinged with the afterglow of hippie dreams, the flamboyance of the gay scene and the glamour of the jet set at play.

"The hippie influence is really basic because the spirit really comes from them – that freedom and wild kind of life," says José Padilla, who left mainland Spain for Ibiza in 1973 and subsequently became one of the island's leading DJs. "That's the heritage and the real spirit of Ibiza – free parties, open air, the moon and the stars, good music, dancing. There are no hippies any more – you see maybe one or two in the market at Las Dalias [a so-called 'hippie market' which is more like a nostalgia theme park]. They started to disappear because society started to change, got more into the business of building, and people started to get more materialistic. Hippies had two choices: either leave Ibiza and find somewhere else they could still live the same way, or stay there and change. The hippie thing is finished, but they've been used in a way to give an image of Ibiza to the rest of Europe – the free island, the island of love."

Since the beginning of the sixties, foreign travel had become increasingly less exotic. People whose parents saw holidays abroad as the sole preserve of the rich were now buying package trips to Spain's Costa del Sol, Costa Blanca and Balearic Isles. Due to the weakness of Spanish currency, these resorts, with their cheap hotels, food and drink, were affordable destinations for many working-class Britons whose income had previously confined them to Blackpool, Skegness or Torquay. Ibiza – and in particular the concrete sprawl of San Antonio bay – became the classic holiday haunt of Brits abroad, with sun, sea, sand, sex and San Miguel in abundance.

In the eighties, as unemployment grew in Britain, a new breed of tourist reached the island. These weren't backpackers or two-week booze cruisers, but bright, inquisitive youths for whom the prospect of slaving for low pay or subsisting on the dole held little appeal; better to get out there, see the world and catch some sun and fun than stay in rainy, depressing Britain. They travelled to Tenerife in the winter, Ibiza in the summer, with perhaps a stopover in Amsterdam en route to sample the *Nederwiet* in the coffee shops. They would survive by doing odd jobs, serving behind bars, giving out promotional tickets for clubs, or running credit card scams, doing petty robberies and selling hash. This bohemian working class update of the hippie trail was hardly a luxurious existence, but better than stagnating at home.

"In Tenerife we met a lot of boys from up north, Manchester and Corby and Sheffield," remembers Marie Marden, a London clubber who spent her first summer in Ibiza in 1986. "From the age of sixteen they left home because they didn't have any careers or anything, and basically they were just thieves. So they used to travel round Europe and do things like dress up in suits and go into jewellers' shops and nick Rolexes out of windows while someone talked to the assistant. I remember they robbed a big safe in the main station in Paris and got £20,000 out. Whenever they weren't doing anything they lived in Amsterdam, they had contacts out there, they had flats out there they'd stay in. When we met them, they took it on themselves to look after us six girls. They used to buy us shoes, give us watches. Whenever they went somewhere they always used to come back with all these presents for us. They ended up living with us and they were doing all skulduggery out there, bits of this, bits of that. They said 'Why don't you come to Ibiza for the summer?', which we did."

British clubbers visiting the island were initially content with quaffing cheap beer in the San An bars, dancing to holiday records in tacky discotheques, then staggering home to their backstreet apartments. But there was another side of Ibiza, another social world which they would eventually discover; a world where the rich would moor their yachts in the harbour at Ibiza Town, enjoy its designer fashion boutiques, expensive restaurants and the outrageous gay bars along Calle de la Virgen before moving on to one of the opulent nightclub complexes inland.

Two of Ibiza's pre-eminent nightspots – Pacha and Amnesia – grew out of the hippie era. Pacha opened in 1973, playing reggae and psychedelic rock for the *peluts*, while Amnesia was

still a working *finca* with no electricity. At night the hippies and
Bhagwan *sannyasins* would gather and dance around bonfires
outside, and you might spot flamenco guitar hero Paco de Lucia
or one of the Pink Floyd crouched around the embers.

As the hippie era was superseded by disco, both venues started
to add bars and dancefloors until they became fully functioning
nightclubs, reflecting the construction elsewhere on the island.
Yet they weren't discos as the British knew them, typified by
tinny sound systems, tacky flashing lights and carpets sticky with
stale beer. Ibiza's clubs had alfresco dancefloors illuminated by
the moon and the stars, bubbling fountains, palm trees, plush
cushioned alcoves, and extravagant, ever-changing decor. And
the clientele! Transvestite floorshows, flash young blades from
Barcelona with sculptured torsos and immaculate hairstyles,
fiftysomething millionaires prancing in their suits, pop stars
sipping champagne, flamboyant gays, people of all ages and
nationalities. There would be theme parties where everyone
would dress in black, or go masked, or where the club would be
pumped full of *espuma*. Amnesia, Pacha and Ku were fantasy
playgrounds, temples to Dionysus designed to stimulate the senses
and accommodate the expression of the wildest desires.

"We'd go to Amnesia but we were the only English in there,
all the rest were Spanish and Italians," says Marie Marden. "You'd
see Grace Jones in there, *Dallas* stars. We couldn't even afford to
get a drink. But we'd go there and see the weirdest people we'd
ever seen and the richest people we'd ever seen, then there was
us, we were like little kids, we didn't fit in at all basically. I used
to think: 'What am I doing here?' When your dad's a painter
and decorator, your mum works in a shop, you've worked in a
dry cleaners, been a dental nurse, done cleaning, you think about
that and you're out there, looking at Grace Jones, you just think:
'God! I never thought this could happen!' "

Amnesia was the best club with the best music. The DJ,
Alfredo Fiorillo, was an Argentinian, a former journalist who
had fled from the right-wing military junta in 1976. "I had

problems. I'd been promoting Argentinian rock'n'roll, and they banned every rock'n'roll group and long hair. They closed newspapers, psychology schools, everything – it was fascist, you know." Alfredo was employed at Amnesia in 1984, and since the crowd had as wide an age range as it had breadth of nationality, he would play a similarly diverse selection of music: soul, reggae, hip hop, European electronic pop, and later the embryonic house tracks from Chicago. "You didn't play music for a trendy group of kids, you played music for human beings."

The classics were emotive songs by Bob Marley and Marvin Gaye, and at the end of the night John Lennon's *Imagine*; but the way Alfredo put it all together captured the indefinable magic of the island after dark, the hippie legacy and the hedonistic present, a style that would later be codified as "Balearic", although, ironically, it would eventually be other DJs and not Alfredo who would capitalise financially on the Balearic methodology. "There were three or four DJs [on the island], but not taking as much risk as Alfredo," says José Padilla. "Alfredo just got the right place at the right moment and he put his balls on the line and said: 'This is how I think it should be.' He had the space – Amnesia was still open-air – he had the Ibiza spirit, he had the sound, he had the people, the new generation – all that together. It doesn't last long, but that's life."

Ecstasy started to come into Ibiza in the early eighties, following the same routes as the international travellers, gays and New Age cultists. Until then, the nocturnal stimulants of Ibiza had been LSD, mescalin and cocaine. The spread of *Extasis* coincided with the first house imports in some kind of weird synchronicity. At the start of the 1987 season, British DJ Trevor Fung and his cousin Ian St Paul from Carshalton, both of whom had been holidaying on the island since the early eighties, opened a bar in San Antonio for the summer. The Project (which took its name from a Streatham club night) became the focus for all the British clubbers on the island, a meeting point for many of the key people who would form the nucleus of the acid house scene in Britain.

These predominantly working-class boys and girls had begun to band together during the summer of 1986. Most of them originated from the southern fringes of the capital, the stretch of London where inner city and suburbs meet, sketchily bordered by the A205 to the north and A232 to the south. This area – completely unremarkable to the eye – had continually been influential in nurturing cultural movements throughout the seventies and eighties. The bohemian milieu that spawned David Bowie was centred around Beckenham; the original punks and the first followers of the Sex Pistols were the Bromley Contingent. Now these teenagers from Carshalton, Wallington, Bromley, Beckenham and Streatham, spurred by the ennui of suburbia and an overwhelming desire to depart this dull, flat landscape for the glittering metropolis, fifteen minutes away by train, found the impetus to invent a new way out.

The pockets of young Brits who had watched in awe from the sidelines at Amnesia the year before were now united in one big boisterous gang. They would meet at bars in San Antonio or Ibiza Town, twenty of them, then thirty, then forty, swelling as the summer progressed, and head out along the main road that links the two towns, to Amnesia, where they would take Ecstasy and carouse till sun-up, or head for the beach at Cala Salada to kick back and see in the dawn, grab a couple of hours of sleep on the beach, and off again to the Café del Mar in San Antonio bay to hear José Padilla play Art of Noise's heavenly *Moments in Love* at sunset, and another night of Amnesia. The summer became an extended vacation in an alternate reality.

Holidays always generate some sense of disconnection from everyday existence. They constitute a special time when normal rules are suspended; an idealised, peak experience that allows space for utopian dreaming and acts as a catalyst for events to come. In Ibiza, dancing in the balmy Mediterranean air with all these fabulous, outlandish creatures around them, all friends together where nothing else mattered, this sense of fantastic unreality was heightened by the drug. Ecstasy accelerated the bonding, creating an extended family, a secret society that no one else understood or even knew existed.

"We were there to dance! And dance, and dance, and dance! And not stop! We got into this ideal, the E'd-up, loved-up thing; we wouldn't have been so close without it. At one stage, eighteen of us lived in one apartment with six single beds," says Adam Heath, then a nineteen-year-old clubber from Bromley. "We all got into the clubs for nothing, they knew us, they called us 'the crazy English' and they loved us. Everyone was quite young and well-travelled. We all had the same mentality, which was to have a really good time and try as hard as possible not to think about anything else. When we all came back to England, it really struck me that we'd got some kind of . . . it felt like a religion."

In September 1987, Trevor Fung and Ian St Paul invited their friend Paul Oakenfold to Ibiza to celebrate his twenty-sixth birthday. Oakenfold, who trained as a chef, had been a DJ since the early eighties, and had a natural antenna for trends and an ear for the pop music of tomorrow. He had run hip hop break-dance clubs in Carshalton with St Paul, been to the Paradise Garage in New York, promoted the Beastie Boys and Run-DMC's first records in Britain. He worked for a record company, DJed at the Project Club in Streatham and wrote a hip hop column for specialist magazine *Blues and Soul* under the pseudonym Wotupski. He and Fung had tried to stage an Ibiza-style club in Purley in 1985, but it hadn't worked; the soul boys couldn't understand why he was playing all these strange pop records amongst the jazz-funk, and of course there was no Ecstasy.

Oakenfold brought two colleagues with him: his friend, funk DJ Johnny Walker, aged thirty, and Nicky Holloway, twenty-four, a cheeky young imp with a keen eye for business opportunities who had progressed from party nights in Old Kent Road funpubs to running the most prestigious of the soul weekenders with his Special Branch organisation. Holloway also asked his mate Danny Rampling along, a twenty-six-year-old former scooter boy from Streatham who played soul on the Kiss FM pirate station and at Holloway's gigs.

What happened next – their Ecstasy conversion experience – has since been elevated to a pivotal moment in house culture, but it and the subsequent events that it catalysed wouldn't have been possible without the footloose young clubbers who had already laid the foundations. "I can still remember the experience as clear as ever," says Johnny Walker. "I had never taken drugs before – maybe the odd puff – and I really wasn't sure about doing it. The others took theirs and after about half an hour I saw them smiling and hugging each other and thought 'that looks all right'. The Es then, people used to say they made you look good and feel good, and that was true, I've still got photos of us on it and we looked great. You could hold a decent conversation, and you felt OK afterwards. It was almost like a religious experience; a combination of taking Ecstasy and going to a warm, open-air club full of beautiful people – you're on holiday, you feel great and you're suddenly being exposed to entirely different music to what you were used to in London. This strange mixture was completely fresh and new to us, and very inspiring."

Holloway's telling of the story is coloured by his characteristically self-deprecating humour. "What you basically had was four wallies with moonboots on walking round San Antonio, going: 'This is great, man!' We used to think we were being cool or not making fools of ourselves, but if we look back at it, we were probably all over the place. The first time I took it I was going: 'Oh it was great but I wouldn't do it every time, we'll only do it a couple of times for the rest of the week.' And what happened was we did it every night for the rest of the week, every night we went to Amnesia, every night lost it. We were basically all loved up – it was a big mind-opener. Standing in Ibiza listening to music, going 'God this is good', going up and asking the DJ what the music was, finding out the band was from Romford, it's just that we'd never have bothered to listen to it because we'd been snobs. We basically came back like salesmen for the stuff . . ."

It was hard not to. Dancing in front of the speakers, holding hands with new soulmates, telling their life stories and their most intimate emotions to people who seemed to *really understand* for the first time . . . and back on the floor, with the music sounding more vibrant than anything their imagination could conceive, whooping and clapping like they never wanted it to end.

streatham high road

**"Author's diary 2.12.75: . . . London suburbia: sterility –
cynicism – boredom ready to spill into violence; incipient right-
wing backlash. Fuck London for its dullness, the English people
for their pusillanimity and the weather for its coldness and
darkness."**
Jon Savage, describing the pre-punk era in *England's Dreaming*

Soon the season was over. Back at Gatwick, they stepped off the plane into a country they'd almost forgotten. *Fuck London for its dullness* . . . Where to go now? Back to their parents' homes to plaster Amnesia posters over the walls of their bedrooms, sit back and drift away in reminiscence. Grey mood closing in. They'd changed, but Britain hadn't.

The country had just entered its third consecutive term of Conservative rule, a period which compounded the break with the collective values of the past. The last battalions of class warriors, the miners and the printers, had been vanquished after long and turbulent strikes, socialism was in terminal retreat, and Thatcher's "economic miracle", a consumer boom fuelled by wild spending on credit and a mood of uninhibited individualism, was entering its final phase before the shuddering stock market crash of "Black Monday" heralded a plunge back into recession.

London clubland mirrored this monetarist climax; the exclusive West End "Style Culture", which writer Jon Savage described as the "cutting edge of Thatcherite materialism", was peaking.[2] Elitism was a virtue, acceptance had to be bought, and those who couldn't afford the price were turned away, their voices denied expression. But there were also signs of what was to come. In the eighties, dance music and electronic rhythm had become live currents within British youth culture; not only the New Romantic synthesiser pop and its rejection of the four-man guitar band format and "rockist" ethics, but the post-punk, avant-garde electronic music of Cabaret Voltaire and Throbbing Gristle, the "rare groove" funk and hip hop fraternities with their outlaw parties in disused inner-city warehouses, and the suburban working-class "Soul Mafia" scene focused on hedonistic weekend-long bashes in holiday camps around the British coastline. These traditions would form the basis for what happened over the following years.

In the autumn of 1987, the only places playing house music in central London were Noel and Maurice Watson's Delirium and gay nights like Jungle and Pyramid. So this is where the Ibiza crew would go, a gaggle of brightly dressed extroverts in baggy sweatshirts, dungarees, ethnic accoutrements, strings of beads around their necks, hair grown long over the summer and caught up in a little ponytail with an elastic band. Compared to the drab uniform of London clubland at the end of the eighties – MA-1 flying jackets, Doctor Martens and Levis 501s – they looked and acted like freaks from another dimension. "There'd be about thirty of us in the club, standing in one corner, all dancing, and the rest of the club would be looking at us like, 'Where the fuck did this lot land from?' We wanted to dance all night and there was nowhere to do it. When it shut we'd be stamping and jumping and screaming," recalls Adam Heath.

"They were all in ponchos, dancing on the speakers, popping

Es. It was like: 'What the fuck's going on here?' I didn't want to have them in the club!" exclaims Noel Watson. "I told some of the door staff: 'Don't let them in, they're thugs from south London, I know they're thugs, they're casuals, we don't want casuals in the club.' Then I started realising that they were cool."

But Delirium wasn't theirs, however great the music was; it belonged to the past, to the trendy West End. They needed their own place, a club that was run for and about the mind-shattering experience of Ibiza, where the inhibitions would drop once more, and, in their own environment, they could gambol and play without fear or stricture. Paul Oakenfold and Ian St Paul began to open the Project Club on Streatham High Road after hours; from 2 a.m., when the club officially closed, until 6 a.m., they would let the Ibiza fraternity in through the back door, and the madness would commence again. It only lasted a few weeks, but before it was raided by police, Oakenfold flew in Alfredo from Ibiza and invited down a contingent from *Boy's Own* fanzine, which would become the mouthpiece of the early scene, and which Oakenfold knew from West End clubs and Chelsea football matches.

Boy's Own was part of another, older tradition, a hip terrace fanzine which itself had been inspired by *The End*, a Liverpool 'zine edited by Peter Hooton, lead singer of The Farm (a band that would also, in years to come, play a role in Ecstasy culture). *The End* colonised the borders between football, pop and fashion with incisive humour and subversive broadsides aimed at the London-centred homogeneity of eighties Style Culture. *Boy's Own* followed Hooton's lead, but attacked from within. Published from Windsor and the dormitory towns to the west of the city, its covers featured cheeky urchins with pit bull terriers, and its prose was by turns hilarious (if you got the in-jokes) and vicious. *Boy's Own* fulfilled the role of *agent provocateur*, telling the scene in no uncertain terms exactly where it was going wrong, carrying a strictly purist ideological line to the point of outright élitism. Run by Terry Farley, Steve Mayes,

Andy Weatherall and Cymon Eckel, *Boy's Own* went on to influence the form of dance culture all across Britain, inspire a wave of similar fanzines, and make DJ stars of Farley and Weatherall. At the end of 1987 it was still eulogising obscure football firms and describing in intricate detail their idiosyncratic stylistic peccadilloes, but it was also adopting increasingly club-based concerns. By May 1988, the cover urchins were mooching under the slogan "Drop Acid Not Bombs", and the editorial talked of "giving out flowers at the [Chelsea FC] North Stand gate".[3]

After the Project closed, there was nowhere to go again, except Delirium and the gay clubs where DJs like Mark Moore and Colin Faver mixed a few house tracks into the Eurodisco and hip hop. Of the four DJs who spent that fateful week in Ibiza, Rampling seemed the most affected; he was also the one who had least invested in the past, as Oakenfold, Holloway and Walker had well-established careers in the music business. "It did change Danny's life," believes Steve Proctor, a key DJ in the scene and, at the time, a close friend of Rampling. "I had been through punk and the New Romantic thing, so from my point of view it was exciting to be involved with something like that again, with the energy and intensity magnified by the drugs, but for people like Danny, who'd only known playing soul records in pubs in the Old Kent Road, it changed his life. He went mad for it."

And so it transpired that in November 1987, Danny Rampling and his wife-to-be Jenni threw a party in the Fitness Centre gym near Southwark Bridge, just south of the Thames. "Sensation seekers, let the music take you to the top," declared the invitation. The name of the night, Shoom (or as it was initially styled, Klub Sch-oom), was said to be a description of how one felt when the first rush of Ecstasy took hold. "The word expressed the feeling of the club – up, positive energy," says Rampling. "The first night was quite nerve-racking. Carl Cox played with me, and another guy that played funk, so it was a real mish-mash really. There was a funk crowd and a house crowd and it just didn't work. It was shaky but it was fun, hence the enthusiasm to do it again."

A few weeks afterwards, Ian St Paul and Paul Oakenfold booked the Sanctuary, a back annexe to the huge gay club Heaven in Charing Cross, for a party entitled Future. One Thursday night, the Ibiza crowd gathered outside the front door, each chipped in £5, had their hands rubber-stamped, and filed through Heaven into the Sanctuary, where Oakenfold played Alfredo's greatest hits of the summer: light and airy holiday music with a touch of house. At this point there probably weren't enough house records in existence to carry a whole night, and anyway, Future was a *Balearic* club.

There has been much conjecture about who was the first to adopt and promote house in Britain – was it Mike Pickering in Manchester, or Graeme Park in Nottingham, or Londoners like the Watson brothers, Mark Moore, Colin Faver, Jazzy M, Kid Batchelor and Eddie Richards? Although house had a hard-core following in the north-west and Midlands, it's safe to say that none of these DJs was playing house alone; they would mix it up with rap and soul, and there was none of the Ecstasy euphoria of Ibiza.

In London, however, house was widely seen as a nasty new strain of gay disco. When Mike Pickering came down from Manchester in 1987 with his box of Chicago Trax, he was verbally abused in the DJ booth, recalls Johnny Walker: "I remember a guy coming up and handing Mike this piece of paper that said: 'Why are you playing this homo shit music? Fuck off!' That was the attitude." Nonetheless, house had already made an impression on the pop charts; recordings by Chicago's Farley "Jackmaster" Funk and Steve "Silk" Hurley had reached the top ten in August 1986 and January 1987 respectively, and British-made house tracks were already beginning to appear. By the start of 1988 London Records were marketing "acid house" as a new pop-cult brand name via compilation albums.

The ascendance of house chimed with an exciting, optimistic new mood within British pop as it became clear how simple it was to make a record using the new technologies of digital sampling and drum computers. For a moment at the end of the eighties it seemed that new horizons of opportunity were opening up and music would never be the same again. The turntable scratch mixes of hip hop DJs and the drum-machine formula of the first Chicago house records pointed the way to a cheap low-tech methodology which nonetheless sounded revolutionary. The way music could now be composed on a four-track recorder, assembled from samples and beatboxes, then cut to a white label 12-inch single and sold through independent dance record stores, was a democratisation of the creative process, just as desk-top publishing had opened up the publishing industry and enabled the rise of the fanzine. Its do-it-yourself, open-access strategy was repeatedly compared to the anti-musicianship ethics of punk rock, but samplers and drum computers also banished the need to learn to play instruments, to rehearse, to book recording studios, to organise gigs or even to seek a record contract.

The remarkable success of the first, rudimentary British DJ records – in late 1987 and early 1988, Jonathan Moore and Matt Black's Coldcut, Mark Moore's S-Express, Dave Dorrell and CJ Mackintosh's M/A/R/R/S and Tim Simenon's Bomb the Bass all scored pop hits with DIY tracks assembled from samples – was a wake-up call. Computers brought the whole idea of "the band" into question: a band need no longer be four men on stage with guitars, drums, bass and a microphone, but something more fluid and volatile: an *ad hoc* collective of any number of people, constantly changing and redefining itself to suit new situations. Naturally, there were new skills involved in programming house tracks, and consequently many of the thousands produced were amateurish or derivative, but at the time it seemed that people could, as the independent labels which grew up in the wake of punk had dreamed, short-cut the suffocating structures of the music business. The events that unfolded over the coming months would raise these hopes to a frantic crescendo.

southwark street

"We're going to teach people to stop hating . . . Start a peace and love movement." Allen Ginsberg, after first taking psilocybin in 1960

The period from December 1987 to April 1988 was a voyage of innocence and discovery, untouched by the concerns of the outside world. The Shoomers had an amazing new music that you couldn't hear on the radio and could only buy in specialist shops, and an amazing drug that turned them into the people they always dreamed they could be. There were so few people involved that friendships became all-consuming. Suddenly all they could talk about was love, togetherness, sharing, the sheer joy of life. In Ibiza they had discovered something they hardly knew how to comprehend, and so they looked for the nearest comparison they could find – the mythology of the hippie era – adopting a simulacrum of what they believed the sixties were like, a hand-me-down, pick-and-mix bag of fashions and slogans – minus the radical politics of the era – all viewed through a prism of suburban working-class aspirations. Yet they sincerely believed that the fabric of their minds was changing. Were they turning into hippies, they asked themselves, was this the beginning of a New Age?

"The way I was feeling at that point was the golden age was dawning, Aquarius was on us, and I wanted to share that with other people – let's get together, bring people together!" says Rampling. "Shoom was a club where anything went. There was such a strong sense of freedom and no restrictions. We greeted everyone when they arrived and said goodbye to them when they left. When the club first opened we'd give away Lucozades and Perriers. We made people feel part of something rather than just coming into a club and paying their money."

The only genuine hippies at Shoom were Maggie and Roger Beard, Stonehenge veterans and old friends of Ian St Paul from Carshalton, who drove a thirty-foot bus left over from their life on the road with the "Peace Convoy". Inevitably they found themselves the focus of enormous curiosity – especially after they turned up at Future in full Indian costume. An excited little huddle would form around them, demanding: "What was it like in the sixties? It must have been better then?" And they would reply: "No, no, it's better now – we didn't have the drugs."

By January 1988, the Ramplings had adopted the yellow Smiley face logo – the symbol of hippies and religious evangelists which had recently been revived by Alan Moore's hip graphic novel, *The Watchmen*. On their new flyer, which introduced "the happy happy happy happy happy Shoom club", Smileys bounced down the page like a shower of pills.

Shoom and Future helped set the agenda for a lot of what was to follow. The claustrophobic cocoon of Future was like being locked in a humid black box where the bass vibrated through bone and sinew – you were literally lost in music. In Shoom, sometimes you couldn't see more than a foot beyond your face as strawberry-flavoured smoke billowed out and relentless strobe lights froze motion into jagged shapes. There would be legs sticking out of the speaker stacks, bodies crammed into the bass bins. People would walk into the mirrors on the back wall, not realising the place was so tiny. The dancing was the antithesis of the funky London strut, with kinetic windmilling arms and kung fu chops; jerking bodies synched to the strobe and the metronomic beat; finger dances where extended digits would choreograph the high-hat patterns. Once Paul Oakenfold played *All You Need is Love* at the end of the night, and everyone just shoomed together, holding hands and hugging.

Ecstasy had opened some kind of psychic trap-door, and all manner of bizarre phenomena were streaming out. Many treated

Shoom like a kiddies' ice-cream-and-jelly party, giving each other presents, little trinkets like Smiley badges or clip-on hearts, anything cute; and everyone seemed to be carrying some crazy accessory, a crystal ball that they'd hold under the lights or a fan to waft cool air and describe geometric patterns in the strobe – all freaking on a communal groove, locked together in harmonic convergence – together, as one, like nothing else mattered in the world.

"It was magical every week, a group of people linked up on this mad friendly buzz," says Spencer Guinere, another Ibiza veteran from south London. "Inhibitions were totally gone. People used to start painting each other Day-Glo or get inside the speakers. They must have wanted to get right inside the sound. People were just reverting back to a childlike way." Everyone had a story about spontaneous acts of kindness or expressions of unconditional love, like the whole club singing "Happy Birthday" to one beaming Shoomer, or making a huge Smiley card for someone in hospital. "We used to have teddy bears," says Jason Hawkins. "We had a teddy bear club in the Shoom – everyone had teddy bears. There's no way of explaining it really, it was like going back to childhood. You used to do all sorts of silly things down there. It was unlike anything else had ever been. It was all drug-induced, totally. The vibe was in the air. For the people that were there, all friends and all on the same level, it was totally wild."

A dealer that used to serve the Hug Club was amazed at what Shoom had made of MDMA. "They'd put it onto a different level. To switch it from people having parties and laying on their backs, hugging each other and listening to *Moments in Love*, chilling out, to somewhere the lights are flashing, it's full of smoke and there's this pumping sound, it was like, 'fuck me!' It showed how bored people were with that Style Decade."

An arcane language developed that was almost impenetrable to outsiders – "on one", "toppy top", "acieed", "shooming" – phrases that attempted to map the indescribable landscape of the drug experience. Beer was replaced by Lucozade, not only because alcohol dulled MDMA's impact, but because it was *their* drink – as Steve Proctor explains: "Lucozade became *the* drink for no other reason than because it was the thing they sold at the Fitness Centre – if they only sold Milk Stout it would have been that."

They had returned with the functional Euro-fashion of the Ibiza summer – shorts, T-shirts, Converse baseball boots and bandannas – and embellished it with kindergarten accessories, the fervent atmosphere amplifying the sartorial experimentation. There was a palpable sense of liberation in throwing off designer clothes and donning a carefree T-shirt and jeans; it was a statement that the holiday wasn't over yet, that there would be no return to reality. It was also an implicit rejection of the rigid style hierarchy that the London scene was based on, a suggestion that the conspicuous consumption of the late eighties was laughable, pathetic . . . there were more important things in life.

Another Shoom member, the fashion designer Nick Coleman, who graduated from prestigious St Martins College of Art at the same time as John Galliano and launched his own label in 1985, gained a unique perspective on the shift from designer cool to utility wear. "Suddenly my lifestyle had completely changed – I didn't want jackets with pleated peg trousers any more, I want something sporty, something easy to clean, functional. The whole restrictive, smart way of dressing gave way to a casual approach. We were among the first to pick up on it because I was going to clubs and seeing what people were wearing and doing my version of it."

The following year, Coleman began to introduce designer clubwear, acting on a hunch that casual clothing would itself become fashionable, a path that many other designers would follow in years to come. "The indications are that 'dressing down' may well have happened anyway," Coleman qualifies. "If people have much more leisure time on their hands, their lifestyles alter, and the type of clothing they desire alters. The thing that affected the clothing business was the recession really; people who bought designer clothes started to have much less money."

Nonetheless, the impact on Coleman was remarkable – he started buying records and turntables, opened his own house club – and an indicator of how effectively Ecstasy could dissolve the social fabric of the Style Decade. Rag trade acquaintances thought he had lost the plot. "I was somebody who was thought of as this business person who worked every hour that God sends, a complete workaholic, really uptight, the least likely person to get involved – it was a complete and utter shock to most people. It started making me think in a way that I've never done before; a very positive way, but not necessarily conducive to working hard or making your business succeed. I was less worried about the business failing or not having the best collection."

The Ecstasy supply in London at the tail end of 1987 was still extremely limited. "Obviously you had to have Ecstasy for those clubs," says Ian St Paul. "Without it, none of them would have worked." London dealers just couldn't supply it in the quantities required, so some of the young blaggers made surreptitious missions to Amsterdam or Ibiza to tap connections they had made during the summer and bring back bags of fluffy white powdered MDMA. Everyone knew the few who were selling and what they were selling, and they knew it was good stuff. Soon supply lines were established around the scene's key figures and venues. At this point there was a generalised, erroneous belief that the drug was legal – in fact, no one really knew much about it at all – but some would soon find out the truth, to their cost.

Although everyone understood the potential of what was taking place, there was no one who could really define this new collective consciousness, and as the impact of Ecstasy is so personal, communal beliefs were sketchy and vague. Ecstasy undercut verbal concepts; you didn't intellectualise about it, you felt it with every cell of your body, without the distortions of language intervening. Because of their very nature, the Shoomers weren't about to write a manifesto, so all they had were reconstructed hippie myths: "peace and love". The prevailing mentality was totally defined by MDMA – empathy, sensation, sound – and the set and setting of the participants, which itself was interwoven with the prevailing economic and social mood of entrepreneurial, free-market Britain. Was this a desire to escape, or just smart kids looking for a good time? Saturday night fever, or a new way of life?

"Danny and Jenni were the more spiritual amongst us, but I think the love and peace thing was when you were in a club off your head," says Lisa McKay. "People were literally walking around a club telling everybody that they loved each other. There was a feeling of unity, there was *something* there, but it's so hard to pinpoint when it's a drug thing, isn't it?"

People did feel they were shedding old prejudices and leaving their past lives behind. "A lot of kids used to be quite bad, a lot are from the terraces years ago," Rampling noted at the time. "But all that has gone out of the window."[4] Some of them may have once been "faces" at Chelsea; some may have been thugs or racists; one, years earlier, had written letters to mod fanzines talking about fighting "wogs"; but now, packed into this sweatbox with people they would never before have come into contact with, gays, musicians and older bohemians, they were changing. Some of them experienced the classic psychedelic epiphany – this drug could change the world! – but they were also astute enough to realise that it was probably better to keep it a secret.

Success brought its own problems. People were bringing their friends, the friends wanted to bring *their* friends, and soon there wasn't enough space for all of them in the same little room. Hundreds would be crushed outside Shoom as people fought to get Jenni Rampling's attention at the door, with the result that she got the reputation of being the most ruthless operator in town. Inevitably, some long-time regulars found they couldn't get in any more. "Jenni was hated, literally hated," says Jason Hawkins. "We used to call her Hitler."

Within a few weeks, the West End glitterati had discovered Shoom. At first they were barred: "There was a rule," says Steve Proctor, "no pop stars, no trendies in the club." But soon celebrities like Boy George, Patsy Kensit, Pete Wylie, Paul Rutherford of Frankie Goes to Hollywood, Martin Fry and Mark White of ABC, dancer Michael Clark, and journalists like Gary Crowley and Robert Elms were introduced to the club, and a chasm started to grow between its perceived ethos and its new fashionableness. Were they turning, so soon, into the people they had conspired to overthrow? "It was odd, because it was like when I was a punk – 'oh, we're not like the old stars' – but they *were* like the old stars, very cliquey," says Boy George.

Steve Proctor believes that the Ramplings were simply overwhelmed by their own good fortune, and didn't really know how to deal with it. "Bear in mind that Danny and Jenni both left school with very little qualifications, Danny was older but Jenni was very young, suddenly thrust into this trendy limelight and heralded. People used to be scared of Jenni because she used to be downright rude and arrogant, but it wasn't a calculated thing – she was a Bermondsey girl who would knock you out if you gave her a hard time. The only way she knew was straight talking."

villiers street and clink street

Ian St Paul was a larger-than-life character who radiated self-confidence, a natural PR man with more than a mouthful of hyperbole. He believed he could take the scene to another level, and convinced Paul Oakenfold that they should book Heaven for April 11th, 1988, a Monday night. "No one had ever done a club that size – 1,500 people – on a Monday night," says Oakenfold. "It was unheard of. Everybody was saying: 'You're fools, you've got a little club going, leave it at that, you can't do Monday night in London.' But Ian was so determined. He believed in it."

"Spectrum: Theatre of Madness", read the flyer. At its centre was a garish eyeball splashed with primary colours and bordered by psychedelic typefaces, the design adapted from a Grateful Dead poster from their Haight-Ashbury heyday. Heaven was the best-appointed discotheque in London, with an amazing sound rig, lasers and automated lighting gantries; no expense or effort was spared on the decor. But on the opening night, the only ones in the club were the Ibiza diehards – little over 100 people, way short of break-even, sharing free Ecstasy in an empty venue. By the third week, St Paul and Oakenfold were deep in debt and thinking of calling the whole thing off. Had they misjudged the city's mood? But Maggie and Roger Beard had faith; success was inevitable, they insisted. "We were on a cosmic hippie one about the whole thing. When we saw the flyer we knew it couldn't fail; Monday was a good day, Shiva's day, and there was a pagan temple near that part of London so the ley lines would have been right; the time was right and the drug was right." And so it proved. On the fourth week, out of nowhere, the queues stretched right round to Charing Cross station, and the curtain rose on the theatre of madness.

There has never been such a spectacular weekly event in London before or since. The wide green beam of Heaven's lasers captured the outstretched arms and convulsing fingers reaching through the dry ice. There would be incredible visual happenings halfway through the night – spaceships descending from the roof, pyrotechnic displays, rooms full of polystyrene balls, explosions of silver confetti, snowstorms blowing over the dancefloor. If Future was about Ibiza memories, Spectrum was about the future shock of acid house. Oakenfold and Johnny Walker pumped the big, diamond-sharp sound system, while upstairs in the VIP bar, where the Ibiza crowd would gather, Roger Beard and Terry Farley played obscure psychedelia and dub under a original, hand-made sixties slideshow provided by one of Beard's hippie friends. "Can you pass the acid test?" demanded the flyers for the first Spectrum all-day party, informing its clientele what was required in terms of drug intake: "On one all day!"

Towards the end of May 1988, the first feature about acid house was published in the youth magazine *i-D*, with photos of some of the core Ibiza crowd, including Spencer Guinere, Nancy Turner and Lisa McKay (who by now were both DJing, under the names Nancy Noise and Lisa Loud). The fresh-faced, barely post-adolescent bunch were dubbed "Amnesiacs", "beach bum hippies". MDMA wasn't mentioned directly, a conscious decision to protect the scene, although there were enough coded references to "the state of dance ecstasy" to get the idea across. "Peace and love mateys and get on one right now," it concluded. "Acieeed!"[5]

Up to this time, the Ramplings had encouraged press coverage on the condition that the articles didn't include the address of the club: "We wanted to keep it special. We wanted to hold on to what we had for as long as we could." They knew that when the youth media picked up on the scene, its development would inevitably be accelerated. What they didn't realise was exactly how much, and how this would ultimately take it beyond their control. Yet the strength of the formula they had helped create – Ecstasy plus house music equals mass euphoria – had its own irrepressible dynamic. It was literally too good to keep secret.

In May, the Ramplings, boosted by their remarkable success, moved Shoom to the YMCA on Tottenham Court Road in the West End and courted a fashionable crowd by giving out flyers at designer boutiques like Browns. They also published a magazine to introduce the new clientele to the club's ethic. Peppered with Smileys and naive poetry, it included snippets of letters to the Ramplings. "The greatest thing that Shoom creates is the freedom in which we can be ourselves," read one. "Shoom has never been a club," declared another, "it's just like one happy family, who care about each other." Yet as "peace and love" was projected as its public doctrine, the scene was fracturing within. The Ramplings had chosen Thursday for their new venture; the same night as Future. The tiny community was forced to choose between the two, and much bitterness accompanied the split. Oakenfold and Rampling fell out. Some believed Shoom had "gone commercial", betrayed its own philosophy. "I felt offended," says Blane Scanlon. "People lived for the club, it was like supporting your favourite team. You started getting the in crowd wanting to be part of it. It started getting plastic."

In Spectrum, too, the Ibiza veterans started to feel isolated amongst the crowds, surrounded by all these people they didn't know, who weren't part of the gang, who hadn't been there from the beginning – all whooping and screaming and dancing like they had the summer before, wearing their Day-Glo shorts and dungarees, even parroting their phrase, "acieed!" It seemed to them that these "acid teds", as *Boy's Own* dubbed them, were a caricature of their original spirit. "I hated it! I didn't even want to go out. We didn't want to go and mix with these people. We seemed to think that we were better than these people," says Marie Marden. "When we were a select few, we had a party, we felt special and everyone was made to feel special – 'oh I love you, you're my best mate' – we were all really really close because there was only a few of us. Once something blows up like that, you know you've lost your scene forever. Because now it was a money-making thing. When I think of it now, I could have had such a good time if I'd have been a little less stuck-up about it all."

As far as they were concerned, that unique, intimate warmth was dissipating. But in a chaotic social situation with no defined beliefs, suggests Roger Beard, it was inevitable that the reconstructed hippie idealism couldn't but be crushed under the weight of numbers. Apart from *Boy's Own*, which was becoming ever more sporadic, no one was attempting to verbalise the complexity of emotions people experienced. Acid house had only developed rituals for the night, Beard observes: "The problem with the scene was that it only really existed for the time that you were in a club, whereas the sixties was a much more all-encompassing thing. If you were a young hippie in the sixties you'd have had *International Times* or *Oz* magazine. All people had then was music magazines, which was a bit sad. It happened so quickly that it was such a short time before things got swamped and started to go wrong."

There were other reasons, too. People who were in it for fun at the beginning now saw it as a form of income. Either they were DJing, or running clubs, or they were selling drugs to the new initiates. The drug distribution system had stepped up a gear and it provided a way of living for and in the scene full-time; the £15 pills could finance a lifestyle of hedonism.

"Everyone was doing it – everyone was a drug dealer. Whether it was three or thirty, they were still selling," says one of the Ibiza crew. "When it started off, the drug was there, the music was there and we had Future and we had Shoom, that was fine. There wasn't a lot of people dealing, there was one person. You all ordered your drug, you'd come in, all stand there, 'one for you, one for you, one for you', all take them at the same time, bang, music on, great. There was no competition. When it did go into Spectrum, there were different gangs who would try to outdo other gangs. There'd be fellers that stood there and give the young kids drugs to sell and bring them back the money. When you've got five different gangs working in a club, things get a bit nasty. People get threatened. Everyone that was dancing at this time and being all this 'peace and love' and whatever, never ever saw this. But we did because it was our friends. Our friends were the five different gangs. So now they're arguing. A lot of friendship was lost over money."

Adam Heath had been arrested the week before Spectrum opened, and subsequently spent a year in prison; he was among the first people in Britain to be jailed for Ecstasy possession. But his imprisonment was no deterrent; one of the enduring narratives of Ecstasy culture is that people become so involved, wrapped up in the experience, that many start dealing, whether it's buying a few for their friends as part of what drug theorists call "mutual societies", or buying in bulk and selling them on; the law makes no differentiation: it's all drug dealing.

When Nicky Holloway opened The Trip at the Astoria on Charing Cross Road on June 4th, the scene officially went overground. Holloway stretched long white drapes across the cavernous hall and projected huge, technicolour images over the walls, with red globe lights glowing far back into the corners of the balcony, and thousands poured through the doors. Holloway, who had continued running his Special Branch soul nights up to this point, had seen a marketing opportunity that was too good to miss. The Shoom and Future élite damned him as a bandwagon-jumper who was cashing in on the acid teds. "Holloway spoilt it," says Jason Hawkins. "That's when it went full-on commercial. There was no style, it was for the masses, the sheep. Nicky Holloway's club was just Astoria, rammed full with people standing on the tables waving their hands in the air. They were acid teds and they didn't have a clue. They couldn't dance, they just stuck their arms in the air and waved them. All right, we might have put our hands in the air but our dancing was sort of like vogueing in a way, it was very fluid. We knew how to dance before we started dancing to acid house."

But The Trip was all that its name promised; it and Spectrum opened acid house out to the inner-city working class and packaged it for the media and record industry, drawing a multi-racial mix that was never really in evidence at Shoom or Future. Every inch of the Trip dancefloor, every table on the balcony, was filled by screaming, writhing maniacs in outlandish costumes. By this time, Ecstasy was everywhere; dealers were even propositioning punters under the Astoria's anti-drug notices and there were banners on the walls reading "acid" and "drugs". When The Trip closed at 3 a.m., the whole of Charing Cross Road would erupt into a street party, with people dancing on the roofs of cars and in the fountains beneath the Centre Point office block.

The police arrived to disperse the raging mob, but hesitated, confused; when they switched their sirens on, the Day-Glo freaks started jumping up and down and shouting: *"Can you feel it?!"* They could hardly have known that the siren and slogan formed the refrain to Todd Terry's raucous house classic, *Can You Party?*

Ibiza, Shoom, Spectrum, The Trip; this is the endlessly repeated, "official" history of acid house, yet like all official histories, it leaves much else untold. Perhaps it's because the people who graduated from Shoom had good access to the pop media and went on to base careers on their own mythology that *a* story became accepted as *the* story. But there was another important strand within London house culture, composed of people who had never been and had no interest in going to Ibiza. Instead they had connections with black dance collectives like Soul II Soul and Shock, and roots in the urban warehouse party phenomenon dating back to the turn of the eighties and legendary illegal events like Dirtbox and the Wharehouse. They also drew on black British narratives from reggae and soul traditions; the sound systems and MCs chatting over dub plates. There was a strong link with north London clubs like Camden Palace, a venue inspired by New York's Studio 54 but set in prosaic Camden High Street, where Eddie Richards and Colin Faver had played electro and early house, and where in the early eighties there was also a small but significant Ecstasy fraternity connected to Marc Almond's Soft Cell. Jazzy M's *Jackin' Zone* radio show on the pirate LWR, which showcased the latest imports from Chicago, Detroit and New York, was also a powerful force in creating an audience for house music in the inner city that was not mediated by Ibiza or what one of its listeners calls "that same old white-boy power".

These people felt excluded by Shoom's suburban south London majority. As Richard West, a former milkman from north London who rapped over Richards' and Faver's records at Camden Palace under the name Mr C, explains, to them the

Balearic records sounded like nothing more than pop music (which, of course, many of them were). "Shoom was very important in the whole thing because at a very early date it showed you the difference between the lightweight fluffy shit and the real deal. Shoom was pop. *Lovely*, if that's what you like," he sneers sarcastically. "It *was* very spiritual down there. Everyone was on MDMA for the first time. You had 400 people completely loved-up to bits. 'Course it was good. 'Course it was spiritual. 'Course it had lots of lovely vibes. But what did it represent? Look at it for what it was. It was a pop club. Musically and socially, it was a pop club, and it was very white. It wasn't mixed, it wasn't integrated, it wasn't raw, it wasn't raunchy, it wasn't dangerous, it wasn't rebellious, it wasn't dark. It was happy and fluffy."

North London couple Paul Stone and Lu Vukovic had been inspired by the first warehouse parties of the Ecstasy era, which took place from February to April out by the Hangar Lane gyratory system on the western fringes of the city and were titled, appropriately enough, Hedonism. They booked some rooms in a recording studio on Clink Street in the shadow of London Bridge, not far from Shoom's base at the Fitness Centre and close to the London Dungeons. Though the area has subsequently been gentrified, in 1988 that warren of streets was dark, dilapidated, desolate and rather scary. The only sign of humanity would be the nearby market, which would spring into life just before dawn, the lorry drivers and traders bemused at the danced-out, dishevelled clubbers wandering home sweaty and exhausted. The inside of Clink Street Studios was a mirror of its exterior: a run-down, dingy, labyrinthine building within which you were never sure where a door might lead, and where the walls were moist with perspiration – or was it rising damp?

Stone and Vukovic's flyer simply stated: "RIP – Techno, Acid, Garage", but the entertainment they provided, week after week until the end of 1988, every Saturday and sometimes Friday and Sunday nights as well, was far more complex and experimental.

As well as the core DJs, Kid Batchelor, Eddie Richards and Mr C, there would be rappers, singers, keyboard players; like the reggae rigs, they turned sequenced music into performance: a formula that would become particularly influential on one of the bands that frequented the club, the Shamen.

"Amazing things happened," remembers Vukovic, "like one morning the sun was rising and everyone was completely tripping on the energy and the emotion and the feeling of it all, someone shouted out 'bring down the walls!' and they all started jumping up, trying to take the room apart, to actually bring down the walls! No amount of words could describe that euphoria, that sense of belonging, that possibility. The bond was tremendous between those people, it was like they were part of your family."

There was no opulent Spectrum decor here, just a relentless strobe light and a dense fug of dry ice that never seemed to clear. The atmosphere was deliciously dangerous. "Every week there were people trying to climb up drainpipes, giving backhanders of £20 to doormen to get in, doormen having to fight people off with baseball bats and dogs because they were going to rush the doors. Complete madness," says Mr C. "The crowd were the most ugly people you've ever seen in your life and the most beautiful people you've ever seen in your life, all in the same room. People with big ugly scars, villains, thugs, and on the other hand beautiful, well-groomed, good-looking, sharp, nice, fashionable people. Then you had your acid housers in Day-Glo, people in tracksuits, people in suits, all sorts. Every colour, creed, combination; it was totally mixed. I've never seen a club like it since."

Vukovic was motivated by naive idealism; coming from an anarchist punk background, she believed the scene had the potential to be a political force for change, that it was inherently anti-establishment. She banned cameras, excluded journalists and discouraged press coverage, and consequently RIP never became a club legend in the way Shoom and Spectrum did.

"Shoom was a bit more accessible from a press point of view.

They felt more comfortable writing about places like that than something like Clink Street, which was a bit too street, too rough and ready," says Eddie Richards. Indeed, the Shoom disciples found it heavy, hard-core, extreme. "Clink Street was slummier, dodgier. Dodgier characters on the door, dodgier characters inside, a dodgier feeling about it. I think it was a bit frightening. Really frightening at times," continues Richards. "They didn't see that as a 'movement', if you like, because it was just people doing their own thing and it didn't look like anything special, but Shoom did because it had that more organised quality about it, and it just seemed to take all the credit."

Yet Clink Street, like Spectrum and The Trip, was instrumental in evangelising acid house, acting out the inclusive ideology which the original Shoom crowd had set in motion, and showing that house culture was an infinitely adaptable experience that changed shape and form depending on who was involved, where and why.

charing cross road

With RIP, Spectrum and The Trip in full cry, the "summer of love" began in earnest. This was the point when house culture ceased, for ever, to be one unified entity, the beginning of a process of diversification which would accelerate, creating innumerable sub-subcultures and sub-genres over years to come, to the point when many of them would no longer be traceable to source. In June and July, scores of West End venues switched from funk to acid house overnight, and the whole hierarchy of London club culture was turned upside down.

"There were people who one day were the hippest in London and literally a week later looked like dinosaurs," explains Sheryl Garratt, then features editor at *The Face*, which like all the youth press struggled to keep pace with the incredible velocity of change. "That whole Wag culture, dressing in dark colours leaning against the bar sucking your cheeks in, trying to look cool, suddenly those people looked like they were ninety years old. Suddenly people were wearing bright colours, huge grins and hugging each other."

The state of grace could not continue. On August 17th, three months after the first press coverage, mass market tabloid *The Sun* published an investigation into the new drug scene at Richard Branson's nightclub, Heaven, complete with a picture of a blotter of acid. "Scandal of the £5 drug trip to Heaven," read the headline. "LSD – a favourite with 1970s dropouts – is now popular with yuppies," it continued. "Junkies flaunt their craving by wearing T-shirts sold at the club bearing messages like 'Can you feel it' and 'Drop acid not bombs' . . . On the packed dance floor, youths in surf shorts stripped to the waist flailed their arms to the pounding beat . . . The youngsters, mainly in their mid-twenties, try to escape the pressure of work by getting high on acid every weekend."[6] The paper took the term "acid house" literally, imagining that acid meant LSD. The naivety now seems laughable – how could they not notice that people were taking Ecstasy, when every other person seemed to be trying to sell you the stuff?

The following Monday, Richard Branson came down to Spectrum and ambled around, surveying the mayhem. As an entrepreneur who had built his business on the hippie movement, he wasn't overly shocked, although *The Sun* subsequently painted this "drug swoop" as a victory for its investigative expertise. "He wasn't pissed off," says Paul Oakenfold, "because if he was pissed off he would have turned round and said: 'Close the club and get out.' He said: 'Don't close the club, but change the name so it looks from the media's point of view that the club's been closed down, have a month's break and reopen.' " In October, the curtain fell on the Theatre of Madness for the last time (although it would reopen almost immediately and run for years as the Land of Oz). "Spectrum had done its job," says Oakenfold.

"It had set the scene up, it had set the youth culture up as it is now."

The tabloid press initially took a paradoxical stance. While insisting that Branson shut Spectrum down, *The Sun* printed an "acid house fashion guide" and began marketing its own Smiley T-shirt. "It's groovy and cool!" the blurb burbled. "Only £5.50, man."[7] Just one week later, however, the paper began a series of articles on the "evil of Ecstasy – danger drug that is sweeping discos and ruining lives". *Sun* medical correspondent Vernon Coleman warned: "You will hallucinate. For example, if you don't like spiders you'll start seeing giant ones . . . Hallucinations can last up to 12 hours . . . There's a good chance you'll end up in a mental hospital for life . . . If you're young enough there's a good chance you'll be sexually assaulted while under the influence. You may not even know until a few days or weeks later."[8]

Hysteria took hold immediately. Rentaquote Tory MPs claimed acid house was corrupting innocent youth; Sir Ralph Halpern banned Smiley shirts from his Top Shop retail chain; the prime-time BBC chart show *Top of the Pops* declared a moratorium on all records containing the word "acid" after D Mob's Astoria anthem *We Call It Acieed* reached number three that month.

Britain's second Ecstasy death (the first was twenty-year-old Ian Larcombe, who had swallowed a bag of eighteen tablets and suffered a fatal heart attack after being stopped by police on the way to a club in June 1988) appeared to validate the panic. On October 28th, Janet Mayes, a twenty-one-year-old nanny, took two Ecstasy pills, one more than usual, at a party at the Jolly Boatman pub in Hampton Court, Surrey. She collapsed and was dead on arrival at hospital. Her parents symbolically burned her Smiley T-shirt, flares and beads, declaring them evil. The man who sold her the drugs was sentenced to 180 hours community service, and *The Sun* dropped its Smiley T-shirt offer and launched a "Say No to Drugs" campaign with a frowning Smiley logo.

The police, although they insisted that acid house did not represent a major problem, began an extensive series of raids on the many illegal acid house parties that had sprung up in deserted warehouses and industrial units all around the capital, culminating in Operation Seagull, a raid on a boat party on the Thames at Greenwich on November 4th. East London-based promoters Robert Darby and Leslie Thomas were subsequently found guilty of "conspiring to manage premises where drugs were supplied" and sentenced to ten and six years respectively. Things were getting serious; acid house was no longer a game. "It was an excellent result," Detective Chief Inspector Albert Patrick crowed. "The first conviction of its kind in the country."

Up to this point, Ecstasy hadn't really been seen as a "drug", not like heroin or cocaine were "drugs". "Heroin," promised a government drug awareness campaign of the eighties, "screws you up." But this wasn't seedy, depressing smack; this was life-affirming, joyous Ecstasy! As John Jolly of drugs agency Release noted sagaciously: "Many of the people who are taking Ecstasy at acid house parties and in other places are the sort who would not normally dream of taking illicit drugs."[9]

No one – tabloids, drug agencies or clubbers – really knew that much about MDMA at all. The only medical information that the clubbers had were ancient scare stories that had somehow filtered through from America, rumours about Ecstasy causing Parkinson's Disease, or draining spinal fluid. The latter tale was embraced as fact. "Everybody was talking about it and everybody believed it, which was stupid – people were dancing so much that they got backache," says Jon Marsh, singer with The Beloved, an indie pop group whose trajectory was transformed by Shoom, "but it was accepted wisdom." The underlying significance was that after a year of taking Ecstasy they had discerned from empirical evidence that this wasn't the free ride they once though it to be; people were feeling burned-out, as if they had fried their neural circuits.

Their experiences were typical of users before and since. After taking the drug regularly for a few months, the body tends to become accustomed to Ecstasy's physical effects and the mind has explored the contours of the experience. In a sequence of diminishing returns and systematically decreasing enjoyment, the high becomes less intense and the rush less euphoric. The after-effects appear more pronounced, less easily negotiated: the blank Sunday comedown, the grey midweek negativity. But when something's so great, you naturally want to do it again. And again, and again, and again. Although it is not physically addictive, the Ecstasy experience can become *psychologically* compulsive, especially when it is linked to such an alluring lifestyle, such wonderful music. For some there is an unstoppable temptation to take more: two, three, four, five, six Es a night (the impulse seems particular to men – drug researchers have even given it a name, "macho ingestion syndrome"). The fact that the British club scene has thrown up so many slang phrases for this condition – cabbaged, monged, caned, etc. – is significant in itself. Bingeing, too, tends to reduce the empathetic effects: the sensation becomes jittery, amphetamine-like.

Unique amongst recreational drugs, MDMA appears to regulate its own usage; it has a kind of built-in "pharmacological limiting factor" that deters long-term abuse.[10] Even Alexander Shulgin has commented: "I am completely convinced, in what I have heard from others and from my own findings, that with repeated exposure to Ecstasy, the extraordinary impact which is its particular signature is lost after the first few uses. I have no idea if this is due to physical changes in the brain making the unique magic no longer expressible, or to psychological learning that makes it no longer needed. The Ecstasy experience continues to be rich and useful, but that special something seems gone. It is remembered, but not re-experienced."[11]

Put simply, once you've reached the peak of human experience, you can't get any higher. After that there's only two ways to go, straight on over the edge or cut down, accept the disillusionment, that things can never be the same again. As Jon

Marsh points out: "The problem for anybody is that if it is absolutely the sum total of all the best things that you feel are happening to you in your life, then that's the slippery slope because you just keep chasing after it and you can't avoid the fact that it doesn't ever become *more* exciting, it only becomes *less* – that's the nature of the human capacity to experience joy and pleasure. It's how people respond to the dawning awareness of that scenario that really matters."

For the original Ibiza crowd, the innocence had evaporated months ago; the honeymoon was over. Now many of them were *losing it* – to use the argot that grew up alongside the condition – particularly those who were dealing and had access to large quantities. Some, who would initially be content with one pill a night, were now into double figures. Others were cranking up the buzz with cocaine; with the amounts of tax-free cash they were carrying, they could afford it. And there had always been a little fraternity at Shoom who would top up their E with LSD, or cruise through Sunday tripping. "Acid in the morning," recalls one. "Going out, doing loads of E, coming home, messing about, then doing a trip for the day. We used to go to all the sights – one week we'd do the Planetarium, Madame Tussauds, then Battersea Park, then the Serpentine, then London Zoo."

Now, as some of them increased their dosage, they were finding it increasingly difficult to return to consensus reality. One Shoomer gave away all his possessions and the following weekend was seen running naked down Portobello Road. Others came to believe that there were supernatural forces of Good and Evil battling for the soul of the city; that the biblical Apocalypse was nigh. "Good people I know lost their minds," says Danny Rampling, "mainly through tripping, losing it on E, over-indulging in good times. But that's always going to be the way, people that take things too far, look a bit too deep into things with acid." A few, lost in Shoom, convinced themselves that Rampling was God, the master of the dance, the orchestrator of emotions. The intensity of feeling directed at him can be seen in a telling photograph taken at the Fitness Centre in August 1988; all you can see is arms stretching out to touch Rampling's skinny body, and the DJ beaming back from behind the turntables: a portrait of unrequited devotion that is reminiscent of a religious tableau.

"Danny and Jenni suffered a massive onslaught of people's demands – people demanding to have their own questions and emotions answered and explained," says Steve Proctor. "Danny and Jenni didn't have the answers; they never said they did have the answers. A lot of people who had very little experience of life prior to that and were not mentally, intellectually or emotionally prepared came down with a hard bump. There's people still out there in the country in homes, who couldn't deal with the reality that the rest of life wasn't going to be like this."

And there were one or two turning to heroin, ex-junkies who had been clean for a year but by the end of 1988 were slipping back into old ways. A Christmas collection for a computer for Jenni Rampling to automate her mailing list was blown by one notorious Shoomer on a smack binge. "To those who stole, spent or borrowed (call it what you like!) EVERYONE'S money," raged the Shoom newsletter, "find yourselves another club to go to – because you're not welcome at ours!" Then there were inexplicable illnesses. Everyone seemed to have flu or some strange bronchial condition. Was it the drug, they asked themselves, or was it paranoia?

Because some people thought that this was all that mattered, that they had discovered the meaning of life, going back to dull nine-to-fives seemed pointless. "Everyone wanted to drop out, no one wanted to go to work," says Marie Marden. "I thought the world was going to stop. People were giving up their jobs, people were getting the sack and just selling drugs. I was frightened about little people doing things they shouldn't be doing, and if they got caught, what was going to happen to them? I don't think anyone realised how heavy the situation was." The Ramplings sent out an impassioned message in the Shoom newsletter: "Don't give up your day jobs." By this time they had realised that you couldn't live in a dream world.

Bigger dealers from outside the scene were moving in on the clubbers who ran the London Ecstasy trade. Football gangs were getting involved, using violence and threats. Club bouncers were exerting their muscle to grab a slice of the proceeds. "Everybody wanted E," explains Adam Heath, "and if you had it, you were earning money, bags of money. That's where the thuggery came in." One of the main club promoters had set up a deal involving 12,000 Ecstasy pills with some of the original Ibiza fraternity from the north. His flat had become open house for post-club champagne and cocaine sessions, and he was increasingly indiscreet about his illegal sidelines. Instead of paying him, the northern boys sprayed his eyes with ammonia, leaving him in hospital with two months of temporary blindness. "I was very bitter," he says. "After everything I'd done, I didn't think I deserved that."

As 1988 rolled into 1989, acid house continued to grow and change beyond recognition. Many of the original participants could not deal with what it had become – "commercial", "mainstream", "overground"; clubs full of acid teds; cheap and nasty "Where's the Acid Party?" T-shirts on Oxford Street stalls. It was no longer *their* scene. Dreams were dashed, disillusionment set in, some just got plain bored. Some of the Ibiza crowd hit the road again, travelling, searching; to Thailand, India, America, Hong Kong. A few, for whom Ecstasy had opened up spiritual horizons, found solace in religion, joining the Jehovah's Witnesses, the Hare Krishnas, getting involved with Bhagwan Shree Rajneesh or other New Age cults.

The majority just rationalised the experience – *nothing lasts for ever* – pulled their sanity back into place and got on with their lives. In the re-entry period after the comedown, many became cultural entrepreneurs, setting up clubs, record companies, shops and small businesses to service the scene, helping to establish a coherent infrastructure for a dance market that would support them for years to come. They were, says Paul Oakenfold, turning inspiration into action: "Ecstasy makes you think: 'I could do this, I'm going to do it.' And you do it." Using the new technologies of pleasure, they were attempting to take control of their own leisure time – and their destiny.

3

magical mystery tour

In this era of extraordinary alliances, few were as unlikely and spectacular as the one between Tony Colston-Hayter and David Roberts. The son of a university lecturer and a solicitor, whose parents had divorced during his early childhood, Colston-Hayter demonstrated his entrepreneurial flair before he had even left school. At Stantonbury Campus, a progressive comprehensive in Buckinghamshire, he not only developed an aptitude for video games but started three companies, Colston Automatics, Colston Leisure and Colston Marketing, to rent out the games machines. He even rented one to his school. The company claimed a turnover of £1 million, then went bust, but not before Colston-Hayter had developed a taste for the adrenalin charge of gambling for high stakes. He became an expert on the blackjack tables, and within a year, so his self-made myth runs, he had won around £100,000 and reached the point where he had to enter casinos disguised in a wig and sunglasses, his repute being such that he was barred from most of them. The young prodigy, with his fresh-faced arrogance and shock of thick, dark hair, loved the subterfuge and the thrill of outwitting the establishment – making money, losing it, making more – not to mention the champagne celebrations and late nights.

Dave Roberts, on the other hand, was a black, working-class north Londoner; his brothers were well-known "faces" at Arsenal's Highbury ground and, he hints, "as a kid I'd done some things I shouldn't have done". Roberts had a forceful, radiant personality and an almost incendiary will to achieve. Like Colston-Hayter, he liked to be noticed; he wore the most expensive clothes, silk suits and shoes from Bond Street, and frequented the West End's most exclusive funk clubs.

In 1987, their paths crossed for the first time. Roberts, then twenty-three, was working in the property business, Colston-Hayter, twenty-one, was thinking about getting into property; both wanted to make money fast and spend it just as quickly, scheming by day and partying all night. They hit it off immediately. Colston-Hayter would come to London and Roberts would take him to illegal after-hours dives like the Cotton Club in Stoke Newington; Roberts would visit Milton Keynes, where Colston-Hayter already got the VIP treatment in local clubs, then carry on carousing back at his house in the nearby village of Winslow. Their blossoming friendship coincided with the first flowering of Ecstasy culture. Although at that time the scene was tiny, the brightest, boldest characters in the nocturnal pantheon were drawn to it immediately. Naturally, early in 1988 Roberts and Colston-Hayter ended up at Shoom. "Amazing weekend," recalls Roberts. "The brilliant thing about it was everyone was on the same thing and everyone was so friendly, it was like you'd known them all your life. The music and the drug worked so well. The music was so crazy. The dance you danced to it wasn't posed, it was joy. It was so powerful when the whole club was doing it."

While this sounds like the typical conversion experience, the kind most clubbers will recount, Roberts and Colston-Hayter were far from typical. Their larger-than-life personalities and insatiable hunger for thrills ensured they made an impact, even in an environment where flamboyance was common currency. Danny Rampling remembers how Colston-Hayter would come down to Shoom after a gambling spree carrying thousands in cash, entourage in tow, guzzling endless bottles of champagne and boasting of his winnings. Initially the Shoomers found his showiness entertaining. "He's a bit eccentric, he likes himself," says Lisa McKay. "He used to say: 'I'm an entrepreneur, darling.' It's funny, he went through a stage of everybody liking him, then everybody absolutely hating him." Colston-Hayter was brash and self-assured, yet retained an almost adolescent eagerness to be part of a scene which had so much vibrancy and colour.

The problem was that, as more people were drawn to acid house, the Ibiza veterans began to close ranks in an attempt to protect their fracturing community from interlopers – and Flash Harrys like Colston-Hayter and Roberts just weren't part of the gang. By this time, Steve Proctor recalls, Colston-Hayter was considered "a loud dickhead, a laughing stock" within the scene. As Shoom's door policy hardened, the duo could no longer get their friends into the club. "The Shoom people just wanted to keep it to their own cliquey little fucking bunch," says Roberts. "They wouldn't let no one in, they wanted to keep it for themselves."

Meanwhile, The Trip had opened at the Astoria; no exclusive door policy here, which suited Dave Roberts and his posse perfectly. "In Astoria we were kings, we used to dance on the tables, leading the whole crowd, buzzing, wild. We used to come outside, pick the car up, turn the sounds on and everyone would have a street party, the road blocked, everyone rocking. Madness, man, pure madness, rocking on bus stops, in the fountain by Centre Point. Purely spontaneous, it just happened."

If Shoom was a great club, Spectrum and The Trip were great *concepts*. Outlandish decor and hypnotic music, awesome sound and lights, and every inch of floor space covered with frenzied, jerking bodies. Hundreds queued eagerly outside, desperate to toss their money into the humming tills. It would be uncharitable to say that Colston-Hayter saw Spectrum and thought profit. Over the months that followed, he would be typecast as a ruthless, acquisitive spiv whose only interest in acid house was business, but – certainly in its initial stages – he genuinely loved the scene. In fact he was probably closer to iconic 1960s pop biz grafters like Rolling Stones manager Andrew Loog Oldham, who turned the chaos of Tin Pan Alley into cash.

Colston-Hayter had already made tentative moves into club promotion, running a few small, unspectacular events. What he had seen at Spectrum and The Trip convinced him that the scene could, and should, be opened outwards – parties for thousands, not hundreds. He imagined all classes, all races dancing together – what it was *supposed* to be all about. "Shoom was a very closed shop, and also it was all white," he says. "I didn't see why it should just be kept to a special few." His first Apocalypse Now events at Wembley Studios in August 1988 drew in a diverse cross-section of London's clubland; not just the West End faces, but a wider constituency cutting across lines of class and colour.

In September, the first wave of tabloid hysteria was breaking, the police were beginning to shut down warehouse parties and the Ramplings were attempting to enforce a media blackout. But Colston-Hayter was so enthused that he made a move that would compound his banishment from the Balearic élite: ITN's *News at Ten* was invited down to document the amazing Apocalypse Now success story. "I remember Jenni Rampling at the door saying to anyone who was at Shoom: 'Don't go in there, there's cameras in there,' " says Terry Farley. "I remember a girl having a bad trip and the cameras trying to film it, and people screaming at the cameras. It was very, very weird." Not only had Colston-Hayter betrayed the scene for his own ego gratification, the reasoning went, but he had sold out something that he had no real rights to in the first place.

"The [police] Club Squad did adopt a softly softly approach until the media 'discovered' acid house. Now though, following last week's ITN News report showing drug dealing and Gawd-knows-what at Apocalypse Now, the boys in blue bandannas are closing every warehouse party they hear of," wrote *Time Out* club correspondent Dave Swindells afterwards.

"It had to happen: the police have to be seen to be doing

something and they're never very pleasant when they're 'forced' to act. Quite why they were let in to film at all is a mystery. Of course, the TV crews weren't interested in a story which chronicles the euphoric reaction to house music and Balearic Beats because young people having a good time in clubs isn't newsworthy. However, that's what they said they were going to do. Paul Oakenfold had a half-hour interview about house music followed by a few pointed questions on the drug aspect of the scene. You can guess which was broadcast."[1]

Afterwards, Colston-Hayter renamed his organisation Sunrise, a name which, he says, came to him at dawn, through a pollen haze, while weekending in Amsterdam. But he immediately felt the knock-on effect of the wrath he had incurred; the first Sunrise party in October was halted by the police and he lost all the money he had made. For a professional gambler, however, this was a setback to be overcome by superior strategy and cunning. If the police were making life difficult in London, he would go elsewhere. He sold a thousand tickets for a Sunrise Mystery Trip and laid on coaches to transport clubbers from central London to Iver Heath in the wilds of Buckinghamshire, where he had hired an equestrian centre. Flares burned along the wooded approach road, and as the coaches drew nearer, lasers flashed into the sky and a low hum slowly became recognisable as the throb of house music.

Colston-Hayter wanted to create a hedonist wonderland; he had even hired a children's bouncy castle for clubbers to cavort upon like weightless astronauts. After the confined intensity of inner-city warehouses, the spectacle was breath-taking, like being freed into a fantasy playground sparkling with the fairy dust of MDMA. At the peak of the night, the lights went off, the building filled with dry ice and in total darkness Steve Proctor dropped the needle on the majestic opening chords of Richard Strauss's *Also Sprach Zarathustra*, the theme from *2001: A Space Odyssey*. As the portentous orchestra swelled, a green laser strafed the clouds of dry ice and hundreds of arms raised in unison, cutting through the smoke; all that was visible from the DJ's raised platform were disembodied hands, reaching outwards as if to touch the heavens, frozen in the strobe lights like a weird HR Giger machine.

"Fucking hell!" exclaims Proctor, still awed by the memory years afterwards. "I'd been DJing for eight years then and I thought I'd seen some crazy things, but to be that far down the line and to experience something like that was fucking mindblowing." As dawn broke, people frolicked with the horses and gathered flowers to weave through each other's hair, while Proctor attempted to capture the feeling in music, closing with the Beatles' *Magical Mystery Tour* and Bobby McFerrin's *Don't Worry, Be Happy.* Although, in chronological terms, this was the end of the first acid house Summer of Love, the Mystery Tour in fact signalled the beginning of the second. A new, technologically enhanced environment for the Ecstasy experience had been invented.

That same week, back in the capital, Janet Mayes had become the second person in Britain to die after taking Ecstasy, and the police were turning up the heat on acid house. But Colston-Hayter was emboldened by success and chose a huge venue for his next party, a derelict gasworks set in waste ground at the mouth of the Blackwall Tunnel where Stanley Kubrick's Vietnam movie *Full Metal Jacket* had been shot. The Sunrise Guy Fawkes Edition promised a huge, opulent production, and 3,000 tickets were sold. But as the event began, the area was besieged by riot police, who roadblocked the approach road and shut down the music. People swarmed over dual carriageways and scrambled over barbed wire fences, and at 5 a.m. the police eventually capitulated and withdrew.

For the Ibiza hard core, the ugliness of confrontation was proof enough that Colston-Hayter had soured their spirit. "I remember walking in and there was a line of guys going 'Es, trips, Es, trips', and very young girls falling over and being sick," says Terry Farley, who DJed at the party. "It was very cold, and it was very obvious that it wasn't right. Something that seemed all warm and cuddly at Shoom suddenly seemed really cold and rather nasty." What was more, the promoters had been captured on film, and now the tabloid press had their demon incarnate: luring in fifteen year olds and making tens of thousands of pounds from an "evil night of Ecstasy" was the "Acid House King", Tony Colston-Hayter.[2]

Although the ritualised sequence of moral panic – exaggerated press reports, misleading headlines, self-appointed moral spokesmen demanding action, and weekend on weekend of police raids – was unfolding around him, he wasn't discouraged. Sunrise teamed up with Genesis, who had a formidable reputation as the East End's most fearless and consistent warehouse party organisers, to stage Christmas and New Year's bashes in Leeside Road, Hackney, under the banner of Sunset. It was here that Colston-Hayter came face to face with a more volatile and dangerous force than the police. A firm of former West Ham football "faces" demanded, with menaces, a cut of the take for a party on "their" patch. Colston-Hayter called in Dave Roberts, who until then hadn't been part of the business. "All I brought into it was the stability to control the football thugs and the people that were thinking wrong at the time," says Roberts. "Tony is too soft, he was being taken advantage of."

The most romantic version of ensuing events has Colston-Hayter slipping unnoticed from the warehouse with a suitcase stuffed with banknotes, leaving the West Ham mob frustrated and fuming. Whatever the truth, the result was another complete strategic rethink. Colston-Hayter had to survive as he had begun, through the power of his imagination. If he hadn't, the following summer would have taken another course entirely.

Acid house was such a seductive leisure concept that everyone wanted in, and it was inevitable that the newcomers would carry it off in unforeseen directions, often to the disgust and disbelief of those who came before them. The tabloid (and broadsheet) outrage of autumn 1988 was virtually an advertisement for Ecstasy culture. Loud music! Drugs! All-night dancing! What inquisitive young person could resist such enticements? Just as in the Haight-Ashbury of 1967, publicity accelerated the evolution of the scene and swelled its numbers, but also attracted the attentions of profiteers. The scene had been founded on entrepreneurialism, but now people who had little personally invested in it were becoming involved in its development. The *business* of acid house was under way.

"Most other people had come from enjoying it, going mad and because of that thinking: 'I can do a club as well.' I came from a completely business angle, thinking: 'There's got to be some money in it.' At first I couldn't stand the music and because I didn't take drugs either I was an outsider. I'd go out in a suit and tie, and everyone at these clubs would be in tracksuits, dancing away, sweating like mad!"

Jeremy Taylor already knew Tony Colston-Hayter through the Gatecrasher Balls, parties staged in the school holidays where upper-class youth ("Hooray Henrys and Henriettas", in the argot of the time) could get drunk, dance and grope each other. They were often "exposed" in the tabloids, which usually pictured a sozzled Henry with his hand up a catatonic Henrietta's skirt. Colston-Hayter would come down and run the blackjack and roulette tables. By the end of 1988, Taylor, then aged twenty-one, had discontinued the Balls and was looking for a new opening. His friend Quentin ("Tintin") Chambers, two years younger with a similar public school background to Taylor, was a face amongst an affluent Chelsea set who had begun to frequent Spectrum. He insisted that acid house had the business potential Taylor was seeking, and the two began to organise small parties.

After a few months without success, they managed to bag a prime Friday slot at a large West End venue, Shaftesburys. Fun City was an instant hit; its resident DJ, Fabio (Fitzroy Heslop), was hammering a harder, energetic, instrumental strain of house that the younger dancers loved. Adamski (Adam Tinley), a former squat-punk who had bought a digital sampler and a Roland drum computer and would soon become the first acid house pop star, supplied stripped-down, spiky live techno. Numbers were swelled further by the involvement of "Anton the Pirate", a genial, enthusiastic white man with long dread-locked hair who had become a ubiquitous club face during the summer of 1988. Taylor and Chambers – alias Karma Productions – were in business.

On May bank holiday weekend, they hired Westway Film Studios and attempted to stage the most spectacular acid house party yet. The promotional flyer for Energy read like a stock-broker's salary scale: 15K of water-cooled lasers, 25K of projections, illuminations and imagery, 30K of turbo sound, plus 12 DJs, five rooms, bouncy castle, helter skelter, dodgems . . . By nineties standards, the ticket price of £15 is modest; at the time, it was more than twice what West End clubs were charging. Fortunately, the decor lived up to the hype: one room resembled a Greek temple with Ionic columns, another looked like a scene from *Blade Runner*. Afterwards, as the last few dancers sat blissed-out in the morning light outside the studios, the consensus was that Energy had set new standards. "Beat this," they seemed to be saying to Sunrise.

Meanwhile, Tony Colston-Hayter had headed back into the countryside to escape the unwanted attentions of police, press and potential extorters. After the nightmares at Greenwich and Hackney he had been doing some serious thinking. Since his video-gaming childhood, he had been a gadget freak; he loved tele-pagers and mobile phones, which had been introduced to Britain three years earlier and were still relatively exotic, carica-tured as a yuppie accessory. How, he mused, could he keep the party's location secret until the last minute and throw the police off his track?

He found the answer in British Telecom's Voice Bank system, which would allow him numerous lines into a single answering machine and enable him to change the message remotely, from a cellular phone at the site. Thus he could direct partygoers to an area, wait until the convoys of cars reached critical mass, then release the exact address over the Voice Bank and fill the venue before the police could intervene. And, of course, the premium-rate lines were also profitable. Just as house music had been born from new interpretations of music technology, Colston-Hayter had invented a new function for communications technology, and it put him one step ahead for months to come.

Dave Roberts was now a full partner, and World Wide Productions, as they called themselves, had two brand names: Sunrise, and Roberts's new Back to the Future. But even though the hysteria had temporarily abated, the tabloid publicity about acid house meant that they were finding it increasingly difficult to book venues. They would send out scouting teams to remote farms, telling the owners they wanted to hire their property for a few hundred pounds for a film shoot or a satellite TV broadcast. Sometimes the police would catch wind of the scheme and pressure the farmer into pulling out; often Colston-Hayter and Roberts would only secure a venue hours before opening time, as at Back to the Future 2 at South Warnborough in April 1989, when they had to settle for a cattle silo half full of animal feed. The partygoers took it in good humour; they thought the reeking mound of pellets made a lovely playground slide.

The next month, Sunrise 5000: Once in a Blue Moon was scheduled for an aircraft hangar at Santa Pod racetrack. By now, Colston-Hayter had a membership scheme and was pyramid-selling his tickets via agents, an idea he had gleaned from society balls, and had built up a mailing list of 6,000. But again, however organised the financial side, the production was fraught; arriving at the site, Colston-Hayter found there was no electricity and no toilets, and had to take risks with a diesel generator running on dodgy wiring right next to a potentially inflammable heap of newsprint, and only four toilet cubicles for thousands of people. But Sunrise 5000 had indeed attracted 5,000, and both partners were jubilant. "By this time no one could touch us," says Roberts. "We knew we'd cracked it."

white waltham, berkshire

**"Sway with the rush, rush with the sway,
It's time to play, hip hip hooray!
Them take cocaine, them blow their brain, them go insane ...
I take an *E*!
I feel irie!"
MC rapping at Helter Skelter rave, September 30th, 1989**

The summer of '89 had arrived, and what a long, fine summer it was, the hottest for over a decade. The days seemed to stretch endlessly into balmy, pleasant nights; a great British summer is so rare that when it comes it seems to raise the national mood and infuse the whole country with an unstoppable will to pleasure. While the events of 1989 would have happened anyway, there's no question that the weather enhanced and prolonged them, and perhaps even altered their very nature. Whereas last summer's scene had been about dark clubs and dank warehouses, meeting places for a secret society with its own language and codes, this year, out in the countryside on the communal mystery trip, it seemed more open, freer, less uptight and exclusive. Anyone could join in for the price of a ticket and a pill; £30 would buy you a journey into the unknown and an opening into a phantasmagorical world of sound and light. This year, or so it felt, everyone was a fellow traveller on Hermann Hesse's *Journey to the East*; perhaps they weren't entirely sure where they were headed, but for now they were just sitting back and enjoying a high, wild ride.

The terminology had changed; the only people who talked about "acid house parties" now were the press. This year, people were calling the bigger, spectacular parties "raves", a term inherited, like so many other aspects of the culture, from the black soul scene (although it had been used as early as 1961 by the *Daily Mail* to describe young revellers at a jazz festival, and countercultural magazine *International Times* had launched itself with what it billed as an "all night rave" featuring Pink Floyd at London's Roundhouse in 1966).

Gatherings seemed to materialise out of nowhere. If you wandered onto Clapham Common on a Sunday afternoon, you would encounter a seething mass of colours, lilacs and greens and oranges: ravers, gathering in their thousands to enjoy a smooth, sun-kissed re-entry from last night's orbit, stamping their Kickers and Timberlands and Reeboks and cheery little Wallabee moccasins to scores of ghetto-blasters, sipping fizzy pop around the Windmill pub, languidly building spliffs and lazing by the pond. Boys on mountain bikes would pass by, offering chemical sustenance. If a sound system managed to crack the police cordon, the tiny cells would converge into a writhing mass around it. The sheer spontaneity of this *ad hoc* be-in was glorious; it felt like something wonderful could happen anywhere at any time.

The new mood could be seen in the way the ravers dressed; brighter, baggier, freakier – like peacocks and scarecrows and clowns and overgrown babies in lilac romper suits. It could be seen on the flyers: beaming suns, shining pyramids, Eyes of Horus and psychedelic Mandelbrot Set fractals rendered in blinding yellows and oranges. It could be seen in the dancing: the rigid arm-waving had been superseded by new moves, the hips funking from side to side as the feet weaved geometric patterns into the earth. It could be heard, too: last year's chant of "acieed!" now sounded like the disorientated yelp of someone staring the unknown straight in the face. This year, there was an unequivocal statement of intent – *"mental!"* The cry seemed to encapsulate the flight from the certainties of everyday life – *"mental, mental!"* On a mission, no turning back – *"mental, mental, mental!!"* Even the music seemed different, as if it had mutated in harmony with the collective consciousness drift. The biggest rave hits of the summer were the revival of Rhythim is Rhythim's emotive classic from 1987, *Strings of Life* and Lil Louis's *French Kiss*, an astounding metronomic mantra which ground down to a series of orgasmic moans before accelerating back into electrospace. Both tracks were instrumental, but they became invested with so much psychic energy that they took on a meaning that was far beyond words. Nothing, it seemed, could stop the dance. Could it?

"The drugs culture took a disturbing new turn at the weekend when the biggest ever 'acid house' party was held," reported the *Daily Mail* on June 26th. "As 11,000 youngsters descended on a quiet airfield in the middle of the night, drug pushers were waiting to tempt them with an evil selection of narcotics."[3]

Sunrise's Midsummer Night's Dream party at White Waltham airstrip, Berkshire, finally took the summer's rave spectacle over the top and into the glare of official opprobrium. The party began as normal: bribing the airfield guards to keep quiet; dodging police Special Patrol Group officers who were having a party in an adjoining building; updated messages going hourly out on seventy Voice Banks, each of which could take ten calls simultaneously; bamboozling local coppers, telling them it was a stage set for Michael Jackson's new video; a skirmish with locals trying to stem the flood of ravers that was streaming down their sleepy rural lane. The aircraft hangar itself was a beauty; the biggest in the country, Colston-Hayter was told, and only £1,500 to hire. His production team filled it with green fog, and suspended enormous spheres from the roof, over which flickered projections of enormous faces, lap-dissolving into eyeballs. The police presence was minimal; outside a young copper kept warm by practising his acid dance steps. But while Colston-Hayter admits that he already knew he was "living on borrowed time", what he didn't realise was that amongst his 11,000 ticket-holders was a brace of tabloid reporters.

On Monday morning *The Sun* set the tone. Under the headline "Ecstasy Airport", it related a grim story about fucked-up, spaced-out girls, "some as young as twelve", rubbing shoulders with sinister dealers while drug-crazed youths writhed to alien rhythms, tearing heads off pigeons in their frenzy as a mere six policemen looked on helplessly. By 10 a.m., when the party ended, the floor was littered with "thousands of empty Ecstasy wrappers" (in fact, the "wrappers" were bits of silver foil from the ceiling decorations and the decapitated birds were nowhere to be seen).[4] The *Daily Mail* followed up with a stern editorial entitled "A New Threat to British Youth".

"Acid house is a facade for dealing in drugs of the worst sort on a massive scale. It is a cynical attempt to trap young people into drug dependency under the guise of friendly pop music events. In fact these parties act as highly organised distribution centres for drugs – cannabis, amphetamines, the hallucinatory drug LSD and the more dangerous form of it called Ecstasy. Those responsible for this gigantic exercise in hooking our youth on drugs must be brought to book and the stiffest penalties imposed."[5]

There had been no drugs arrests at the party, and naturally Colston-Hayter denied everything. "I don't take drugs, I don't sell them, and we don't have them at our parties," insisted the twenty-two year old, although few believed the last claim.[6] Home Secretary Douglas Hurd ordered an enquiry into unlicensed parties, a move backed by his Labour counterpart, Roy Hattersley. Back in his Camden High Street bolt-hole, Colston-Hayter was scared, but he was also getting a kick out of the attention. "He was quite excited about it but he didn't know what he was in for," says Dave Roberts, who had realised that a young black man with a dubious past would get short shrift from right-wing journalists, and wanted to keep well clear of long lenses and notepads. "*The Sun* put in the paper: 'You can never stop me, Tony Colston-Hayter tells police.' What a lie! It makes a policeman who sees Tony think: 'We're never going to get him, let's stitch him up.' "

In its early stages, the moral panic over acid house seemed to be just another scripted outrage about wanton youth, a ritualised denigration of nonconformism and teenage freedoms which echoed scares about teddy boys, mods, rockers, hippies and punks in previous decades. The tabloid media compared the ravers to the other folk devils of the period, "lager louts" who staged drunken punch-ups in the central squares of country towns; both were symbolic disruptions of the Thatcherite consensus, a colourful story, but hardly a genuine threat. However, although the sensationalist copy of Britain's tabloids is often written, and read, with tongue in cheek, it can also signal, even inspire, the launch of more serious assaults on marginal cultures. By the summer of 1989, coverage had taken on a sterner tone. The police had realised that there was more at stake – raves were accelerating the spread of the drug trade – and used the media panic to prepare the ground for a wider mobilisation of control resources.

The backlash hit Jeremy Taylor and Tintin Chambers first. Their second Energy party was scheduled for the weekend after Sunrise, in Membury, Berkshire. All the surreal props were in place – a twenty-foot-tall model of Stonehenge, a row of laughing houses – but the police sealed off a twenty-mile stretch of the M4, blocking every exit off to halt the party. They stopped five others that night. Biology, run by Jarvis Sandy, had staged a huge event in open fields near Elstree Studios in June. Now he found his venues falling like dominoes under police pressure, and after shepherding his punters down miles of motorway, ended up in a tacky nightclub in Birmingham, where the doors eventually opened at 8 a.m. All that way . . . for this?

The problem was that if you wanted to stage something really special – and most of the major promoters, striving to outdo each other, genuinely did – you couldn't just roll in a sound system on a curtain-sided truck, plug in and let rip. You needed lights, generators, projection screens, fairground rides, inflatable castles, a whole panoply of technological gimcrackery, and somehow you had to assemble it all without being spotted. Then you needed a good lawyer to stave off the police and keep the landowner's resolve solid, and you had to make sure you'd advertised on the right pirate radio stations – otherwise they might well start broadcasting that your party was cancelled. But what you needed above all was nerve – and the ravers, celebrating their release from restrictive licensing laws, had more than enough of that.

Energy tried to revive their fortunes three weeks later, in a warehouse behind Heston Services. Almost immediately 1,000 police with dogs and tactical support vans surrounded the area, blocking off the M4. This time, however, the ravers weren't to be deterred. They simply parked their cars on the hard shoulder, scampered across six lanes of motorway in front of speeding cars, and finally massed enough numbers to force the police to back off. The tabloids and police had helped to define an outlaw identity for the scene, one that was readily embraced.

It was time to recruit some tough lieutenants, check your gunpowder and mass your forces. The battle was on now, for sure, and the only weapons that counted were technology, strategy and sheer weight of numbers. Colston-Hayter still believed he could turn the negative coverage around, or at least parry it, and called on an old video-gaming friend. Paul Staines, a former Harrow schoolboy with an extrovert demeanour and a caustic wit, had met Colston-Hayter at an Atari Asteroids championships; Staines came in first ahead of his new friend. At university, he was drawn to the radical libertarian wing of the Federation of Conservative Students, and was soon working as a political aide to the rightwing maverick, wealthy property developer and adviser to Margaret Thatcher, David Hart. Hart's philosophy was complete freedom of the marketplace and rabid anti-communism. He had played a key role in the Conservatives' 1983 election victory, been a member of Thatcher's so-called "alternative cabinet", and during the Miners' Strike of 1984–85 had used his cash and forceful personality to build a clandestine network of disaffected and strike-breaking miners, which eventually contributed to the defeat of Arthur Scargill and the National Union of Mineworkers.

A "conspiratorial . . . somewhat bizarre figure", Hart moved among the higher echelons of the security services, received substantial funding from Rupert Murdoch, and would go on to advise Michael Portillo, the darling of the Tory right in the nineties.[7] Hart's organisation, Committee for a Free Britain, published two periodicals, the Cold War bulletin *World Briefing*, which was overseen by former CIA spook Herb Mayer, and *British Briefing*, a "monthly intelligence analysis of the activities of the extreme left". The latter's major impetus was to smear Labour MPs and left-leaning lawyers and writers. It had previously been run by MI6 veteran Brian Crozier and Paul Staines now helped produce it.[8] The twenty-one year old was having the time of his life.

"I was a fanatical, zealot anti-communist. I wasn't really a Tory, I was an anarcho-capitalist. I was lobbying at the Council of Europe and at Parliament; I was over in Washington, in Jo'burg, in South America. It was 'let's get guns for the Contras', that sort of stuff. I was enjoying it immensely, I got to go with these guys and fire off AK-47s. I always like to go where the action is, and for that period in the Reagan/Thatcher days, it was great fun, it was all expenses paid and I got to see the world. I used to think that *World Briefing* was a bit funny. The only scary thing about those publications was the mailing list – people like George Bush – and the fact that Hart would talk to the head of British Intelligence for an hour. I used to think it was us having a laugh, putting some loony right-wing stuff in, and that somebody somewhere was taking it seriously. You've got to understand that we had a sense of humour about this."

He also had misgivings about his boss. "He's completely

charming and can charm senior people like Thatcher and appear sane for a while. But any close proximity to him for a prolonged period of time, you know he's completely off his fucking head."

Between forays for Hart and work for the similarly right-wing Adam Smith Institute, Staines had begun to attend his friend Tony's parties. "The first E I took was at Apocalypse Now at Wembley Studios. I thought it was fantastic, I was down there, Smiley face T-shirt, shorts – never done acid, never done E, I'd never even heard of this MDMA. I had the E, it was pure MDMA, and I was so out of it, so in love with everybody, I had a little windowpane of acid, and that was it, I just tripped out. Wembley Studios has got those white walls with the curves, and I was lost, I was a wisp of smoke; it was a brilliant, fabulous experience."

Libertarian jet-setting was fun, for sure, but this was a better buzz altogether. After White Waltham, Staines became Sunrise's publicity officer – at first running the operation out of Hart's premises. "My credibility was slowly going down in politics. One minute I would be on News at One saying 'there's no drugs at these parties', and the next minute I'm supposed to be talking about civil war in Angola. It wasn't working."

As Sunrise raised their game, so did the opposition. Chief Superintendent Ken Tappenden had also been involved in the grand political showdown that was the Miners' Strike; he had been censured by civil liberties lawyers after preventing flying pickets entering the Kent coalfields via the Dartford Tunnel. Now Divisional Commander of north-west Kent, an area bisected by the recently completed M25 orbital motorway, he found that his patch was prime real estate for raves, or "pay parties" as the police and Home Office preferred to call them.

Tappenden opened a small office in Dartford to monitor this new phenomenon, but was immediately overwhelmed with enquiries from other forces. Taking over the main conference room at Gravesend police station, he instigated the Pay Party Unit with a staff of six and four computers, at a cost of around

£100,000. Within a few months, there were sixty staff and thirty computers hooked into the HOLMES database, the national police computer network set up in the wake of the Yorkshire Ripper fiasco, and Gravesend had become the party intelligence unit for the whole of England and Wales.

Tappenden was eager to take on the ravers on their own terms. As he'd shown during the Miners' Strike, he wasn't afraid of getting his hands dirty, maybe stretching the spirit of the law a little. Like Colston-Hayter, he was excited by the publicity he was getting (he still keeps videos of all his TV appearances and operations). If this was a high-tech war, he wasn't going to be the one fighting with obsolete hardware. If they used phone lines, he'd counter with phone taps; if they used pirate radio, he'd monitor it; if they sent out spotters to find remote ware-houses, he'd have helicopters and light aircraft out after them. "I wasn't particularly a party pooper," Tappenden insists now as he did then. "I would have liked these parties to have gone legal. But what the organisers didn't want to do was spend their money on safety and infrastructure. They wanted the money in their back pocket."

At first, he admits, he was chasing the game. The party organ-isers were sharp and ruthless, and the police didn't have any idea what or who they were dealing with. "I admired their organisational ability. If they were lieutenants in a military outfit they'd be brilliant at it because of the way they could move people. We'd spend weeks briefing and planning and they could do it on a Saturday night in an hour."

This initial naivety is apparent from the Pay Party Unit's confidential briefing papers. The first, published in October 1989, described acid house ("a combination of black dance music, electronic effects and weird vocals") and concluded that "the atmosphere at acid house parties is reminiscent of the hippie days of the sixties, with a philosophy of peace and love". But another, a few months on, attested to improved intelligence and greater resources, outlining its success thus: "After three months we had started 20 major investigations. The HOLMES database held 5,725 names and 712 vehicles. We had monitored 4,380 telephone calls and made 258 arrests." The work went on all week, relentlessly. "We weren't using the lads on the ground, we were using very experienced, hardened detectives," says Tappenden. "At any one time we were running over 200 intelligence officers through the country. Now that is a colossal amount of intelligence, and it was banging down those computers 24 hours a day. We never stopped, we went through the night, through the day. The database was unbelievable."

By the end of the summer, the main rave organisations, Sunrise, Energy and Biology, had been joined by scores of others. Coming out of any London club, ravers would be assailed by flyer teams handing out bundles of ever more opulent publicity sheets, in full blazing colour with endless lists of attractions. Energy lurched from triumph to disaster, emphasising the precariousness of the situation. In August they trumped the police by putting out on their phone lines that the first 5,000 to arrive at their Summer Festival would get in free; within hours there were over 20,000 dancing in a Surrey field. A month later, the chosen venue for their Dance '89 party, intended to raise money for families of those who died on the *Marchioness* riverboat disaster (which included some of Tintin Chambers's Chelsea friends), was discovered by police helicopters. After a frantic day-long chase around the countryside searching for a new site, they ended up illegally occupying a hangar at Raydon Airfield in Suffolk long after dark. Their star-studded line-up of performers failed to materialise; crops were trampled and vehicles burned out; Chambers and Taylor were arrested for causing a public nuisance, excoriated in the tabloids, damned as crooks and ghouls, and disowned by the *Marchioness* appeal fund itself.

Tony Colston-Hayter, meanwhile, was jubilant after beating a charge of running an unlicensed party at White Waltham in Maidenhead Magistrates Court. He had proved that the membership cards that came with Sunrise tickets meant that it was in effect a private party. "So now they were really angry," he says. "It was the height of summer, and we were looking to do an outdoor one. This really was the high point, this was where it all ended."

longwick, buckinghamshire and gravesend, kent

If there was one day upon which the extraordinary energy of 1989 finally peaked, it was August 12th, outside the village of Longwick in the midst of serene Buckinghamshire countryside, at the Sunrise/Back to the Future Dance Music Festival. This is where Colston-Hayter triumphed in the ultimate battle of wits, and pulled off the most spectacular party Britain had ever seen.

"After the publicity, no one wanted to give us a site," says Dave Roberts. "By luck we found this farm, did the deal and got our crew off there really early in the morning. By this time the police were following our crew around, following our sound company, our lighting company, following our security people from their houses, trying to outsmart us. They followed our scaffolding people who build our stage and they found the gig. The farmer doesn't know what to do; we're saying to him: 'You don't have to stop it, we aren't breaking any laws, we're a private members' club.' They're saying to him: 'Stop it, otherwise we're going to prosecute you.' "

But the smooth tongues of Colston-Hayter and his lawyers prevailed. "There is nothing we can do," local Chief Superintendent Pauline Coulthard said afterwards. "Parliament should change the law."[9] They had sold 17,000 tickets, and nothing was going to sour the revelry.

From the stage, the E-Zee Possee declaimed the refrain of their summer hit, *Everything Starts With an E*: "Drop a tab of E and rub up with a stranger!" No one wasted any time doing just that: the girls in baby rompers, the teenies in track pants, the cowboys and the superheroes and the dreads and the bad boys, the girl in the silver sci-fi make-up and the man flailing and hopping on crutches, the groups of three or four stepping in unison as if telepathically linked together.

The party encapsulated all the virtues of this new entertainment format. Tearing down the M40, buzzing with anticipation, not knowing where the final destination would be; it was a thrill without equal, enhanced by the knowledge that this was forbidden fruit. Through side roads and country lanes, then, over the hilltop, the throb of the bassline and the flash of lasers in the sky – and the people, so many people, fired up with excitement and chemicals, garbed in all the colours of the rainbow, all joined in common purpose. The very dynamic of the rave itself felt so liberating – democratic rather than hierarchical. The dancers' focus was not on the stage, but on each other. The hegemony of the performer was usurped; the energy was coming from the participants themselves. They, no one else, were making this happen! And at the far edges of the crowd, dancing alone under the glittering sky, you could feel yourself cutting loose into the fantasy.

"Don't the police care about enforcing the law of the land?" *The Sun* demanded the following morning. "Are they not troubled about what is happening to our young people? Just when will they decide to smash the evil drug pushers in our midst? Only when the drug habit has spread to all of Britain? When the party stretches from shore to shore?"[10]

Time seemed to have accelerated; the scene was growing by the week, almost by the day, and the stakes were getting higher and higher. Locked into a crazy dream, intoxicated by the thrill of the chase and the audacity of the game, could the ravers cross the borders of the impossible before their pursuers caught up with them? The end of the summer was just over a month away. How far could it go, how much higher could they get, before the chill set in?

On October 1st, three of the summer's rave anthems, Black Box's *Ride on Time*, Technotronic's *Pump Up the Jam* and Sydney Youngbloood's *If Only I Could*, were ensconced at numbers one, two and three in the pop charts. The night before, the storm had finally broken. To the north of London, the Helter Skelter party brought an awesome line-up of performers to a muddy, ploughed field in Oxfordshire. The incongruity was sweet, seeing these house icons climbing up a rickety ladder onto the back of a flat-bed lorry – in open farmland! – to sing and play. There was Loleatta Holloway, the lead singer on scores of classic Salsoul disco anthems, who seemed almost scared of the mob of brightly coloured lunatics thrashing in front of the "stage". There was Ce Ce Rogers, whose utopian lament *Someday* was virtually the national anthem of the house nation. There were post-punk pranksters, The KLF, who demanded their £1,000 fee upfront, in Scottish pound notes, upon each of which they scribbled the message "we love you children" before throwing them to the crowd, a dress rehearsal for their burning of 1 million pounds in a situationist art statement a few years later. Despite the drizzle and the turn-out (*only* 4,000!), the mood was elevated.

But on the same night, to the south of London, stand-off finally flared into violence outside the Phantasy party near Reigate, as Strikeforce security guards with Rottweilers and CS gas fought a pitched battle with police, leaving sixteen officers injured and seven in hospital. Outsmarting rural plod was one thing; physically beating the police, right in front of the TV cameras, was unacceptable. Home Secretary Douglas Hurd promised action, and soon, in time for the Tories' autumn conference where there would, as ever, be a willing audience for tough talk on law and order.

Ken Tappenden knew what was coming. The fact was, at many of the hundreds of parties that took place over the summer, the profits weren't only coming from ticket prices of £15 or £20. They were coming from the huge amounts of Ecstasy being sold on site. Whether or not the organisers were directly involved themselves or franchising out the dealing – some of them will admit it now, off the record, of course – there was a colossal demand for MDMA that had to be satisfied. The Ecstasy distribution network had expanded exponentially in the eighteen months since Shoom opened, shifting from small-scale operators to serious criminals who were able to finance huge import shipments. At the end of 1989, Customs and Excise reported record seizures of not only MDMA but also the other dance drugs, amphetamines and LSD. Customs chief Douglas Tweddle put the increase down to "the rapid rise in popularity of acid house parties".

At first, like many in authority, Tappenden couldn't even comprehend how such an insatiable appetite for drugs existed. "These were nice kids – my son, your son," he says. But they were gobbling the stuff and coming back for more. Reviewing surveillance videos of one particular party, he was astounded: they were rolling bags of pills off the back of a low-loader in costermongers' barrows! "We did a sweep of the field after they'd gone, you could see the pockets of drugs all over the place. Most of the kids were spaced out. You can't dance six to eight hours to fairground music the way they were. When we started to tell MPs and the Home Office what was really going on, they wouldn't believe it. It was always denied by everyone, including the government." And where illegal drugs became big business, organised crime would inevitably be involved. Who else would have the organisation, the daring and the financial clout to trade in such great quantities?

"It became very apparent," says Tappenden, "that although there may have been fairly legitimate organisers in the beginning, criminals that we knew had extensive criminal records for violence, murder, robbery, and those that were involved in extensive drug operations, had started to take the pay parties over." Indeed, many promoters admitted it: hard men were getting involved, putting in their own security teams and taking off with the profits, or advertising fake parties and disappearing with the ticket money. Ultimately, this was what kicked the authorities into action: not rumblings in the shires, but the fear of crime syndicates racking up enormous financial power and influence.

"The whole problem was because the activity was illegal," says Paul Staines. "It's the same as drugs, because drugs are illegal, you're going to mix with unpleasant people – so you have to hire your own kind of protection." As law enforcement stepped up a gear, organisers had to employ security teams that were tough enough, if necessary, to physically fight to defend the party against the law or anyone who tried to muscle in on the takings: boxers, bouncers, body-builders, ex-squaddies, and hard, fearless bastards.

"In those days you paid the security to keep the police out. It was mad, you didn't even ask them to, they just saw it as their duty. They didn't give a fuck, those boys. They used to get paid a lot of money and I'm sure they all made their fair share, but they did do a lot of dodgy things," says Tintin Chambers. Inevitably, sometimes they turned on their employers, using the same menaces that they had been hired for. "That was always a worry," admits Chambers. "They were bad boys and we were two little public school Chelsea boys promoting parties for 25,000 people. There were a lot of rip-offs going on; we once got taxed for quite a lot of money by someone. There were always people jumping down your throat with a shotgun, going: 'Give us 20 grand or we'll kill you.' " At one point, Jeremy Taylor claims, he was forced to hire an armed ex-SAS team to fortress his flat and give him round-the-clock protection from extorters. Taylor's fears proved well-founded when, a few years later, another of his business partners was shot dead in a London nightclub.

With hindsight, the strategy that the Home Office adopted appears meticulously thought-out, but at the time they were just scratching around for anything that might work. The decision was made not to pursue the parties on the grounds of drug use, but to concentrate on environmental offences, noise and fire regulations and obscure local bylaws. "If you took it as a hard issue on drugs, I don't think you'd have got the support of all the other authorities," explains Tappenden. "Health and safety means a lot to a local authority, drugs don't. Health and safety took on board every conceivable public authority we could get involved. The fire brigade came on board and all the district councils. Why health and safety? Why emergency lighting? Why noise? Because it was easy, drugs was difficult without thousands and thousands of men." Furthermore, at that time Ecstasy was not considered to be a major public health problem by the government; the "war on drugs" was invariably a war on heroin, and raves were seen as a law and order issue.

The Pay Party Unit's lawyers scoured the statute books, digging out any piece of legislation that could, even vaguely, be applied to raves. They were building up lists of anyone who was involved, from DJs and production teams right down to ticket sellers. They were collecting flyers, buying tickets, listening to pirate radio even more ardently than the ravers themselves, then networking all the information via the HOLMES computer system and attempting to serve injunctions on any organiser they could track down. But making charges stick was an altogether harder matter, as Tappenden admits. "I'm open enough to say that we didn't have many secure convictions. We had lots of arrests, we charged a few, not many; the courts really weren't prepared. As many people as we arrested we let out the door, which wasn't doing our image any good. So we set about stopping as opposed to prosecuting." Roadblocks, stop-checks and petty arrests were all part of a drive to discourage the ravers from even buying a ticket. Twenty pounds for a party that might not even happen? They might enjoy the thrill of the chase for a few weekends in a row. But month after month, and still no party? It wouldn't be worth the effort.

The Pay Party Unit even staged its own phantom raves, phoning in to pirate stations and giving imaginary locations for nonexistent events, pulling convoys of ravers away into the wilderness only to find darkness, silence, and a copper with a loudhailer shouting: "Go home, there is no party." "Pirate radio would be saying – you know how they do it to music – 'It's Brands Hatch tonight, Brands Hatch tonight, Old Bill don't know, Old Bill don't know, starts at twelve, starts at midnight,' " Tappenden chuckles, imitating a cockney MC's rhythmic patter. "But of course what they didn't know was we'd conjured it up." At one point Thames Valley police pulled up road signs in an attempt to confuse party-goers, and in Hampshire in October, officers responded to a lawyer who confronted them on behalf of rave promoters by simply arresting him. The police were stretching the boundaries of legality, Tappenden admits. "[Civil liberties lawyer] Michael Mansfield didn't like what we were doing; he said we were exceeding our limits, and in a way I always thought we were."

In return, Sunrise poked fun at Tappenden and his team by sending them joke faxes. Paul Staines claims that they were also being fed inside information from the Pay Party Unit's Gravesend headquarters. "One of the guys on the Sunrise team was bonking a secretary working down there," he laughs, "so we knew the score."

The police launched an attempt to knock out the communications network that the scene was built upon. In the month following the Reigate clash, London's leading pirate radio station, Centre Force, was raided. The telephone watchdog ICSTIS ordered the withdrawal of the premium-rate 0898 and 0836 phone services that rave organisers were using to transmit party locations, claiming that their code of contact forbade the use of lines to "encourage or incite any person to commit a criminal offence". Was Home Office pressure applied on this supposedly independent organisation? ICSTIS claimed it wasn't; Tappenden hints that it was. But Sunrise's Voice Banks were scuppered. "They cut the lines on us; they were trying everything to nail us down," says Staines. "It was reasonably co-ordinated, there was a Home Office unit on the case. I remember being at something at the Home Office, I ended up in this blazing row [with a Home Office official]. He said, 'look, I know who you are, we know all about you', because I had a Special Branch record from being in politics, working in extreme groups. They couldn't work it out: 'You're a right wing Tory, why are you doing this?' Because I'm doing loads of E and having a great time!"

Realising that Douglas Hurd was due to announce new measures to clamp down on raves, Staines convinced Colston-Hayter to launch a Freedom to Party campaign at the Conservatives' annual conference in Blackpool. "I said: 'Tony, you've got to come up here, we'll cream it, it'll be the most sexy story of the day – acid house Tories, they'll be all over us.' " The campaign focused on the licensing laws: in Europe, clubbers could legally dance all night. Britain, with its arcane legislation dating back to Lloyd George's Defence of the Realm Act, brought in to curb the drinking of munitions workers during World War One, was pushing its fun-loving youth beyond the law and into the arms of criminals, the only people who would dare stage a party if the government brought in tougher rules. Freedom to Party was a loose alliance of all the main organisers: Sunrise, Energy, Biology, Ibiza, World Dance and others. They sold themselves as true free-market entrepreneurs, giving the kids what they wanted; according to prevailing libertarian capitalist ideology, they deserved applause, not censure. This was the government, after all, that had turned greed into a moral virtue. "Maggie should be proud of us, we're a product of enterprise culture," said Colston-Hayter.[11]

In December, the task of bringing in a Private Member's Bill was passed to Graham Bright, MP for Luton South, the man who championed the Video Recordings Act against "video nasties" in 1984. Although *The Guardian* called Bright "the most inappropriately named MP"[12] and claimed that some Tory colleagues referred to him as "Mr Dim", he had been a long and faithful servant to Home Office ministers, and would soon afterwards become the new Prime Minister John Major's Parliamentary

Private Secretary, a trusted aide and friend who was ultimately rewarded with a knighthood.[13] Bright's Entertainments (Increased Penalties) Bill wouldn't create a new criminal offence or give authorities new powers, it would simply raise the maximum fines for unlicensed parties from £2,000 to £20,000 and six months' imprisonment.

There was no serious opposition within Parliament. The Labour Party was in powerless minority, and in any case its reservations stretched only to how far the Bill would affect rock gig promoters or the Glastonbury Festival. No one could be seen to be soft on drug culture, especially during that summer's panic about a crack epidemic supposedly being imported from the States. "I want to make it absolutely clear to the House that the Labour Party believes that tough action must be taken against those people who organise illegal acid house parties," said Stuart Randall MP.[14] Staines hoped that right-wing MP Teresa Gorman would come out in vocal support ("she's a fun girl"), but nothing came of it.

Bright and his colleagues had done their homework, even to the extent of joining one of Ken Tappenden's teams at a rave. In the five-hour-long debate over the second reading of the Bill in March 1990, Bright threw in references to conversations with Adamski and Jeremy Taylor of Energy, quoted *The Face* and *Melody Maker*, outlined his version of the origins of the phrase "acid house" ("the term derives from Chicago slang"), and told of fly-by-night organisers "doing a runner with the money", leaving ravers holding tickets for nonexistent parties. The Pay Party Unit had briefed him thoroughly; he knew how much it cost to get into a rave, and what a can of Coke cost inside. He picked holes in Freedom to Party's manifesto: did they want purpose-built structures for raves in the countryside, or longer opening hours in urban nightclubs? And no MP could disagree when he voiced fears about drug-dealing, organised crime, violence against police and the safety of the young. Echoing Ken

Tappenden, he insisted: "No one wants to be a killjoy or a party-pooper. I certainly do not."

To compound matters, Home Office Minister John Patten announced that he intended to implement an order under the 1988 Criminal Justice Act for confiscation of "criminal proceeds" from illegal parties, which he described as "deeply corrupt", and called for the Bill to be rushed through before the spring brought a new wave of raves. "The country will be shocked if the Bill does not make speedy progress in Committee to become law before the summer." He also promised to tell his "right honourable friend", the Chancellor of the Exchequer, to set the Inland Revenue on tax-dodging organisers' tails.[15]

How much were the organisers really making? £10,000 per party? £100,000? And how much cash was flowing in from the premium-rate phone lines? Exact figures are impossible to come by, and most promoters remain vague, either fearful of the taxman or chary at being labelled a profiteer. "The youth press saw us as a bit slimy," admits Staines. "There'd be stories: 'They're doing a great thing but they're making a few quid out of it as well.' We never made half a million on a party. We did not skimp on the production at all, because we were into it as much as anyone else, so it was like: 'Fuck it, we've got to have 80,000 watts.' We had horrendous production costs. I can safely say that we never ended up with more than five figures in cash – we'd make 40, 50 grand, not 500 grand. Which isn't bad. We were nice middle-class boys having a whale of a time, stretch limos and all that, living *The Great Rock'n'Roll Swindle* number two. We were saying, 'this is the Malcolm McLaren scenario' – making money and having a laugh."

Sunrise's parent company, the Transatlantic Corporation, was registered in the Virgin Islands tax haven. "The authorities could pursue it as much as they liked, it was an absolute dead end," says Staines. "We couldn't get done on tax or anything. We were safe." What was certain was that gains could turn into losses if a party was busted. This undoubtedly hardened the resolve of those who were determined to pull a party off – little wonder that some of Ken Tappenden's raids netted shotguns, knives, baseball bats, iron bars, CS gas and other offensive weapons from security teams.

slough, berkshire

Judge: "What is acid house music?"
Inspector Brown: "I have seen it on *Top of the Pops*. It is just a din, a noise which goes on and on. No rhythms, no words, but it seems to be the current trend."
Judge: "If he had played country or Beatles music, would it have made a difference?"
Brown: "Probably."
Judge: "What did you intend to charge them with?"
Brown: "After I heard what kind of music was being played, I intended to charge them under the Misuse of Drugs Act."
From trial of party organisers in Dundee, September 1989

Endgame. The final showdown. Sunrise versus the law. HM government versus acid house. New Year's Eve: if ever there was a night for a celebration, this was it. End of the decade – end of the eighties! To spice the occasion, most clubs weren't even allowed to sell alcohol after 12.30 a.m. as the date fell on a Sunday; no wonder the ravers had rebelled against such a drab, joyless country with its restrictive licensing laws.

Despite the encroaching gloom, Colston-Hayter and Roberts were so confident of success that for the first time they printed the venue for their New Year's Eve Mega Party on tickets: a former army depot in Halls Green Road, Harlow, Essex. Perhaps they had gone too far down the line and had started to believe their own myth – romantic outlaws, untouchable, unstoppable: "At one point I was beginning to think I was the next Jerry Rubin and Tony was the next Timothy Leary," says Paul Staines.

"We had lost it." Although, as part of the Home Office push, the Association of District Councils was urging its members to adopt the Private Places of Entertainment (Licensing) Act 1967, which forces private parties to apply for a licence in the same way as public ones, Sunrise had chosen an area where the council had not implemented the Act, so the rave would be completely legal. Fireworks would see the millennium's final decade in. They had even invited Graham Bright.

With hours to go, the landowner broke down and called the party off, and the fall-back venue in Norfolk was injuncted by the local council. There was nowhere left to run. At eight o'clock that evening, things looked desperate, and many of the 10,000 ticket-holders started to make other plans. Around 11 p.m., the Sunrise message line directed the remaining ravers to head for Heston Services on the M4. As the chimes struck midnight, a few thousand reached the National Panasonic building in Slough, where Colston-Hayter had negotiated with Biology and Genesis to join in their party. But this, surely, wasn't how it was meant to be; this dirty old warehouse with its locks bolt-cropped off wasn't the hedonist paradise they had dreamed of. After eighteen crazy months, Sunrise were right back where they had begun. Although a World Wide Productions newsletter promised that Colston-Hayter would soon be applying for a licence to hold a 1990 Dance Music Festival, privately he must have known it was finished. There would never be another Sunrise.

"Ecstasy! The party's over," crowed *The Sun*, triumphantly ushering in the year of the Bright Bill. "Acid house parties have been merely a cloak for mass drug-taking. They were a constant menace to our youngsters. The evil craze belonged to the complacent eighties. We hope and believe it has died along with the decade. The party is over. And that is great news to start 1990."[16]

What a year it had been, long months of magic and madness which seemed to collapse into a filmic barrage of images and emotions: innocence, passion, frustration, disbelief, but above all *ecstasy*. The year had also been riddled with rip-offs and false promises. As Dave Swindells wrote in a *Time Out* end-of-year review, "1989 was the year when the scam became almost the norm – you could never be entirely sure whether your £15 ticket would lead you to a fabulous all-night party in beautiful countryside or an all-dayer starting at 8 a.m. in a tacky Birmingham disco . . . In amongst the hype on the flyers was plenty of entertaining nonsense. There was a security firm who called themselves Big Buggers and Their Pets, a leaflet which proudly stated 'This'll be the living bollocks' and raves like Planet E which didn't happen at all."[17]

The comedown was severe. Anton the Pirate, who had endured the nightmare of a thwarted party with World Dance, felt empty and disillusioned: "I remember feeling very drained by it all. I remember a lot of people saying: 'Maybe this is the last year? Can it survive to the next summer?' "

In January, Colston-Hayter, Staines and another David Hart associate, Douglas Smith, opened up another front. The Association of Dance Party Promoters was launched to provide them with a respectable front and dissociate them from the scammers and gangsters while, they hoped, making themselves eligible for licences later in the year. "We desperately want to be responsible and operate within the law and are prepared to make ourselves accountable," stated Smith. "The only thing our party-goers get high on is Lucozade and music."[18] But by this time it was the authorities who held all the cards and the organisers who were casting around frantically for anything that might work.

David Hart, seeing it as a populist libertarian campaign for the free-market rights of the entrepreneur, offered help and resources. During the first Freedom to Party rally in Trafalgar Square later that month, an impromptu pirate radio station even broadcast from the Committee for a Free Britain office. Hart didn't raise the issue with his chums in Downing Street, says Staines, but "he was attracted to the glamour of the whole thing. He thought it was sexy. He saw himself marching down to Parliament Square with the youth of Britain behind him."

However, the demonstration showed just how far the rave scene was from an organised campaigning force, confirming many observers' belief that the only overt political statement that came out of acid house was a declaration of the entrepreneur's right to make money. A few thousand gathered to listen to a shambolic series of rambling speeches, raps and a cappella singing. One woman who tried to link the campaign with wider social issues had the microphone snatched away from her. Loud, pumping house music, which was what the crowd really wanted, was forbidden. Unity dissipated into a sense of frustration.

"The imagination, excitement (and investment) that has gone into some of the raves was nowhere in evidence here," commented Dave Swindells. "Yet the rally should have been successful, because it did attract around 4,000 ravers, because the campaign does address serious issues of individual liberty and because under existing regulations even properly organised raves that comply with all the relevant fire/safety/noise and police regulations are being stopped . . . Most of the ravers were understandably unimpressed by the 'speeches' and only wanted to dance. This was the main message of the afternoon too. Protesting by post to your local MP was frequently suggested: 'Write a letter. Say "Maggie! Maggie! I want to dance!" Put it in an envelope (you don't need a stamp – they can afford it) and send it. Bosh!' If only it were that simple . . ."

Later that night, rhetoric gave way to action as a warehouse was cracked in Radlett, Hertfordshire, by a covert crew who styled themselves the Freedom Fighters to disguise their supposedly respectable Association of Dance Party Promoters identities. But for one of them, Biology's Jarvis Sandy, it was a futile gesture; he had just about had enough of the grief. "The heart had gone out of it. The Old Bill was on top. It knocked the wind out of us."

The second Freedom to Party demonstration in March, just before the Bright Bill's second reading, reflected how low spirits had fallen during this winter of discontent. A mere 1,000 traipsed from Hyde Park past Buckingham Palace, more of a rabble than a mob. The Pay Party Unit, on the other hand, was becoming increasingly efficient. In its report dated April 14th, 1990, it detailed the monitoring of 336 parties, of which 167 didn't take place, 106 were stopped by police and 68 were allowed to run. "Don't worry," laughed a crossed-out Smiley face sticker on Tappenden's office door, "be happy." Energy's Live Dance Concert at the Docklands Arena seemed tantamount to total capitulation. Although the line-up was superb – Black Box, Guru Josh, Adamski, Snap, 808 State, The Shamen and Orbital, all the top names of the moment – it was an all-seated venue that had to close by 11 p.m. This wasn't a rave, it was rock show, an inferior form of entertainment substituted for the genuine article; things were going backwards, not forwards.

Who dared throw a party now? Only the brave, the foolhardy or the criminally minded. The ten- and six-year sentences that had just been meted out to the organisers of a Thames boat party rave under the Misuse of Drugs Act were intended as a warning, one that did not go unheeded. As David Piccioni, owner of the Soho record shop and rave ticket outlet Black Market, notes: "At first it was middle- to upper-class boys who knew what they were doing. And then the riff-raff element came in – gangland types, boxing promoter types. It changed from being double-barrelled names to double-barrelled shotguns."

Colston-Hayter stated his intention to do "rave concerts", but was never granted a licence. The Freedom to Party campaign rolled on without any hope of victory. They were just squeezing a few last pounds out of their premium-rate phone lines and merchandising. "We were making money out of the hats and T-shirts," says Staines. "That was the real reason at the back of my mind I was carrying on with it, because it was never going to be a successful campaign. All those demos cost us a fortune. It sounds money-grabbing, but we were there for business as well."

In July 1990, the Entertainments (Increased Penalties) Bill received royal assent and the profit confiscation measures were enacted. The police, flushed by their good fortune, immediately staged one of the biggest mass arrests in British history – 836 ravers were detained in a 5 a.m. raid on the Love Decade warehouse party in Leeds, filling the cells of thirty police stations in West Yorkshire (although only eight would subsequently be charged). The civil rights organisation Liberty censured them for using "intimidatory arrest" to discourage party-goers but the police cared little; they would, they said, be doing it again and again. Satellite Pay Party Units had been set up all over the country, as illegal raves spread far beyond the M25's ambit. But sooner or later it had to end. The sheer cost of the operation was depleting police resources, and forcing them to return again and again to the Home Office for increased budgets to deal with the parties.

"We were on top of it, but we were spending an awful lot of money," says Ken Tappenden. "Just in the fabric of setting up the Pay Party Incident Room we'd spent £94,246, which was starting to alarm people. That's not including the operational work on the ground. Everyone was asking the Home Office for additional money to run it and they were fighting shy of it, they were saying: 'No, you've got to run it out of your contingency funds.' The cost was colossal to the county and the government. We were spending money like water."

And rave culture showed no sign of disappearing like the passing fancy it was initially thought to be. If anything, it was growing. There had to be some sort of *rapprochement*.

By the end of 1990, a few central London clubs had been granted licences to open beyond 3 a.m.; one, Turnmills in Clerkenwell Road, was able to open twenty-four hours. Raves like Raindance, on the A13 near Barking, took place with official approval. Ken Tappenden was holding seminars with party organisers who had set up the Association of Legal Promoters to thrash out a series of guidelines for raves, of which he is still proud. The liberalisation of licensing laws, which soon began to spread throughout the country, didn't happen by chance; the police could not go on running huge operations weekend after weekend. "It wasn't a coincidence, it was part of the drive," explains Tappenden. "It was actually fairly well planned, not only at local authority level but at government level, because they knew we had to get out of it somehow."

The two-pronged assault – cracking down on illegal raves while allowing nightclubs to stay open longer – was intended to undermine the basis of the scene. "I think the youngsters got fed up of paying £15 a ticket and have the Old Bill trap them on the M25, turning them round, sending them back, making them come up this motorway and off that motorway," says Tappenden. "Licences were being given and we were acting as a springboard. Once you started getting them legal and giving them longer hours to open, it started to crumble, didn't it? And I'll tell you what else it did – it cut the fun out of it, the fun of cocking a snook at the law, getting away with it and making £150,000."

Slowly, raves became integrated into the infrastructure of the entertainment establishment; shepherded back into licensed premises, contained and commodified if not eradicated. In September 1991, the Pay Party Unit finally closed down, its work done. The main players began to drift away; Colston-Hayter back to the gambling clubs, Roberts into the music business, Staines to the City, Taylor to manage the Crinkley Bottom theme park with TV presenter Noel Edmonds, Chambers to become a DJ, Tappenden into retirement – but not before this extraordinary period left lasting impact.

At the time it seemed that the government had won, handsdown, TKO in twelve bloody, month-long rounds. But with hindsight, this was the beginning of the implementation of the Freedom to Party manifesto's demands for liberal, European-style licensing laws. Leisure patterns in Britain were changing, and no law could stop them. Young people were no longer satisfied with boozing in pubs and staggering home at closing time. The government had either to bend their rules or break under the sheer weight of opposition. To avoid conflict, they had little choice but to go with the new flow, to sway with the rush. Even their core concerns – stemming the spread of drug culture and preventing organised criminals from consolidating their power base – went unresolved. And elsewhere, out in the countryside, a new breed of outlaws was massing for action.

4

journey to the east

"Well I had the little magic tablet mate, and I fucking just *fwooor* . . . I remember coming up on it and that was it – it was a yellow burger and it tasted like pepper and it fucking knocked me. I'd heard all this about Ecstasy, I'm getting a guy come up to me, used to be one of my close pub mates, who's now wearing an orange fucking shirt, a Smiley bandanna, only got half his teeth in his head, telling me how much of a good time he's had down King's Cross. I'm thinking, three months ago you were down the Old Kent Road with me at the Thomas A'Beckett getting lagging, I wondered why I hadn't seen you for a little while. I remember this yellow burger, I took it, I walked around, and then I got this feeling from the tip of my toes to the top of my head – like this burning rocket fuel – and I got scared because I wasn't used to the buzz, three pints of lager I could handle but an E, I didn't have a clue . . . I remember literally running to a wall, and it had nothing to hang on to, and I just slid slowly down. I was running round this fucking place with my shirt inside out, shouting 'I'm on one!' because I'd fathomed it out, and everybody was shouting 'mental!' and clapping their hands – I fucking loved it man! This girl came up to me and said: 'Wouldn't it be good if the whole world was on E?' She was sweating it, I was pissing sweat – I didn't know what was going on – and all I could think of was: 'Yeah, you're so right love.' And this is so unlike me. I came out of there in the morning, and I just sat in a car in Peckham all day, just watching people – I was just

karma'd, I couldn't believe what had happened to my body. I've got a big blue lion tattooed on my arm, and MFC on my arm like a mug – I used to go to Millwall when it was at the Den – I had to spit at a pig, I had to call a guy a Paki because monkey see, monkey do; it was Neanderthal man going down the Den, it was programmed. E changed my life completely – if I saw you walking down the street and you were from north London and I was from south London we would supposedly have to have a scuffle, which is bollocks, but we all lived by that, we didn't know no better. You couldn't get east, south, west and north London kids in the same warehouse without having a fight – you're fucking asking for miracles to happen, and you didn't get miracles in the eighties – but you did with the miracle drug." Tommy Cockles, London DJ

East London: a flat, grey expanse stretching out beyond the City along the Central and District Lines, bisected by the A102 (M) Blackwall Tunnel approach motorway, covering miles of concrete estates and ill-lit streets. Wealth has always poured through the area, from the colonial Port of London in the nineteenth century to the Docklands developments of today, but has continually failed to enrich its inhabitants. The property boom of the eighties passed it by and unemployment in the area runs at twice the capital's average. Much of it was bombed out by the Nazis during World War Two, and the slum dwellings rebuilt as tower blocks and low-rise estates that generations of neglect, deprivation and underfunding have allowed to decay. The East End has always been London's psychic bogeyman; impoverished, dangerous and threatening.

All of which made it fertile ground for acid house to thrive. Hundreds of buildings left empty by recession, a closely intercon-nected community and established criminal networks, plus a young population with hopes and aspirations that Thatcher's "economic miracle" inflated yet left unrealised. On top of this ran the deep tribal loyalties of the area's football clubs – Millwall to the south, West Ham United to the east, and pockets of Arsenal and Tottenham support to the north.

"People who haven't experienced the thrill of football do not understand what makes a hooligan tick, but if any one of those people who condemn people who fight at football could experience the feeling then perhaps they would begin to understand," wrote Colin Ward in *Steaming In*, his pre-acid house insider's account of London's football mobs in the mid-eighties. "It is said that the brain can create its own drug to beat any of the most powerful opiates. If the substance created within a football hooligan to give that feeling could be marketed, then it would be called an ecstasy pill."[1]

The term "football hooliganism" came into popular currency in the mid-sixties, but it wasn't until the early eighties that soccer thugs were seen as more than an anarchic rabble and became genuine folk devils; typified as well-organised regiments of fighting men led by generals with organisational genius, dressed in expensive casualwear and adept at outsmarting the police. Foremost amongst them were West Ham United's Inter City Firm, who caused mayhem across the country, leaving their victims with "calling cards" announcing: "Congratulations, you have just met the ICF."

In 1985, Scotland Yard's Public Order branch, prompted by a hysterical media, instigated undercover operations on the country's leading "firms": amongst others, Chelsea's Headhunters, Millwall's Bushwhackers and the ICF. Officers were given false identities and ordered to live the lives of hooligans (some even went so far as to get arrested whilst fighting themselves), lengthy surveillance was conducted, and in 1986 and 1987 there was a series of dawn raids on suspected thugs' houses. Seized weapons were laid out for press cameras and the arrested were accused of being master tacticians of violence.

The main charges laid were those of conspiracy to cause violent disorder or conspiracy to make an affray; these were thought easier to prove. However, many of the trials began to collapse, for reasons of insufficient, unreliable or even forged evidence from the police. In the most high-profile of the ICF cases in May 1988, the judge stopped proceedings after fourteen weeks and ordered the jury to clear the eleven defendants of all charges; stating that prosecution evidence was "fabricated", and that police had faked log books.[2] The ICF "ringleaders" went free; one of them, a key face called Cass Pennant, stated that the police had "set criminals to catch criminals, and got caught".[3]

One of the grand myths of Ecstasy culture is that it put an end to football hooliganism. Instead of fighting, the thugs genially buzzed on E and danced with each other, subsequently taking the carnival atmosphere onto the terraces; many of the "top boys" began to channel their energies into clubs and drugs, creating new weekend rituals based around dancing – and making money – rather than violence. As if confirming the utopian idea that Ecstasy could somehow raise human consciousness to a higher level, thuggery seemed to be outdated, finished, almost embarrassing. "It's almost as if hooliganism is not fashionable any more," commented John Stalker, Deputy Chief Constable of Greater Manchester Police in 1990.[4]

Arrests at English matches fell by 22 per cent between the 1989/90 and 1992/93 seasons, and continued to fall during the nineties, although violence never really disappeared; many began to stage set-piece showdowns away from club grounds. But while this apparent sea-change coincided with the rise of Ecstasy, there were other social and economic factors involved. Changing police tactics after the collapse of the ICF trial, which culminated in the establishment of the National Football Intelligence Unit, made an impact. Forces acquired a whole armoury of new technologies, closed-circuit television, mobile video cameras, surveillance by plainclothes "spotters" who recognised known faces by sight, and a computer database for names and mug-shots. Another determinant was the change in the culture of football, a growing nausea at hostilities in the aftermath of the disasters and deaths at the Heysel stadium in 1985, Bradford in 1986 and Hillsborough in 1989.

As the terraces were replaced by all-seater stadiums and the lucrative Premier League was established in 1992, clubs began to place greater emphasis on the commercial side of the sport, selling themselves as a total leisure concept. Television coverage, satellite media contracts, sponsorship and merchandising increased in importance at the expense of the fans, who became little more than background atmosphere for TV broadcasts. But did the "miracle drug" truly alter consciousness and somehow contribute to the changes within the sport? Or was it simply a moment of euphoria that illuminated the end of what the Football Trust called the "dark days of the 1980s", a temporary diversion, as football became just another commodity controlled by the forces of a free-market economy?[5]

Acid house's transition from its original suburban and bohemian provenance to an inner-city audience was effected early. Tony Wilson was a soul scene veteran, a DJ who played his funk and hip hop collection in disco pubs around his birthplace, Stepney, east London. He was also a friend of Paul Oakenfold, had been holidaying in Ibiza since 1983 and playing alongside both Oakenfold and Trevor Fung, first at the Project Club in Streatham and then, at the end of 1987, at Future. His trademark style was a mixture of white pop – like his anthem, the Gaelic mysticism of the Waterboys' *Whole of the Moon* – with slow, pounding Belgian "New Beat". Wilson became a conduit for the introduction of acid house to his east London constituency; soon Spectrum, where he also played, was the haunt of what were patronisingly labelled "love thugs" – proletarian E-heads.

At first the influx of outsiders was a novelty; much was made of former football hooligans from Millwall, Arsenal and West Ham dancing together at Clink Street, Spectrum or Camden Palace, necking Es, shaking hands, grinning like loons and passing each other spliffs, a complete reversal of the mass street fights of the mid-eighties. Ecstasy, people muttered, what a wonder cure for intolerance! "I was chatting to Andy Weatherall at a Spectrum all-dayer," recalls Dave Swindells, "and he was pointing at this bloke: 'Oh this geezer, he used to be a real hard nut at the [Chelsea] Shed End.' And there was this guy, this skinhead, with all these flowers laced like a daisy chain in his hair. And then he went on: 'And so was he, and so was he, and so was he . . .' "

But by the autumn of 1988, these new recruits who had never seen the sun set over the Ibiza shore or been part of fashionable West End clubland were being damned as "acid teds" clad in their uniform of bandannas and dungarees, shirts off and tattoos out, gurning and shrieking "acieed!" in chorus like they were still on the terraces. Yet the vision of an identikit "love thug" was a caricature of reality with a distinct undercurrent of class tension; the uncouth hordes from the council estates were viewed as a joke or a threat, or both. Nevertheless, the flow could not be stemmed, and the scene spread inexorably outwards. In October 1988, Tony Wilson launched the first acid house club in the East End, Adrenalin, establishing a new point of departure for the scene. He'd brought the East Enders into the West End, now they were taking the scene back east with them.

"I don't regret it," says Andy Swallow. "People say: 'Why did you do it?' I don't know really. I don't suppose there is a real reason. You're brought up in something, an era in football; I was fourteen, I either went with the hooligans or I went with the mums and dads and the normal people. I chose to go with the hooligans so from the age of fourteen I didn't know any different. So from the time you're fifteen, sixteen, seventeen, you think it's right anyway. When you're twenty, you enjoy doing it. There ain't any explanation for it. Nobody can say why you go chasing a geezer down the road. There ain't a logical reason for it! Why do you beat a geezer up if he's got a Norwich scarf? There ain't a logical reason! It was a trend. You become a gang, feel part of it. Everyone says to me: 'Why?' Fuck me, I couldn't tell you mate. Why does anyone go to church? You believe in it, I suppose. And that was it, it was as strong as religion."

Andy Swallow was one of the West Ham supporters whose case was thrown out of court during the Inter City Firm trial of 1988, although he would soon find history repeating itself. After the trial collapsed, Swallow, then twenty-eight, moved out to Essex where he ran a series of market stalls selling T-shirts and jumpers. He also started going to acid house clubs. At Future, he befriended Tony Wilson and began organising after-hours parties in Mile End and Hackney with his football mates John Eames and Danny Harrison, and DJing under the pseudonym Mr Pasha. By the start of 1989 they were ensconced in what would become one of the key clubs of the summer, Echoes, a small discotheque set back from the A11 at the foot of Bow flyover, in the middle of some of London's bleakest scenery. Friday nights were Tony Wilson's Adrenalin, Saturdays Swallow's Pasha; the crowd were young, working-class locals, and in the euphoria of the honeymoon period, the East End seemed to be rising from its grave.

The area was also becoming the centre of the warehouse scene, primarily through the efforts of Genesis. Genesis was run by Wayne Rockwood, Andy Pritchard and Keith Brooks. Rockwood, twenty-two, was an East Ender with music business connections; he had worked with Stock Aitken and Waterman girl pop duo Mel and Kim, and had enjoyed his initiation at Spectrum. He immediately rushed back east and started spreading the word. "My immediate friends thought I was totally off it. I used to go to this East End pub with all these villain-type fellers and say: 'I've found these clubs, come out.' They were like: 'Leave it out!' These were hard-core villains who'd start fighting and have a major punch-up just for looking at them. One day I got them to come to Camden Palace, they popped a pill and that was it, after that they were running around loved-up in acid T-shirts. Every one of them totally lost it."

From their first party in October 1988 onwards, Genesis

developed a prodigious reputation for cracking huge warehouses, week after week, from Aldgate to Hackney, Tottenham to Walthamstow, a reputation that led Tony Colston-Hayter to collaborate with them at the end of 1988. They would break into a building, change the locks, copy a phony leasing agreement onto an estate agent's letterhead, and Rockwood would stand on the door with a clipboard and a fake guest-list of celebrity names, telling police he was running a reception for George Michael or some other rock star. Few thought he could be lying. "I've had commissioners of police signing snide leases, saying: 'Here's my number, if you've got any problems, just ring,' " he smiles.

The east London police, familiar with the area's tradition of illegal late-night drinking clubs and blues parties, appeared unconcerned about acid house in its initial stages. "The police were always more than happy," says Tim Strudwick, who ran Hypnosis at The Dungeons; dank, claustrophobic cellars beneath a biker pub on Lea Bridge Road. "They knew there was no trouble guaranteed, there might be some noise complaints, but as far as they were concerned, if there was something happening in east London and no one was getting killed, it was a good night."

On May Bank Holiday weekend, Andy Swallow helped launch the first acid house pirate radio station, Centre Force. What seems commonplace now was ground-breaking in 1989: house music all day and all night long, seven days a week, interspersed with advertisements for raves and "shout-outs" to callers who rang in to the station's mobile phone. Centre Force was instrumental in fostering the sense of community which illuminated the summer of 1989; its rattle and hiss a constant background, whether at home or in the car, it shot static and sparks through the drab cityscape. The combination of off-the-wall DJ babble and superlative music was unprofessional, unpredictable, and completely inimitable, and not only made the station's owners the biggest players on the East End scene, but set the blueprint that all house pirates have followed since. Over the summer of '89 it was essential to "keep it locked" to 88.3 FM. "Are you ready London?!" screamed the most memorable Centre Force advert over the rising chords of Rhythim is Rhythim's *Strings of Life*. "Let's go . . . MENTAL!!!"

The "studio" – two turntables, a tape deck, a cellular phone and a list of telephone numbers scrawled on the wall – was moved around regularly through empty high-rise flats in Stratford and Poplar. Centre Force was part of a long outlaw tradition, but it was also more than that: it set a tone, a kind of ruffian bravado, which fed on and contributed to the mood of the times.

In 1964, Radio Caroline began pirate broadcasts from a ship off the British coast, playing rock and R&B, music that was rarely aired on national radio at that time. Since then illegal stations had continued to fill cultural gaps, particularly for black musics like reggae and soul. This continued with house, which was little heard on legal radio until 1990; as with many other aspects of the house scene, the pirate format was adapted from the urban black community. The house boom of 1989 sparked an upswing in pirate broadcasting, and 1990 saw an all-time high in Department of Trade and Industry raids on pirates, 647 in one year. Technological developments had made it not only cheaper to set up a transmitter, but easier to conceal it from the DTI. In fact, pirates usually had more to fear from other pirates, who would steal or smash their transmitters in internecine conflicts, than the DTI. In 1990, the government brought in a new Broadcasting Act which provided powers to seize equipment, including DJs' precious record collections, and pass sentences of up to six months in prison. Trade and Industry Minister Edward Leigh cited pirates' interference with emergency services transmissions: "This is no joking matter," he commented. "It could cost lives."

At the end of 1989, many pirates ceased broadcasting in order to apply for legal status. Kiss in London and Sunset in Manchester won the first licences to broadcast dance music twenty-four hours a day to their respective cities. They subsequently adopted more commercial daytime programming in order to reach a wider listener base and raise advertising revenue, saving the specialist DJs' shows for the evenings. BBC Radio One soon followed their lead with Pete Tong's weekly national dance show, the *Essential Mix* DJ slot, the poaching of Danny Rampling's show from Kiss and the launch of jungle and soul programmes, making it a major player in the dance market. Even stiffer fines for pirate broadcasting were introduced in 1992, yet still the radio outlaws proliferated, fulfilling new demands for genre dance music – specifically ragga, hardcore and jungle – which the legal stations could not satisfy. Although Britain now had national dance radio, it still needed its pirates to speak for and to the heart of the scene.

plaistow and canning town

Things started to go wrong very quickly in east London, for one major reason: drugs. It was a reflection in microcosm of the wider rave scene of 1989. Everyone wanted Ecstasy, and Ecstasy was illegal; a huge black market was created almost overnight.

Throughout 1989, rave promoters and the police had expressed fears at the encroachment of organised crime on the scene, drawn by drug money and the chance to establish new empires of influence. By the end of the eighties, organised crime had become synonymous with drug distribution, and, seeing a booming market in Ecstasy, LSD and amphetamines on the rave circuit, growing numbers of traditional villains were leaving crimes like armed robbery behind and entering the trade. The idealistic, hippie cannabis smuggler of the seventies was a thing of the past. As former London gangster Dave Courtney pointed out: "Nowadays, you can say that most people who are involved in crime are really involved in drugs. Villainy revolves around money, and there's no better, easier, quicker way to make money than drugs. People who wouldn't have touched drugs a few years ago are well into it. The stigma's gone. No one looks down on it."[6]

The stakes had been raised; according to Customs and Excise statistics, the amount of Ecstasy coming into Britain multiplied by 4,000 per cent between 1990 and 1995. Criminal gangs became involved in importing the drug from Europe, running clubs as outlets for drug dealing, operating rave security firms, and taking protection money from other clubs. Club culture is perennially negotiating the grey area between legality and illegality, and staff in most house venues have to deal to some extent with criminals: if there are no drugs, the atmosphere will suffer and numbers will dwindle. In London, some clubs are run by prominent criminal families, and in others drug sales are controlled by teams of bouncers who franchise out the right to trade within the venue and use their muscle to evict rival dealers. "When the Ecstasy thing started, in the early stages you had rival drug gangs fighting it out on the dancefloor, which went against the whole peace and love thing," explains Bernard O'Mahoney, a former doorman and member of a gang which controlled the Ecstasy trade in Essex during the early nineties. "So club managements were faced with a stark choice: they either allowed dealing and controlled it, or they threw all these people out and ended up with an empty club. Obviously no punters would go in a place where there was an air of violence, so it was agreed that doormen were a necessary evil and that they would control these people. That's when the money started rolling in. If you stand on the door, you control the club. If you control the club, the money comes your way." In Northern Ireland and Eire, Ecstasy supply is often controlled by Republican and Loyalist paramilitaries. The murder of three Ecstasy wholesalers (one of whom also ran a club security firm) in a professional contract killing in Essex in 1995 was just another indication of how lucrative and serious the Ecstasy trade had become. The result of the explosion of Ecstasy culture during the summer of 1989 was that the lifestyles of British youth became inextricably bound up with criminal activity.

Joe Wieczorek, then thirty-two, was a veteran of the rock gig circuit, working for everyone from the Bay City Rollers in 1974 to Live Aid in 1985, and had owned a pub on the Hackney Road. At Clink Street Studios in 1988, he bumped into some of the faces he knew from football – Millwall and West Ham boys. Wieczorek was Tottenham; years before he had been stabbed in a feud with Millwall, maybe even by one of the "proper fucking enemies" who was dancing in the warehouse alongside him. But now, nothing. MDMA had worked its miracle cure again. Wieczorek saw the Clink Street format as simple yet perfect: just four walls, smoke, strobe and rhythm. He began running parties under the banner of Labrynth, taking the misspelt name from the warren-like venue in Bow – "ten rooms of madness" – which he occupied for ten weeks early in 1989. Unlike the opulent productions of Sunrise and Energy, this was no-frills, no-nonsense entertainment; a quick glimpse of heaven, then away again into the darkness.

"Warehouses were the best. If it had a toilet, lovely. One minute it's empty, deserted, no one wants to know, the rich fat businessmen have finished with it, the sign's up 'for sale', and all of a sudden, in the space of eight hours you've brought so much happiness and enjoyment into so many lives and it didn't really cost people too much money. And sometimes, just sometimes, you got a little pot of gold at the end of it. I call that a dream."

Kingsland Road, Shacklewell Lane, Essex Road, Homerton High Street, Ferry Lane; Wieczorek, his girlfriend Sue Barnes and partners Brian Semmens and Tom Larkin took their guerrilla revue all over the area, busting in, partying hard and getting out fast, notching up an amazing tally of 112 illegal raves. But within months they found that others wanted to take advantage of their success. Before a warehouse party in Silvertown Way, Canning Town, their security team demanded more money than usual.

Wieczorek refused. During the night, a gang of men slipped into the warehouse unhindered and attacked the ravers with machetes. "They attacked every black person in there," says Wieczorek. "It was not a racial attack although it was made to *look* like a racial attack – racial attacks in Canning Town happen all the time so another one at an acid party would not raise any eyebrows with local Old Bill because it's fucking normal. But this wasn't normal – they wanted to take us over and that's all there is to it. If I had been in that warehouse I don't think I would be alive today. I mean that."

Wieczorek insists that it was a nucleus of ex-Inter City Firm men who were involved in this and other such attacks over the summer – demanding protection money, ordering people not to stage parties in their area unless they delivered a cut of the takings, and taking over security in order to control drug sales. "If you've got the promoter in your pocket, all the Es are down to you," he explains. "That was the thing, the Es, and they were flying out."

One night, he says, they treated him to a night on the town to show off the riches at their disposal, treasures that could be his if he offered up Labrynth to them. "They took me out, gave me the red carpet treatment, took me to all their clubs, said 'this is owned by so-and-so but we run it', that sort of shit. It was all protection of one form or another. Probably exactly the same thing had happened to the people who ran these pubs and clubs as was happening to me in acid parties. I got taken to Orpington, to the West End, to the East End. No money changed hands but there were drinks put in front of us every time we walked in a gaff.

"When I came back, I felt sick at how much of a foothold these cunts had. Feet firmly under the table, running things. All the old firm, the same geezers who would be standing across the road, throwing bricks and having silly fights over football, had realised there was no money in football. I realised: 'You cunts have got your act together, haven't you.' "

When Wieczorek refused to co-operate, a deputation turned up at his Bethnal Green flat to threaten him with a gun. This was when he realised it was time to get out of the warehouse party game, and soon afterwards moved Labrynth into a permanent home, the Four Aces club in Dalston, where it would remain for years to come.

He wasn't the only one living in fear. Around the same time, another prominent East End promoter was kidnapped from his home by a gang he describes as "the new Krays", demanding 25 per cent of his business in return for protection. He, too, gave up running parties but was forced to let the extorters carry on using his organisation's name.

Police intelligence suggested that incidents like this were instigated by people connected with Centre Force – West Ham thugs turned party pirates, using the station, its club nights and warehouse parties as a base from which to take over the East End scene. Andy Swallow insists that such rumours were just that: unsubstantiated accusations based on fantasies about organised hooligans striving to dominate the area's black economy:

"There were a lot of myths going about that we were involved in taking people's doors, taking over their clubs, that every time somebody put a party on we demanded 25 per cent. If that's the case, I don't know where the money is, because I obviously didn't get it! No, there were a lot of false statements. We were big in east London for parties because we lived in east London. At that time everybody seemed to be scared of east London and we were an east London radio station. You do get people who say it was run by gangsters, but that's only people who don't really know. The myth was it was all ICF. I've heard all the rumours about the parties we took over – I don't remember it although I was there. People like a bit of that. It's like the Krays; people love that, but if you look into what they did it wasn't that clever anyway."

Nevertheless, ugly stories proliferated in east London's pirate underworld: racist graffiti scrawled on the walls of pirate HQs, one DJ attacked with a Stanley knife, his fingers slashed so he could no longer mix records, another hung by his ankles from a bridge over the Thames because he had played at the wrong firm's rave, a team of bouncers stabbed, one of them scalped. Acid house had transformed the East End, but as thousands danced in blissed-out ignorance, their pleasures were facilitated by violence and terror.

The police were convinced that a major drug-dealing network was operating out of Centre Force and its Bow Road club, Echoes, and at the end of the summer of 1989 set up Operation Tiger at Plaistow police station to investigate. The team, headed by Detective Inspector Toby Charles and Detective Sergeant Craig Stratford with a dozen officers under their command, had heard about assaults at various warehouse parties in their district, and began to monitor Swallow and others associated with Centre Force. "When we gathered more intelligence on these incidents, we found that it was more than just an isolated party at an isolated venue, and that they were being organised by a number of groups, one of which appeared to be centred around the East End area, Plaistow and Canning Town in particular, and some of the people were ex-ICF members, and we had information that these particular people were into drugs themselves in quite a large way," says Stratford.

The Ecstasy trade, Stratford believed, had united London's once warring football gangs: "It seemed that a group of people who had started as football hooligans were then getting into some sort of organised crime situation, and they obviously had contacts throughout London and the south-east with other football-oriented people. It certainly appeared that drug dealing was taking place within the requests of the punters on the radio as well as the people who were running it, the DJs."

The team set up phone taps, surveillance on half a dozen core suspects, and worked with the DTI to monitor the station. (This was the part Stratford enjoyed: "You found yourself getting into the music," he admits.) But illegal parties and unlicensed broadcasting weren't what Operation Tiger was all about. Its purpose was to prove that Swallow and his colleagues were involved in the large-scale supply of drugs. They wanted to collar them with Es. Tiger, however, was flawed from the outset. It was, says Stratford, a "rag, tag and bobtail squad" with a serious lack of resources, little expertise in the drugs field, and unskilled in observation techniques. Undercover officers were spotted and the investigation was leaking like a sieve. Swallow quickly realised that Centre Force's base was being watched and its staff followed, if only because they had been allowed to remain in the same place for so long without DTI interference.

On October 20th, 1989, police raided Echoes, Centre Force's Plaistow studio and a dozen houses simultaneously. It was Friday night, just after the club had opened; some thirty constables dressed in jeans and T-shirts had paid at the door and were waiting inside, and at 10.30 p.m. another hundred stormed the front door and swarmed through the fire exits. But the raid was also botched. Swallow, leaving his house, was jumped by eight men. He wasn't in the least surprised; he had been tipped off about the proposed raid a week beforehand. The bags of drugs and wads of banknotes that the police hoped to find were nowhere to be seen. "You can either blame the non-success of the raid on their intelligence, or us being unlucky or totally wrong," says Stratford.

The police were still convinced that they could make a case against the twenty-two people charged with conspiracy to supply controlled drugs, based on previous undercover observations of drug deals within the club. "Their definition of the charge," says Swallow, "was that we at Centre Force Radio were sitting there guiding people to these parties and at the parties we had all our drug dealers selling all the drugs, and we made the money from the drugs, money from the parties, and extortion from the parties that weren't ours."

However, the evidence, already circumstantial, was further weakened when, just as in the ICF trial, the judge ruled much of it unsound and inadmissible, and after a few weeks it became obvious that the main charges were not going to stick. "At the end of the day we could have proved lesser charges on a number of them, but because the main people were obviously going to be found not guilty, it was decided that there was no point pursuing the lesser charges against the others," says Stratford. "The whole case was dropped."

Swallow, again, was vindicated: "The judge basically threw it out. It was a load of old bollocks like we said it was from the off." Stratford admits that even if they had proved the case, it would have had little impact on the new criminal networks that had built up around the Ecstasy trade. It was just a manifestation of something much bigger, a phenomenon that they didn't have the resources to combat and that he is still dealing with as a Detective Inspector on one of east London's Area Drug Squads. "We never really got on the end of it at all," he says. "It was so large."

The only thing that Operation Tiger did achieve was the end of Centre Force. Tainted by rumours, wearied by the stress of court and custody, with many of its DJs having left to join the new pirate Dance FM, there was no longer the will to carry on. The station that had soundtracked the illicit rave era of 1989 finally closed the following year. "We came back on for about another four months, scattered periods, but within hours of coming back on we would be taken back off," says Swallow, who would eventually re-emerge in the mid-nineties as a successful dance record label boss. "It wasn't the same any more. The fun had gone out of it."

The "dark days of the 1980s" were over. But had a miracle truly occurred, or had it all just been a dream?

5

freaky dancing

In 1980, Ian Curtis, the twenty-three-year-old lead singer of Joy Division, mired in a depression that was more than hinted at in his unremittingly lugubrious lyrics, committed suicide. It was the end of an era for independent rock, and the beginning of another. Within a few months of the tragedy, the remaining members of the band, Bernard Sumner, Peter Hook and Stephen Morris, were gigging again. They recruited Morris's girlfriend Gillian Gilbert to play keyboards and, crucially, augmented their sound with electronic sequencers and drum computers.

The Manchester quartet – renamed New Order – were signed to Factory Records, a local label run by Granada TV presenter Tony Wilson, a charismatic motormouth with a love of Comme des Garçons suits and soundbites from the Situationists. Although Factory's prevailing image was one of grey northern earnestness, its roster included numerous bands who were experimenting with electronics, funk licks and percussive grooves – an early release was *Moody* by ESG, a classic at New York's Paradise Garage. New Order had considerable success in the States, and whilst in New York had been deeply impressed by the vitality of the city's dance clubs. This would ultimately result in collaborations with key American dance producer Arthur Baker on *Confusion*, and a minimalist, technotronic behemoth of a single, *Blue Monday*, the best-selling British 12-inch record of all time. Of all the independent rock groups of the eighties, New Order were the furthest ahead of their time, an early indication of the textural, technologically enhanced rock'n'roll of the future.

1980 was also the year that another band formed that would shape not only the culture but the public image of Manchester right into the nineties. Born in 1962 in Little Hulton, a tight knot of streets in a working class area to the north-west of the city, lead singer Shaun Ryder had been in and out of youth custody and had first taken LSD at thirteen. Before long, he and his best friend, Mark Berry, would be swallowing three or four microdots at a time and walking down to the Arndale Centre to watch the colours unravel. Berry, nicknamed Bez, had also been inside for robbery after being turned in by his father, a Detective Inspector in Liverpool. They made a comical pair: Ryder with his absurdist turn of speech and extra-dry wit, Berry with his exaggerated loping gait, both of them blaggers and thieves with a restless intelligence, continually searching for the next thrill and preferring to travel to Amsterdam or London than stay in small-minded Salford.

Their band, the Happy Mondays, played its first major gig at Factory's Haçienda club in 1983. The Haçienda, largely funded by New Order, had opened the year before with a party featuring the incongruous partnership of obese Mancunian "comedian" Bernard Manning and disco divas ESG. Designed by Ben Kelly as a utilitarian space, it was a former yachting showroom, a monolithic warehouse with raw steel and brick exposed, girders and bollards around the dancefloor, columns painted yellow and black in imitation of factory hazard warnings. *Industrial*, it was called, a word in vogue at the time.

The man who booked the Happy Mondays into the Haçienda was Mike Pickering. Born in Manchester in 1958, Pickering had a perfect c.v. for the job. He had danced to Northern Soul at the Blackpool Mecca, seen the Sex Pistols' seminal Manchester debut at the Lesser Free Trade Hall, mixed Chic with industrial dance-rock records in Rotterdam clubs, and as a member of mutant funk band Quando Quango, had scored dance hits on

New York's black gay scene and been remixed by Mark Kamins, the American DJ who discovered Madonna. Pickering was brought in to the Haçienda by New Order's manager, Rob Gretton, an old friend from the Maine Road terraces. Like Paul Oakenfold in London, Pickering had extraordinary foresight; he believed that the Haçienda could emulate the Paradise Garage, where Larry Levan had alternated psychedelic dance with opulent disco and European electronic pop.

At the time, Hewan Clarke was the resident DJ, playing raw soul, jazz-funk and heavy Latin percussion work-outs. Clarke was a recruit from Manchester's thriving black soul underground: clubs like Legends, Berlin, the Gallery and the Reno, an after-hours where the real hard core would bump and grind, wreathed in cannabis smoke. In a city most often celebrated for its white independent rock, it's worth noting that this other tradition existed, a tradition that would later provide the backbone for electro, hip hop and house music.

Mike Pickering produced the first Happy Mondays single, *Delightful*, which was released in 1985. The band were beginning to hit their groove, a ramshackle thrash with a submerged under-current of funk and Ryder moaning free-associations over the top. "Our sound's all sorts really," Ryder would explain later. "Funkadelic, *One Nation Under a Groove* . . . Northern Soul . . . punk rock . . . Jimi Hendrix . . . Captain Beefheart. And a load of drugs on top of that."[1] "People tend to forget that the Happy Mondays were always a dance band," adds his father Derek, "but people couldn't dance to it until E came along."

They looked the part too: shaggy haircuts, ragged goatees, huge, flapping denim flares and training shoes. Gaunt, spindly Bez was their talisman, playing no instrument, just cavorting insanely on the stage with a pair of maracas; no other indie band had a member who did nothing but *dance*. The Mondays looked like football casuals, Perry Boys, scallies; lads from the estates, but *clued-up* lads who knew where to get an ounce of weed and had all the right records in their collection. Maverick impresario Jeff Barrett promoted their first London gig:

"It was a real shock, because I went down to the soundcheck and they were sat outside – at that point it was a bit of a meeting point for winos, so I went up to these guys sat round the side of this club with their snorkel parkas, flares and bottles of cider, and was just about to say to them, 'Would you leave?', when I smelled hash. I suddenly thought, who are these guys? They actually looked good in a peculiar way – and it was the Mondays. What made them different from casuals down here was they took acid. That night, Shaun Ryder came up to me and asked me: 'Can you get me any draw?' I'd never heard it called draw before. His dad came over to me, Derek, who was their sound man, and said: 'Jeff – our Shaun, he didn't ask you for acid, did he?' 'No, he asked for puff.' 'If he asks for acid, don't give it to him, he's got a gig to do . . .' I was totally hooked. I put them on six times."

In November 1984, Mike Pickering started DJing at Nude Night at the Haçienda, which would run every Friday for almost six years. Initially the venue was, as one regular of the time describes it, "a freezing Arctic warehouse, the domain of arty group cliqueyness, all dark and dismal indie music", but now it had begun to widen its social horizons. Pickering and his partner Martin Prendergast would mix electro – speedy, synthetic rap built on the innovations of Kraftwerk – hip hop, funk, techno-pop, New York dance imports, anything which moved the crowd, in fact, a crowd which was increasingly mixed in race, and included some spectacularly extravagant dancers – the Foot Patrol – wearing zoot suits with white spats and spinning intricate patterns around the floor.

By 1986, Pickering and Prendergast would also be playing the early Chicago house records on Trax and DJ International. The raw jack-tracks chimed with the prevailing mood and slotted right in amongst the hard-edged, modernist sounds that the dancers preferred, as they also did at Nottingham's Garage club and Sheffield's Jive Turkey parties, where DJs like Graeme Park, Parrot and Winston Hazell were programming similar selections. Stu Allen's *Bus Dis* shows on Piccadilly Radio – an hour of hip hop, an hour of house – focused this futurist agenda. The big tours of 1987 were the Chicago House Revue and electronic hip hop duo Mantronix: both radical, avant-garde applications of technology with a fierce, energetic kick. Every progressive musician in the city sat up and took notice. If the Sex Pistols' visit inspired Manchester's first punk bands, these gigs helped inspire a new explosion.

whitworth street west and oldham road

"In Ibiza there was a big contingent of people from Sheffield and Manchester, about the same number of them as there was of us," remembers Shoomer and Ibiza veteran Adam Heath. "Really cool people. They came from a different place. We all pretty much had working class parents but none of us was poor. But suddenly we met people who had a background that was poor. That struck me. They were very much people who got out of where they came from. They all lived around Europe, they didn't really go home a lot. What work they did was thieving mainly. There was a name for them – Interpol call them 'international tourist thieves'."

Ibiza, London, Amsterdam. From this working-class hedonist's hippie trail, with its built-in itinerary of sun, drugs, clubs, thieving, football and music, Ecstasy first came to Manchester. The story that gets told and retold is of Shaun and Bez driving back from London with a car boot stuffed with pills and setting the town alight. But some of the original Balearic community from Spectrum and Future were involved too; connections were made, networks established, based on old football ties, Ibiza acquaintances, and followers of the Mondays.

There was already some mad dancing going on in the

Haçienda on Friday nights, but by the start of 1988 there was some *very* mad, very *strange* dancing too. *Freaky Dancing*, the Mondays' second single had been called, and here it was in action. In one corner of the room would be Shaun and Bez – his eyes rolling and limbs pumping like a broken doll in electro-shock – plus a gaggle of mates, rocking with an intensity that seemed almost unnatural. They were already infamous in their home town, but now people were staring at them, fascinated. What? Why? *How*? And each week the group got larger, the dancing more freaky, until one Friday, Bez left "E corner", climbed onto the stage and began to *conduct* the crowd, which by now had locked into his chemical wavelength.

Manchester's Summer of Love was inaugurated by a new Wednesday night at the Haçienda. Hot started on July 13th, 1988: "The original idea was to do a tacky Costa del Sol beach party theme with sand and umbrellas," says former Haçienda promotions manager Paul Cons. "I'd been down to various acid house parties in London; Shoom and Hedonism. The acid house thing had been building in the Haçienda anyway on Friday nights, a little E crowd in the corner. So it all coincided and mutated into an Ibiza thing. On the opening night everyone was off their heads, we had a swimming pool, seaside lights and all that. The stage got completely taken over by people off their faces on E who didn't want to know about anything else but dancing. The whole thing felt right – it was summer and it was very Ibiza." The DJ, Jon Dasilva, would string together acidic textures with recordings from the BBC sound effects library, babbling brooks and crashing waves, which gave Hot an exotic ambience; a sunspot at the heart of the Rainy City.

At Friday's Nude Night, Martin Prendergast had departed and Mike Pickering was joined in the DJ booth by Graeme Park, an extrovert Scot who had introduced house to the Midlands at Nottingham's Garage, and excelled at creating a joyous narrative out of his mixes. The two had collaborated on the Northern House Tour in February 1988, where Pickering's Latin-influenced house band T-Coy had topped the bill. Now they stood together at the end of the night, high above the crowd, T-shirts soaked in sweat, arms raised, eyes skyward, like pagan deities, while the banshee wail of Byron Stingily's falsetto reamed out of the speakers: "I want to give you . . . *devotion* . . ." And the crowd, fingers reaching towards the booth, murmured the a cappella refrain in unison: "Oh, *devotion* . . . oh, *devotion* . . ." It was, someone pointed out later, a feeling so intense that it could not be expressed in mere words.

The summer was brief but seemed timeless. The Mondays and their mates were now into Ecstasy retail, and made it their mission to turn on Manchester; one weekend they had a party and gave it away gratis. The Haçienda had become a place where normal laws didn't apply. It was common to see someone sitting on the stage, nonchalantly serving up from a bulging plastic bag of pills. People were changing overnight. Stephen Cresser, roadie with both the Happy Mondays and Stone Roses, recalls how his friend Eric Barker – one of *the* club faces in the city – "in literally three weeks went from nice side parting and checked shirt and chinos – dapper – to wearing a goatee beard, sunglasses, a pillbox hat, Aladdin slippers that turned up at the ends and baggy silk trousers with a whistle round his neck".

Whereas the venue had been a place for students, trendies and soul boys, now it was also attracting a new demographic, youths from the sink estates of north Manchester. "It seemed like a really eclectic mix, everyone rubbed shoulders and got on really well whether they were students or scallies or whatever," remembers Paul Cons. "The scallies that were at the Haçienda were the more progressive ones, more sussed; it was more bohemian working-class kids – maybe they went to Amsterdam or were doing a bit of part-time drug dealing to have a good life, not get a proper job."

Acid house, for a few brief moments, seemed to unite the city: the outcasts from the north side of town, the scammers and grafters and chancers and characters mixing with the pop stars and students and fashion-conscious club kids. "In London there was a lot of that hippie vibe. That never really happened in Manchester," says Justin Robertson, then a student, one of the dancers on the stage, but later to become a celebrated DJ. "In Manchester it was quite close to what acid house was about – people from council estates and students, not particularly trying to promote some image of togetherness, but just getting on with it. And certainly not being élitist – that's the funny thing. All the early stuff you used to read about the London acid house scene was love and peace, but then they had the most strict door policy."

After the Haçienda closed at two, the diehards would head off into the wastelands of Hulme, through the concrete crescents of the area's huge low-rise estate (now demolished), to party on at an after-hours blues dance. The Kitchen in Charles Barry Crescent was actually two council flats with the walls knocked through into one and converted into a studio. At first there were video games and beds in there, and people would sit around a huge table talking themselves down with a beer and a spliff, or carry on dancing on a makeshift floor downstairs. Some weekends there would be hundreds packed inside.

By the end of the summer, Manchester had its first major illegal warehouse party under a railway arch near Piccadilly Station. The prime movers were the bohemian blaggers Paul Cons refers to, people who would become the driving force in Mancunian house culture over the next two years: Anthony and Chris Donnelly, siblings in their early twenties from the estates of Wythenshawe, plus Eric Barker and his younger brother Andy, who was one half of the Spinmasters hip hop mixing duo. On the corner of Store Street, around the corner from the Donnellys' father's scrapyard, they spraypainted a huge Smiley face and the words: "Sweat it Out." If you look hard enough, you can still see it, faded but optimistically grinning. New Order were still right at the centre of things, too. One night they held a debauched illegal rave in the Haçienda's basement; they had just completed recording their *Technique* album in Ibiza, and later that year Bernard Sumner would do a fair impression of Bez's demented choreography on *Top of the Pops*.

In October, the Happy Mondays strengthened their links with London at a press launch for their second album at Ian St Paul and Paul Oakenfold's Spectrum club. *Bummed*, says Shaun Ryder, was first and foremost an Ecstasy album. During recording, they had kept producer Martin Hannett stoked with the stuff. "The thing about *Bummed* to us is when we were taking E we didn't initially know how to handle it and would shag everything in sight," explains Ryder. "The phrase we used, which we don't any more, is 'Did you bum her?' So bum was like our term for fucking."[2] By this time Spectrum was running a franchise in Manchester, too – the Mondays filmed a strobe-lit video for their *Wrote for Luck* single there – but the London jaunt demonstrated their ragamuffin charisma to the music press in a conducive environment. These crazy Mancs, marvelled the invited journalists, they just can't stop dancing! Naturally, the band's entourage was more than happy to provide chemical enlightenment as to why.

Within a few months, the Haçienda, a burning ball of energy, wasn't big enough to contain the scene: sheer physics – not to mention chemistry – decreed that it was going to bubble over. And sure enough, it did. The Osbourne club was a former rock venue on Oldham Road in Miles Platting, a grid of streets just north of the city centre, one of the most deprived and depressed parts of town, a landscape of boarded-up shops, broken glass and half-occupied council terraces; "car thief city", as one local called it.

The Osbourne looked like a working men's club, dark and low-ceilinged with foul-tasting beer that stank like home-brew. When Eric Barker, Jimmy Sherlock ("Jimmy Muffin") and his partner John Kenyon ("John the Phone") – another two infamous local characters with a background in the marginal trade of flyposting – booked the place, it was hosting Irish dances and wedding receptions. It was renamed the Thunderdome, and never was a club's description so apt: in this close, crepuscular hall, the music raged and boiled like heavy weather; whirlwinds and thunderbolts, hurricanes and hailstorms. The resident DJs, the Spinmasters, Steve Williams and the Jam MCs, cranked up the pressure. In the Haçienda, it was all bliss and beauty and ecstatic disco diva anthems; here they preferred metallic funk from Detroit and the steamhammer pulse of Belgian hardbeat.

By this time it was increasingly difficult to get in to the Haçienda if you weren't a regular; the Thunderdome drew the youth from the surrounding estates of Miles Platting, Ancoats, Clayton and Newton Heath, people who were desperate to get out, or simply out of it. "There's a north/south divide in Manchester," says Gary McClarnan, a photographer from Wythenshawe who documented local clubs. "The south is cosmopolitan – students and media types. The north is rough and barren to look at. People have had a hard life. It's an exploited area, a sad case for housing, there's more unemployment and therefore less respect and more to kick back at. The Thunder-dome was a very vicious sort of night, very hard-edged. You couldn't walk in there and be comfortable unless you were com-pletely out of it. Heavy music, hard, dark. Cheaper drugs. Acid and speed."

To outsiders, the Thunderdome had a scary reputation; from the inside, it was a paradise. People would meet a few hundred yards down the road at the Angel pub – and before long, the pub's sign had been modified, the letters of its name ripped away, leaving only a simple, significant "E".

Manchester was built on initiative and invention. Its textile trade was central to the Industrial Revolution, a crucible of Victorian entrepreneurialism and development commerce: Cottonopolis, the "chimney of the world". Friedrich Engels lived there in the nineteenth century, and its dark, satanic mills provided some of the inspiration for his and Karl Marx's *Communist Manifesto*. It also played a part in the birth of the Information Revolution – the first commercially available computer was built there. Although the Victorian architecture remains as testament to the affluence of its cotton kings, in recent years the city has undergone considerable regeneration, and the focus of innovation has shifted from manufacturing and engineering industries to cultural produce and leisure goods in an attempt to counteract industrial recession.

Manchester is perhaps the only city in England, excluding London and Liverpool, to create metropolitan mythologies which resonate beyond its limits. The quaint nostalgia of *Coronation Street* is the best-known of these: an idealised memory based on lost notions of community and cultural homogeneity, of honest working-class folk, cobbled streets and a warm welcome in the Rover's Return. "I knew it wouldn't last," *Street* creator Tony Warren once said, pining for the city of the late fifties. "I wanted to preserve it, like flies in amber."

If this is Manchester past, science fiction writer Jeff Noon strives to imagine Manchester future, transmuting the landscape into a claustrophobic, nocturnal sprawl populated by robocrusties, bass addicts, dole-fed thrill-seekers and sink estates used as rubbish dumps where half-human, half-canine mutants scavenge amongst broken bottles. Like all science fiction, it's an extrapolation from contemporary reality; Hulme and Rusholme projected into a dystopian parallel world. Then there are the rock myths – the wryly humorous but at the same time miserable, rain-soaked Mancunian psychogeography of the Smiths, and the one that superseded it at the turn of the nineties, which is typified by Sarah Champion's breathless eulogy, *And God Created Manchester*: the city as pop-cult central, where all cultural roads begin and end. "Why? Why? Why? Why?" Champion asked rhetorically, replying: "It's in the air, the water and the architecture . . . Manchester where the streets are paved with rock'n'roll. A land of possibilities where forming a band can bring instant fame."[3] What typifies all these disparate visions is the idea that Manchester is a city apart, unique. Things happen here that could happen nowhere else.

Manchester is big enough to have economic clout – to make things happen – yet small enough to retain some sense of community. The city has a cocksure swagger, an arrogance born of the knowledge that although London may be the capital of Britain, it is indisputably the capital of the North, a mythical principality which starts at Watford or Nottingham or Leeds, depending on whom you listen to.

This self-belief and community spirit, coupled with the musical infrastructure that already existed in the city, would contribute to the extraordinary burst of creative activity which spewed forth from the Haçienda and the Thunderdome. In 1987, Mike Pickering's band T-Coy had written the theme tune for Manchester's nascent house enclave, a loose-limbed Latinate shuffle called *Carino*. This was followed by two records which announced the city's new generation to the globe: *Voodoo Ray* by A Guy Called Gerald and *Pacific State* by 808 State. The same personnel were involved in both: Gerald Simpson, Martin Price and Graham Massey. All had been through electro, hip hop, the avant-garde fringes of rock, before being shocked into action by the raw Chicago trax. As 808 State, the trio brewed up harsh acid jams by day, bunged the demos in carrier bags and took them down to Hot in the evening, where Jon Dasilva would roll the tapes to the bewitched assembly.

Early in 1988, Simpson split from the group, to be replaced by Spinmasters duo Andy Barker and Darren Partington, and took on his own identity, A Guy Called Gerald. His debut, *Voodoo Ray*, was just that, electronic voodoo, a disembodied soprano incantation set to digital talking drums. It would take a year for it to spread to every club in the country; for now it was a cherished local secret. 808 State's *Pacific State* was intended as a homage to the technomeisters of Detroit, but turned out warped and weird with a machine-jazz sax coda. Its impact was awesome. "It was like writing the National Anthem," says Massey.

"I know it sounds like an ego thing but it wasn't, because it felt like that tune belonged to the whole culture. Something that a whole collective of people put a new value on." Indeed; both *Voodoo Ray* and *Pacific State* were simple series of musical tones transformed by communal will into invocations of freedom; alchemical spells which could unlock wide open spaces in the mind.

"The empowerment of people was an important part of it, people doing things in groups," Massey continues. "It felt strange, it was the first sense of community there'd been in years. We could define the culture, we could push the boundaries of the culture. We were very much feeding off what was going on around us because there was so much energy around, we could never run out of ideas and never run out of purpose. There was an atmosphere of 'you can do it, you can do what you want'. I just feel incredibly lucky to have been there at that point because music happens on a very personal level, but this happened on a collective consciousness level."

It wasn't just Manchester any more; it had spread out beyond the boundaries of the metropolitan district and into the outlying mill towns and rural villages of Lancashire. Blackburn, a small industrial town with a population of just over 100,000, once the biggest cotton-weaving centre in the world but now more reliant on engineering, became the focus for the events of the summer of 1989. Like many northern towns, its manufacturing industry had been decimated by recession and it was dotted with empty warehouses. It was also a convenient access point between Manchester, Bolton, Rochdale, Blackpool, Liverpool and Preston, and within easy reach of West Yorkshire. As Greater Manchester Police, headed by the religious fanatic James Anderton, a man who once claimed he had a direct hot-line to the Lord, harassed anyone who attempted to stage an illegal rave within the city limits, Blackburn became the focus for parties characterised by evangelistic beliefs as strong as those of the police chief himself.

"The drum was beating and people were tuning in on it, it was something primal inside us. You had euphoria spilling out all over the place, genuine happiness. Wow! Smiles the size of the Mersey Tunnel! There's something inside when you dance, you're into another dimension, you've got a whole new view. And if you're doing this en masse you just thrust forward with the power and energy. The law of the dance was stronger than the law of the land. What Ecstasy and hallucinogenics did was give people access to other levels of the brain that normally would be shut down, they weren't even aware of their existence. Not only had they got a new life but they'd got a new mind. It would be a shame to just say 'we were all on drugs, it was mad and we had a good time, it was a fashion', because it wasn't."

Tommy Smith has had a few years and a lot of time alone to ponder the events of 1989 and 1990: locked in a cell for twenty-three hours a day facing a potential twelve-year sentence, then travelling in India, and later camping out in the trees for nine months as part of eco-activist protests against the building of the M65 motorway in 1995. Looking back, he believes that acid house was an unstoppable force; that it was inevitable that youth would stand up and demand pleasures beyond the restrictive leisure opportunities that they were supposed to be content with.

In 1988, Smith, whose Scottish brogue gradually became infused with a latterday Celtic mysticism, returned to Blackburn from a theatre company tour of Europe. The first night back he went to an acid house party, and within months he was organising them himself. Outside London, licensing laws decreed that clubs must close by 2 a.m. It was too early: at 2 a.m. the whole club would be riding on a peak – then lights on, music off, sharp jolt back into the mundane, regulated, ordered world. No, Smith thought. The dance must go on. He and his partner Tony Creft started small, with parties in a tiny club, a shop, a factory unit, then moved into the Sett End club on Shadsworth Road, Blackburn. This would become the operational base; after the venue closed, hundreds would mass outside, waiting for the generals with their mobile phones to lead the car convoy out into the surrounding industrial estates.

These weren't rave spectaculars; Smith and Creft preferred to crack a warehouse, charge up a cheap PA and forget the frills. The charge was a mere £2 or £3; the parties didn't even have a name. Unlike Sunrise and the southern entrepreneurs, insists Smith, they were less interested in financial returns than simply giving local working-class youth access to pleasure. Once inside the venue, they would lock the doors, preventing the police from gaining entry. Even if they did break through, they wouldn't capture the sound equipment, as Smith and Creft would build kamikaze rigs hooked together with butterfly clips, so if the lawmen grabbed the PA, the electronics could be smuggled out of the building under jackets.

Power generators were more difficult: hard to hire, expensive to lose. But Smith's team of helpers were fearless; once they borrowed a car, ram-raided a shop window and escaped with the generator in their boot; another time they hijacked a power cable from a set of temporary traffic lights and fed it into the warehouse – just as, on New York's hip hop scene in the seventies, block party organisers would wire up the sound system from a lamp-post. Nothing would deter them from their goal. At another party, the police had captured the DJ's record box and slung it in their van. As ravers and police stood baiting each other, they simply wrenched the van's doors open, grabbed the records and ran back inside.

Within months, word had spread throughout the north-west. Blackburn town centre would be busier at 2 a.m. than it was on a Saturday afternoon. If you missed the convoy you had to drive endlessly round the outskirts of town, looking for the rave. Not everyone endorses the glorious myth that grew up around the town; journalist Mandi James recalls one party in the depths of winter where it was so cold, people danced with crushed Coke cans stuck to their shoes to avoid the below-zero concrete; as it became light, she felt disgusted and depressed, realising that the cause of the overpowering stench was the fact that they were dancing in an abattoir.

That summer, two parties in the north-west made national news, but neither was staged by Smith and Creft. Nor were they cheap and cheerful guerrilla raves. Joy, in Rochdale in August, and Live the Dream, in Blackburn in September, both run by the Donnelly brothers, were modelled on Tony Colston-Hayter's Sunrise, right down to the artwork and £15 ticket price. Anthony and Chris Donnelly, with their crazy schemes and crazier chat, made an infamous and inimitable double-act, and yet they had the nerve and the verve to pull off the seemingly impossible. Part of their local celebrity was inherited: "We're supposedly sons of the Quality Street Gang [a family firm from the rough end of Wythenshawe that was notorious in the seventies]." In earlier years they might have been called spivs, but Ecstasy had turned them into evangelists.

"The estate where we come from, drinking's the thing, get proper out of it and have a top chuckle with your pals," explains Anthony Donnelly. "We had a base in Wythenshawe where every activity in the world was going on from. One hundred young lads in there on beer, but all of a sudden five or ten of them have gone wayward, they're coming in with fucking bandannas tied round their heads. From 1988 to the end of 1990 we didn't touch a drop of alcohol, not one fucking drink. After Sweat it Out, for two years we went on a fucking mission from God, we were like Jehovah's Witnesses going out promoting it. Telling our parents it's going to change the world and all that."

They retained the entrepreneurial spirit, however, and at Joy brought around 3,000 to Stand Lees Farm despite the efforts of Rochdale council, the imprecations of local MP Cyril Smith and the injunction served on DJ Mike Pickering to keep him out of the area. The party that followed, Live the Dream, was equally impressive, a natural amphitheatre filled with glowing lights and marquees throbbing with bass. The Donnellys were also the prime movers in Manchester's contribution to the protest against

Graham Bright's Entertainments (Increased Penalties) Bill. They booked Albert Square in the centre of town, and 1,500 rallied around a Freedom to Party wagon from which the Jam MCs played records under the banner "Expression Not Oppression". Later that night, they kicked down a warehouse in Hasling, which, significantly for the ultimate failure of the anti-Bright Bill campaign, attracted more than three times as many people as the demonstration.

Back in Manchester, there was madness everywhere, every night: the Haçienda, the Thunderdome, the Venue, Precinct 13; in the surrounding districts of Ashton, Middleton, Ancoats and Hulme. "Manchester vibe in the area!" as the dreadlocked extrovert-about-town Fonso Buller would scream over the PA whenever he got hold of a microphone: "Manchester vibe in the area!" Or as the Spinmasters would constantly repeat on their deranged Sunset Radio show: "Big shout going out . . ."

By the end of the summer, the rest of the country was waking up to what had happened in Britain's largest village. *Pacific State* and *Voodoo Ray* were anthems in every club in the country, and the triumvirate of bands that represented what would soon be labelled "Madchester", the Happy Mondays, the Stone Roses and the Inspiral Carpets, had gained in status in the eyes of the London music media. They now commanded front covers in the two national rock weeklies, *NME* and *Melody Maker*, and would continue to do so for years to come. How did these three indie rock bands (and the imitators that followed them) become so entwined with an electronic dance-drug scene? The Mondays' link is obvious: they drank and drugged in the Haçienda, and had established a friendship with the prime movers of acid house in London which resulted in a radical remix of *Wrote for Luck* by Paul Oakenfold and Terry Farley. The Roses and Carpets frequented the Haç too, but were less influenced by its culture. "You can't say that it hasn't done some good, Ecstasy," said Roses frontman Ian Brown when asked exactly how the drug had affected his band. "Ecstasy has loosened people up who maybe weren't really in touch with their true spirit."[4]

The combination of house music, indie bands, Ecstasy, and the terrace chic of the north-west created a synergy between rock and dance that was perhaps only possible in a city where most musicians had worked in the same studios and were connected somewhere along the line, and where the main players could often be found on the dancefloor of the same club. Yet even within the context of indie rock, all three bands displayed marked differences. The Mondays played a crazy, stoned, mutant funk; the Roses an oceanic sixties psychedelia enhanced with backwards guitar and studio trickery; the Carpets were a straight-forward Hammond Organ-driven beat group with pudding-bowl haircuts. There were differences in attitude, too: the Mondays were full-on hedonists, "twenty-four-hour party people", in their own words; the Roses, with their cool, arrogant, pouting lead singer Ian Brown, saw themselves as rock messiahs in waiting (they refused to support the Rolling Stones on tour; the Stones, Brown insisted, should be supporting them). The Carpets, well, they were simply a pop combo who had struck a lucky chord with the times.

"The Roses aren't really working-class estate kids – although they are – but not in the way that the Mondays are; the Mondays came from Salford, the Roses are from Timperley, so they had a different perspective in the way they would enjoy themselves," explains Stephen Cresser, who worked for both bands. "The Roses were about art, the Mondays were more situationist. Just do it now, fuck it, twenty-four hours, no days off."

"If you want a punk analogy," suggests Jeff Barrett, who by now was the Mondays' publicity agent, "the Mondays were the Pistols, the Stone Roses were the Clash, and the Inspirals were the Stranglers."

Like the Pistols, the Mondays brought their own entourage with them – not so much fans as mates, an extended family which at its core was real family: Ryder and his bass player brother Paul, their dad Derek, their cousins Matt and Pat who ran Central Station Design and coated the Mondays' record sleeves with sleazy glamour, plus a host of blaggers, dealers and hangers-on. It was their own black economy in microcosm, a "freakshow circus", as Ryder described it. At one gig they bought around 200 tickets for this delinquent entourage. "It was one big party from 1983 on," explains Derek Ryder. "It wasn't about making money, they spent money, loads of it, and they spent it because it was there. It was about having a good time, with all your mates around you."

Everything came together in the last week of November 1989, just after the Roses had played a triumphant gig to 8,000 at London's Alexandra Palace. The Mondays and Roses made their *Top of the Pops* debuts; 808 State and the Inspiral Carpets were also in the charts. The Mondays' EP of remixes, *Madchester Rave On*, had given the scene a perfect marketing slogan; the scallies in their twenty-inch-bottom flares and brightly coloured hooded T-shirts had given it a style; the Haçienda had given it a focus. What was a scene had become a *phenomenon*, and now everybody wanted in; there was a sharp rise in applications to Manchester colleges at the start of 1990.

Yet as it was translated for a wider constituency by the music press, as happened with punk, "Madchester" had become simplified and reduced to a formula: Haçienda, flares, scallies on E, indie-dance, a caricature that was more easily commodified but overlooked both the diversity and history of the city's intertwined communities. "Why are we hearing so much about Manchester now?" questioned local ideologue, Haçienda DJ, journalist and record promoter Dave Haslam. "Why is it so surprising that a city like Manchester could be so innovative? The London-based media industry is comatose. It was only once the groups involved could afford London-based press officers and pluggers that they were taken seriously. There is a definite, identifiable surge in the amount of coverage given to the city's music once professionals like Philip Hall [the Roses' PR man] and Jeff Barrett became involved. This is a sad, but revealing truth."[5]

The homogeneity of "Madchester's" public face also irritated some of its key figures. The rock press version of events excluded the role that black subcultures had played and understated the importance of house music in its desire to elevate the rock bands to star status; a scene it could celebrate and sell to its readers simultaneously. It looked at the town and saw white boys playing guitars to throngs of ecstatic white youth; the more complex reality didn't fit into its world-view. This rankled with dance partisans like Graham Massey and Martin Price, who were friends and collaborators with some of the indie bands, but considered themselves in totally different terms; as Third Wave techno-rebels rather than sixties revivalists assembling homages to their record collections.

"I was surprised by how people like the Inspiral Carpets got attached to that scene – it was very confusing," says Massey. "The music that rode the back of that scene, even things like the Stone Roses, it wasn't connected to the culture that was driving everything forward. We used to get quite bitter about that at the time because we were very much futurists, whereas a lot of that stuff is to do with pastiche. The Mondays joined in the scheme of things by doing those remixes; it didn't matter because they were special, you knew the party went where they went."

A year later, Shaun Ryder would agree: "What was the Manchester scene anyway? It was a few people going to a few clubs and taking a lot of E. The whole Manchester thing was nothing to do with the actual bands – it was the E scene that started it all off."[6]

The *idea* of Madchester, however, provided a backdrop over which people, both in and outside the city, could project their own fantasies and aspirations. Though the British winter was, as ever, dull and bedrizzled, it was as if someone had switched on fairy lights over Oldham Street. The key colours of the year – lilac, orange and lime green – combined with T-shirts decorated with hearts, flowers, smiling suns and half-ironic slogans like "On the Seventh Day God Created Manchester" or "Born in the North, Live in the North, Die in the North"; outlandish denim flares trailed unconcerned through muddy puddles. The image proffered a message that was more than civic pride, it was a celebration of the knowledge that here and now was all that mattered, that the city was surfing the peak of the rush. And that it had to be enjoyed *right now*, before the moment passed. "You felt like anything might happen," says Graham Massey. "Maybe this is my warped view because I was riding on the crest of that wave, but there was a collective energy and hope around at that point, and you just thought everything was going to get better and better."

Nothing exemplified this better than *Freaky Dancing*, a photocopied fanzine packed with comic strips that was given out free in the Haçienda queue from the summer of '89 onwards. Innocent, sometimes amateurish but infused with passion and belief, it captured the feeling of being right in the eye of the storm. It was pencilled by twenty-year-old Nick Speakman and ten of his friends, and they made themselves and their Haçienda circle the central characters of the strips – Fish, Ste, Mr Big, Amir, the Skanking Moocher and co., their day trips to Blackpool, bonding and hugging on the beach ("I wish the whole world felt like this"); tripping on acid on a park bench in the centre of town ("our eyes were opened and we saw the whole universe"); jumping and yelling in a tent at Live the Dream ("tear it up, Stevie Williams!"); meeting old school friends on the bus who just don't understand how they've changed ("I'm not talking to this weirdo again"); back at work on Monday dreaming of Friday past and Friday coming.

"Nobody was really recording anything that was going on, and to us it genuinely seemed like the dawning of a new age or something – that after this, everything was going to be different. We were just trying to find some way to express ourselves," says Speakman. "Now it seems normal, but at the time, you'd be the lone one with a hooded top, E'd out of your face, when everyone else was coming out of the pubs pissed, shouting at you in the street and taking the piss out of you. You felt you were in on the start of something that was going to be really big." The subject matter was simple: friendship, dancing, drugs, drugs and more drugs. Lips pursed with the onset of an E rush, human faces transmuting into Smileys as the buzz took hold, heads exploding; *Freaky Dancing* plotted the trajectory of the Ecstasy experience and, simultaneously, the trajectory of the scene.

fennel street

As with every strand of Ecstasy culture, the substance that made the scene so special also contained the means of its destruction. The sequence of honeymoon period giving way to excess and comedown repeats itself endlessly from 1988 onwards – not just chemically, but culturally too. On July 14th, 1989, a sixteen-year-old girl from Cannock, Staffordshire, whose mother had borrowed another girl's birth certificate so that she could get into the Haçienda, was given an E by her nineteen-year-old boyfriend. After swallowing the £15 capsule, she perched on the stage and started sweating heavily, breathing uneasily, vomiting and losing her balance. She looked like she was having a fit; internally, she had begun to haemorrhage. Thirty-six hours later Claire Leighton was dead.

Her boyfriend, welder Tim Charlesworth, was sentenced to six weeks' detention for supplying her with the drug. The coroner reported that death was due to an unusual reaction to an amount of the drug that would not normally have had this effect. "This should not make anyone feel complacent," he cautioned, prophetically. "Although the drug has not been associated with deaths in this country, it is only a matter of time before we will hear of other cases. This is the first but regrettably it is not likely to be the last."[7] A verdict of misadventure was recorded, and

Haçienda manager Paul Mason warned: "Anyone taking or dealing – stay away from my club."

"In all honesty," former Haçienda PR man Paul Cons admits now, "it was only a matter of time before that happened because everyone was going so crazy. It's amazing when you think what went on that first summer that no one died. I think it was because initially it was the more sussed people, whatever their background, they were a little more intelligent, more cutting-edge, either so used to drugs that they could cope with it or knew how to handle themselves, whereas what then happened was you had this huge new generation of kids that read about it in *The Sun*, who didn't really know what they were doing, who maybe came from backgrounds where they'd never really been clubbing before. They'd suddenly get an E in the Haçienda, and that's where you started to get the casualties."

Greater Manchester Police had already made some significant seizures of Ecstasy in 1989. Now they were to focus their efforts on the Haçienda. A team of undercover police were sent in to monitor drug dealing on the premises. "They're cool," a Haçienda employee would later report. "The right clothes, the right dancing. They look sorted. You just can't tell."[8] Dealers had been taking liberties, getting cocky, and the freedom they'd enjoyed was now rebounding on them. "The drug dealers that they carried out of the Haçienda were all soft targets," says former bar manager Leroy Richardson. "When you read about it in the paper it was a twenty-two-year-old student from Wilmslow who had twenty Es on him and was selling them to his mates. They never got anybody [important] besides one person who was extremely stupid – you don't stand in a club shouting: 'If you want an E, I'm your man!' He thought he was invisible; doing the drug himself, he thought nobody would touch him. The police don't arrest you, they want to see if you can take them to someone bigger. And because nothing's happened to you, you get a false sense of security, and all of a sudden, bang!"

But it wasn't just about under-age girls dying of drugs. The police knew it, the Haçienda knew it, and by the end of the year everyone in the club knew it. The New Year's Eve party at the end of 1988 was a rapturous celebration of the year's joy ride. By New Year's Eve 1989, the mood had darkened. In the passageway behind the DJ booth, some very scary characters were hanging around. People whispered to each other about gangs from Cheetham Hill, Moss Side and Salford. Young dealers were being beaten, their bones broken and their money and drugs taken from them. "All of a sudden you'd notice a menacing Cheetham Hill contingent in the corner and you'd have eight guys round you on the dancefloor," says one. They either had to fight back, get themselves protection, or give over their business to the hard men.

As dealers built up firepower to protect their turf and profits, the conflict escalated. The likely lads with their bags of E were replaced by gangs of ruthless criminals with nothing personal invested in the welfare of the scene, and the quality of the drugs decreased – another recurring narrative of Ecstasy distribution. At one time the chancers and characters seemed like entertaining local colour – bad boys on E, loving and hugging – but now many were saying that the profit motive had reverted them to their true, pre-Ecstasy personalities. Of course it wasn't as simple as that, some were genuinely transformed by their experiences. Others, however, simply saw the scene as a business opportunity. "Sometimes in Manchester it's hard to differentiate between the criminal element and the legitimate element, because it's all commerce," says Graham Massey. "Some of the criminal elements had real fronts – clothes and all kinds. Everyone had a few numbers going and a lot of people had a lot of dodgy numbers going on top of legitimate things."

Leroy Richardson claims he can pinpoint the shift to May 1989, a few weeks before he left the Haçienda to manage Factory's new bar on Oldham Street, Dry. One night he refused to let one of the most prominent gangster "faces" from Cheetham Hill into the club without paying. "I said: 'You know where I am. I'll die before you'll be let in.' And he said: 'You'll most probably have to.' It was 'White Tony' – Tony Johnson."

The Haçienda couldn't stop gang members like the notoriously volatile Johnson coming into the club. The staff were scared. The gangs would demand champagne and sandwiches; no one dared refuse. They weren't afraid of showing they were armed, as a series of shootings of bouncers outside the Thunderdome (which soon shut down) demonstrated. Richardson tried to reason with them, calm them, accommodate their wishes without backing down – never show weakness else they'd be all over you. "The police should have been protecting the club," he argues. "They should have been saying to the club: 'We will get these people.' Instead they were actually saying to the club: 'We want *you* to get these people for us; tell these people they can't come in.' I said: 'Why don't you have two officers on the door when we tell them? You only come round to pick up the pieces.' "

It was worse at Konspiracy, a new club that had been launched in November 1989 by businessman Marino Morgan and Chris Nelson, a DJ with the Jam MCs. Konspiracy on Fennel Street was intended as a response to the increasingly stringent door policy of the Haçienda – "the street people's reaction," says Nelson. It was a labyrinthine warren of rooms, alcoves and dank caves decorated with swirling psychedelic frescoes. It felt underground, edgy and dangerous in a way you couldn't quite put your finger on, a spiky little frisson of fear. "Konspiracy was some kind of global village," Nelson recalls. "People hanging out all over the place. There were so many dark corners. A lot of people tripping out until midday sometimes."

Upstairs in what was known as "Salford's room", harsh techno, the rhythm of amphetamine psychosis, battered at the walls like the Thunderdome revisited; down in the caves, Justin Robertson and Greg Fenton spun pretty Balearic tunes and indie-dance hybrids. For five months Konspiracy was a new meeting point between the scallies and the students, seething with sweat and smoke; 1,500, sometimes even 1,800 people on a space licensed for 800. Then the gangsters began to take over, running the door staff and treating the club, said one staffer, as if it was their own private fiefdom: "They'd want their people at the door, all their people in for free, to order drinks and not pay for them, and to openly sell drugs in the place. The owner used to tell me we were losing £300 a night in liquor off these guys, then it got into £400, and in the end they'd just walk behind the bar and take a bottle of vodka or six bottles of champagne."[9]

According to regulars, guns were pulled, DJs were Maced, employees attacked. Nelson, the licensee, was trying to keep an increasingly lawless situation under control whilst DJing at the same time. And here, too, undercover police were watching and taking notes. "There was a set of stairs downstairs where you'd find a lot of the crews – I'd rather use that term than 'gangs'," says Nelson. "It would be lined with about ten kids on each side just shouting out 'Ecstasy! Hash! Acid!' to anyone indiscriminately. If you tried to inform them that they were actually trying to ply their wares to plainclothes police, their reaction was: 'I don't give a shit, fucking back off!' That's the way a lot of them were. They were troopers. I was enlightened – I'd known people that didn't give a shit about the police, but these kids . . . I was not able to do anything about it."

In Blackburn, the same scenario was unfolding in parallel with events in both Manchester and London. Tommy Smith and Tony Creft were being squeezed by gangsters on one side and policemen on the other. The numbers had grown massively, from a couple of thousand to almost 10,000 each weekend, pouring into the town, tearing around the back streets looking for the rave. Suddenly Smith and Creft were being threatened, first by men from their home town, then men from Liverpool, then another gang from Salford, all of whom wanted a piece of the action.

"They just came into our house and a few other houses here in Blackburn and did unspeakable things, like a dog would do in new territory, just go and shit on it and say: 'This belongs to me.' That sort of mentality. They were threatening us, saying that we work for them now, that's it. When it gets to the stage where they know where you live and come and threaten you, it's scary. But you know that they're not going to run it like it should be run, suddenly it's going to be £10, guns will be in – it's lost it then. At the time me and Tony were so innocent; whereas we were on a spiritual dance buzz, we were having to deal with this extreme ugliness. It was hard to balance it out but you had to be aware of it because suddenly it was in your face. A long while after it happened I saw them somewhere and they apologised, saying: 'We really ruined something there.' For someone of that mentality to realise that and to dismiss his ego so he could admit it, for me that was quite something, although it was too late."

By the start of 1990 the *Lancashire Evening Telegraph* had commenced a campaign against Smith's raves. "Enough is enough," an editorial fumed. "The acid house anarchy has to stop. The acid house criminals are laughing at the law."[10] East Lancashire councils and MP Ken Hargreaves were demanding penalties in excess of those proposed by Graham Bright's Bill. Outlining the safety risks of raves in derelict, "death-trap" buildings, Hargreaves warned Parliament: "It is only a matter of time before someone dies – and, regrettably, it will not just be one person but many. I find it hard to understand why those who attend such parties cannot see the danger into which they are putting themselves. I find it equally difficult to comprehend how parents can write to local newspapers defending the parties, and suggesting that the organisers are providing some sort of service that livens up the area."[11]

Although Smith would scan police radio transmissions, this wasn't the complex techno war that was going on in the Home Counties; it was more of an old-fashioned fist fight – sometimes literally. When police officers attempted to seize equipment, they would be physically prevented from doing so. One week an officer was captured and beaten and his radio stolen; soon police frequencies throbbed to the sound of house music. Another week, the record decks were confiscated. "Someone ran to a house and kicked the door in – it had to be done in those days – kicked the door in and got a stereo out, an Amstrad. They wired it up and played tapes until somebody could go and get another pair of decks."

The deciding conflict came on February 24th, 1990. The gangsters were still encroaching; the police were becoming more determined; there had been an ugly fight with riot squads a few months earlier when two patrol cars were set alight outside a party. Now, in Nelson, just north of Burnley, a battalion of 200 policemen marched on the biggest warehouse Smith had occupied, with 10,000 people inside.

"I was sitting on the roof revelling in the beauty of it all," he remembers. "It was dreamlike, *Strawberry Fields Forever* was playing on the decks, there was a blue wave coming in and when I looked closer it was a wave of shiny blue riot helmets. They laid into everyone there. We got outside and were throwing stones at them. It was like a cowboy movie, six in the morning, everybody spaced out and mellow and having a wonderful night, and they're there on the horizon, more of them, shields drawn. They were well briefed, they had photos of us so they knew who they were looking for. Fortunately I got a disguise on and got out of there."

Smith crossed the county line to West Yorkshire and attempted to carry on as before. But the Yorkshire police, well prepared for mass conflict after the Miners' Strike, were ready and waiting. Smith helped organise the Love Decade party in July 1990 which resulted in one of the biggest mass arrests in British history. Police in riot gear with horses and dogs surrounded the warehouse, beating the ravers with truncheons as they fought to get out, leaving many injured and 836 in the cells. It didn't seem worth it any more, Smith and Creft pondered sadly. "Me and Tony looked at each other and knew in each other's eyes and hearts that something beautiful was being destroyed. We just disappeared. I went to America."

It wasn't over yet. On his return, Smith was arrested and charged with possession with intent to supply 70,000 doses of LSD. Some of the people who had been involved with the parties were indeed dealing. "They were known for the parties and they were known for selling drugs as well. Such was the energy and the thrust of what was going on that you felt untouchable, or invisible, and it was dangerous with the things they were doing. The police tried to set me up, although in the end they couldn't prove I was selling drugs because I wasn't." Out of the original collective of eight, six were found guilty of various charges. "John got five years. Joe got two and a half years. Steve got twelve years. Tony got eight years. Brian got ten years. Nick got seven years. I got a 'not guilty'."

salford and cheetham hill

1990 was the year the Happy Mondays peaked. The Stone Roses were caught up in contractual wrangles with their record company; the Inspiral Carpets were worthily plodding around the country, selling records but signifying little, while the wave of bands that sprang up in their wake, like Northside and the Paris Angels, seemed to owe more to the laddish "Madchester" caricature than the spirit of Ecstasy. The Mondays were heroes, walking on the wild side and coming back to tell the tales, week after week, in an endless series of music press front covers and lurid exclusives that they themselves sold to tabloid newspapers.

The band had something genuinely new to offer, not just a reworking of old formulas. The Roses and Carpets were essentially warming over the four-man beat-group blueprint which had been the basis of every Brit-rock boom since the early sixties, and they visualised themselves as "artists" in the rock tradition. The Mondays, on the other hand, were fusing all Ryder's influences – Northern Soul, Motown, Bowie, Roxy Music, Funkadelic, the Beatles, the Rolling Stones, New Order, hip hop, house music – and had a refreshingly irreverent attitude to rock heritage; hence they embraced dance culture while others were sceptical. While their albums were ragged and imperfectly formed – the instinctive chaos of their gigs far better represented what made them special – their self-made myths placed them in the tradition of iconic British pop groups like the Rolling Stones and the Sex Pistols. They were an archetype of Ecstasy culture: working-class refuseniks, delinquent bohemians – "Thatcher's children," insisted Ryder.

"Thatcher turned straight people into criminals," he explained later. "We dealt. They called us criminals, but the way we saw it, we were enterprising business people. She laid the cards out and people had no choice but to play her game. Me and millions of others. But I never voted Tory. I tell people I vote Tory because it winds them up, but I've never voted in my life."[12]

The other key element that set the Mondays apart was Ryder's surreal lyricism. He would steal phrases from classic songs, twist them, lace them with lascivious slang, then slur them out in his obscene groan of a voice. In print, however, Ryder was often painted as a stupid Northern oik, his Mancunian accent mimicked and, by implication, mocked: "fuck" written as "fook", like he was a retard from the provinces who had barely learned to speak. "I always come over double thick, I sound brainless in a lot of interviews. How they're written makes me sound thick," he says. "If they're interviewing a black guy, they don't start writing in patois, do they? It's just how we talk."

Yet when speaking with journalists he would play up to the stereotype, disingenuously claiming that his lyrics were meaningless nonsense, exaggerating or making up stories, retelling them over and over but slightly differently each time, perhaps to entertain the writer but more likely to entertain himself. He may have been, as he has said himself, a working-class blagger with no other talents save thieving, selling drugs and writing songs, but he also had a sharp wit and a restless urge to create, had travelled widely, boasted a broad knowledge of music, and had tried almost every drug known to man. "If Shaun hadn't been and done what he did, he wouldn't have written the songs, lyrically, that he did," his father Derek points out. "You don't write stuff like that if you're just a local band in Manchester, you've got to have been out there, somewhere else, and seen a lot of things."

Their gigs brought Ecstasy culture to the rock community. Although they still adhered to the standard rock gig format, the atmosphere was more like a rave. It was down to Ecstasy, insists Ryder: "Everyone was E'd up. Everyone in the place was on E and it made us look better and sound better. I know they were all on E because we used to go out in the audience selling E like T-shirts. You've got a few hundred people, they've all had an E, it makes it look really cool, it makes it sound right, the vibe is right; we were all on E as well so we had a good time and the venue had a good time."

The Mondays' gig at the cavernous G-Mex exhibition centre in March 1990 was the zenith of Madchester. Jimmy Muffin and John the Phone were promoting, 808 State were supporting, and the 8,000-capacity hall was sold out. "To everyone involved in that scene it felt like The Night It Climaxed," says Graham Massey. "It had risen and risen and risen and that night seemed like some sort of pinnacle. It was an incredible atmosphere – imagine all those nights at the Haçienda condensed into one building."

In May, the Stone Roses responded with a 30,000-strong open-air concert at Spike Island, near Widnes. The baggy hordes frolicked in the grass as Paul Oakenfold, Frankie Bones and Dave Haslam shook the speakers. The Roses took to the stage as night fell, fireworks and feedback concluding a set which seemed to enthrone them as the Last Great Rock'n'Roll Band – yet after this triumph, they wouldn't release another album for five years, and would split up soon after that.

That summer, Manchester's ascendance was confirmed in some remarkable ways, none more so than when New Order recorded the theme song for England's World Cup campaign in Italy. On first hearing, *World in Motion* was barely believable; so audacious that you had to play it again immediately to make sure you hadn't misheard. That chorus! Did the England football squad, who joined in on backing vocals, comprehend its connotations? It was the biggest in-joke of all time: "It's E for England! England!" Number one in the charts: *E for England* . . . of course . . .

The Mondays hits kept coming. *Pills, Thrills and Bellyaches*, co-produced by Paul Oakenfold, was voted the album of 1990 by the *NME*. They filled Wembley Arena and at the end of the show ignited a huge illuminated "E" over the stage, to delirious applause. Yet something wasn't quite right. During a jaunt to Ibiza that summer, while the rest of the band lounged and pranked around the beach like boisterous lads on an 18–30 holiday, Ryder was holed up in his hotel room, unusually taciturn and moody, only coming down to squint in the sun for a brief photo session. His press agent Jeff Barrett dropped thinly veiled hints about "bad drugs".

A few months later it became obvious that Ryder was addicted to heroin, maintaining himself on methadone whilst recording the album. In December, he was admitted to the Priory Clinic in Cheshire for treatment. The Mondays' premise – a human incarnation of Ecstasy – was undermined at a stroke. The fans who thought they were merely laddish love puppies were devastated: smack, the Bad Drug, the last taboo in town. Ryder admitted he had been taking it "to chill out" since his teens. The dream had begun to sour.

It felt as though, one by one, the cornerstones of the scene were crumbling. The sixteen-month police surveillance of the Haçienda and Konspiracy resulted in a move to revoke the clubs' licences. The Haçienda's management was furious – instead of tackling the gangs, the authorities were trying to close the clubs down. The management fought back. First Tony Wilson hired the renowned QC George Carman, who had represented politician Jeremy Thorpe and comedian Ken Dodd, to argue the Haçienda's case, demonstrating to the police that they weren't about to give in easily. Then Paul Cons contacted the Labour leader of Manchester City Council, Graham Stringer, who pledged his support to the club, stressing its importance within the civic fabric of Manchester and its contribution to the city's raised international profile.

Finally, the management announced its intention to eradicate all dealing and, as much as possible, drug-taking inside the venue, handing out a flyer to customers which read: "Please do not, repeat, NOT buy or take drugs in the club." Stringent searches were instigated at the door, regulars turned away, and £10,000 of video cameras, metal detectors and infra-red sensors installed; a first indication of how closed-circuit surveillance would spread through the club culture of the nineties.

The result was devastating. Numbers dropped immediately, the atmosphere evaporated overnight and the Haçienda was no longer a fabulous pleasuredome, just another bare industrial warehouse again. The club – which had only really started making money for the first time when acid house hit – was heading for dire financial straits. "It was very depressing," says Paul Cons. "We had no choice about having to crack down on the drugs, but in a way it was totally hypocritical, because they were important to the club – if no one was doing E, no one would go there. So we were sort of going halfway, taking a lot of the fun and excess out of it without killing it off."

To remodel the club's image, its doormen also started turning away people who they thought looked undesirable – even fanatical devotees. The August 1990 edition of *Freaky Dancing* depicted one of its writers at the Haçienda's door with a bouncer barring his way: "Not tonight." To people who had invested such powerful emotions in the club, this was overwhelming. "The worst thing is how much I believed in it," says Nick Speakman. "You really did feel like saying: 'Don't spoil it, don't let it go wrong.' You thought it was transcending everything, you didn't realise how much of it was the drug – you thought it was deeper than that. With hindsight I realised that a lot of the people I had as friends were full of shit. That was a blow as well; you were convinced that everybody was going to be your friend for life, and even that went sour, not just the whole scene but you started getting in-fighting within groups of friends. A lot of that was drug-related too, because people were getting a bit psychotic and paranoid through going over the top. A lot of people became casualties. *Freaky Dancing* never came out again. It just died."

At Konspiracy, Chris Nelson and Marino Morgan couldn't afford a George Carman and they didn't have the national profile to get the council and *NME* – which ran a cover story on the Haçienda, "Britain's most famous club" – on their side. They couldn't even control their own doormen or prevent Cheetham Hill gang leaders like the feared "White Tony" Johnson making the club their base. The *Manchester Evening News* painted a sensationalist picture of a dangerously humid and overcrowded dive: thousands of innocent youths rubbing shoulders with violent, dangerous mobsters who refused to pay to get in and demanded free drinks all night; black gangs from Cheetham Hill fighting white gangs from Salford; hundreds openly smoking cannabis; police officers being offered LSD for sale.[13] At the licence hearing, Chris Nelson was declared "not a fit and proper person to hold a licence", and by the end of 1990 the club was shut, just one year after it had opened.

"Tony Wilson certainly knew what he was doing and was able to secure his business interests; we didn't have the cards to play that kind of angle," says Nelson. "We had a great time, though, I'm not bitter about it at all. It did a lot for me in lots of ways, and I'm glad I got out before anyone died in there or anything.

The fire exits weren't open, there wasn't enough control, the place was too big and too hot. It was getting too much – too much pressure. We bit off more than we could chew."

With "their" club, Konspiracy, closed, where were the gangs going to go? Back to the Haçienda. Three weeks after being given a short reprieve by the licensing authority, the Haçienda, too, shut its doors after the head bouncer was threatened with a gun. "We are forced into this drastic action to protect our employees, our members and all our clients," read Tony Wilson's statement to the press. "We are quite simply sick and tired of dealing with instances of personal violence."[14] The gangs were also drinking in Factory's Dry bar; when the Mondays and Roses debuted on *Top of the Pops*, recalls local journalist Mandi James, "they were buying champagne as if it was their record and they'd actually nurtured the bands". But they were also demanding free bottles, two one week, four the next: "I've seen them drink champagne for free and then use an empty bottle of Moët to beat someone senseless," one of the bar staff told the *Manchester Evening News*. "I've got used to them flashing guns to get what they want. No one, not even the police, seems to be able to do anything about them."[15]

These gangs from Salford and Cheetham Hill didn't really constitute "organised crime", rather they were loosely affiliated groups and delinquent families from those areas, who were driven by ego and bravado – the urge to prove that they were harder than the rest – as much as by greed. In 1989, London's East End Ecstasy gangs had been content with controlling their own patch outside the city centre; in Manchester, the situation wasn't necessarily more extreme, but more visible.

Since the end of 1989, Shaun Ryder had been hinting that the drug of choice amongst the city's prime movers had changed. When he first discovered Ecstasy, he said, he'd pop pills all day, constantly euphoric. But once the experience had been explored, the honeymoon period passed and he was bingeing on the stuff just to try and recapture the original buzz, it was time to move on. "You do twelve months on it and that's it, finished," Ryder observed.[16] But he still wanted to take drugs, so he started in on cocaine. Police and customs seizures of cocaine reflect how the drug was gaining in popularity through the late eighties and early nineties; it was no longer a "champagne drug", the property of affluent yuppies and music biz players. It was on the streets, in the clubs. "E were great two years ago, y'know . . . It made everything peaceful. But now the violence is comin' back in the Manchester clubs," Ryder warned at the height of the Madchester boom. "There's too much freebasin' going on. It's takin' over in Manchester . . . like everyone in Manny had a binge on E, right, only the people who had a binge on E from the start are now having a freebase binge on cocaine. All the lads we know in London . . . it's the same."[17] The Donnelly brothers had launched a casualwear company called Gio Goi, and their first T-shirt designs documented the atmosphere. One was emblazoned with the word "Gibraltar" – "because everyone's smoking rock these days"; the other simply stated: "Dodgin' the rain and bullets".

The ones who were selling, taking and fighting over cocaine were the gangs. "It was never E that was a problem with them," says Leroy Richardson. "It was always coke and crack. On coke, the amount they had access to, you would certainly go past the enjoyable stage into the psychotic." After taking over the small-time dealers in the Haçienda, the gangs were squabbling amongst themselves. In the last week of February 1991, "White Tony" Johnson was killed outside the Penny Black pub in Cheetham, shot once through the mouth and twice through his body, the result of a feud between Salford and Cheetham Hill factions. His friend, "Black Tony" McKie, was also shot, but survived. Johnson usually wore body armour, but on this occasion he hadn't. The twenty-two year-old father of a three-month-old child, "White Tony" was a suspect in one murder, various shootings and robberies. "Tony Johnson was the most significant one," says Leroy Richardson. "It was his murder that led us to think it was going to be easier to reopen the Haçienda, because he was *the* major force."

In the week following the killing, police and Haçienda management held secret negotiations with other gang members to persuade them that the club could only reopen if they stopped the intimidation, and gave them free tickets as a peace offering. A date was set: May 10th. At the relaunch party, clubbers had to pass through a metal detector at the door. But to no avail: six weeks later a knot of men from Salford slipped in through a side entrance and stabbed six bouncers in well-planned retribution for not being allowed entry. At other clubs over the summer of 1991, doormen were beaten, intimidated and shot as the gangs pillaged their way across town. Tony Johnson was dead, but nothing had changed; the illegality of, and huge demand for, drugs like Ecstasy and cocaine had created an enormous black market, easy pickings for the criminally minded. The honeymoon period seemed years away now, and the city was enduring a heavy comedown.

"The aftermath of the scene seemed very bleak, when all that enthusiasm was crushed," says Graham Massey. "It was down to things like greed – everything became dangerous, too much trouble. There was less energy in the air, it was almost like everything was exhausted." The Haçienda retained its licence, but has rarely since displayed the magic it once flaunted so joyfully. Some people, in Manchester as elsewhere, tried to prolong the buzz by bingeing on E or cocaine or combinations of both and other drugs simultaneously, charging into destructive sessions of prolonged polydrug abuse. Ecstasy just wasn't enough any more. "People started taking any drug that the dealer turned up with," says Mandi James. "The club became the meeting place, and the party afterwards was where the serious drug-taking happened. There was a period when you went to clubs to meet the people who you carried on afterwards with. Going out on a Thursday night was dangerous – you wouldn't see daylight until Monday morning. There used to be a hard core of twenty people who you'd always end up with."

"That was the strangest and least enjoyable period," says Gary McClarnan. "We had a clique and we were known for having these hedonistic do's that went on from the Friday till the Monday where we'd lock ourselves away in a house in Biddulph and just go completely off it, continue to take pills. It was weird, psychotropic. We never really came down. I was getting electric shocks up my spine. I was trying to sleep and I'd have these sparks going off in my head. It was definitely abuse." McClarnan, suffering from depression and paranoia, ultimately had a breakdown and was only able to return to clubs after a long period of recuperation and re-evaluation.

In this context, the subsequent downfall of the Happy Mondays was inevitable. It was as though it had to happen; it was written into the script – the set-piece climax of a long and crazy tale. First Ryder went into rehab, then the band posed with cheesecake nudes in *Penthouse*, talking about shagging and porno movies. Although the band didn't see anything wrong with larking around with topless "birds", their music press admirers were less than keen.

Finally, there was a watershed interview in *NME*. Journalist Steven Wells held the Mondays' hedonist philosophy up to the light of his own socialist principles, and found the band severely wanting. They looked like "glue-sniffing Wombles" in £400 jackets and £1,300 watches, he wrote. They didn't protest about the condition of the working class under the Tories, they celebrated their money and the success that had bought them expensive clothes, smart cars and unlimited pharmaceuticals. And worst of all, Bez ranted on and on about how "faggots are disgusting . . . not right". Homophobia, sexism, materialism: guilty on all counts. They were proletarian conservatives, Wells concluded, reactionary mores thinly concealed under a patina of outcast chic – rebels without a brain. "Working Class Zeroes," ran the headline.[18]

But it wasn't just the build-'em-up-then-knock-'em-down of a rock press backlash. The Mondays had built themselves up, and they could knock themselves down quite adequately, thank you. In January 1992 they flew to Barbados to record their fifth album, with Tina Weymouth and Chris Frantz of Talking Heads as producers. The island was chosen because it was believed that there was no heroin there, only weed; Ryder could clean up and get down to work. But at Manchester Airport he dropped his bottles of maintenance methadone, 1,500 mills of the green sticky stuff oozing all over the floor. On the plane he began to feel uncomfortable, sweating and twitching: withdrawal setting in.

The trip became a disaster. Within a week of touching down, two cars had been written off, Bez had broken his arm badly, Ryder was swallowing tranquillisers and rum punch as methadone substitutes – and he had also discovered that Barbados had a plentiful, dirt-cheap supply of crack. Journalist Miranda Sawyer witnessed this conversation between the singer and his manager Nathan McGough:

" 'I've just done thirty rocks,' states Shaun in a matter-of-fact don't-give me-any-shit-about-this-one style.

"Nathan gapes: 'What?'

" 'Thirty,' Shaun gives him a side-long grin. 'I'm tanning the stuff, man.'

"Nathan can't believe it. He reasons with Shaun, knowing that he's never been that bothered with crack in Manchester. *Why? You just used to smoke the occasional rock at home, you're stupid, you've come off smack, you've come off methadone, what's the point of this, you know you're not doing yourself any good . . .*

"Shaun half-listens, half-agrees.

" 'I know, I know, man,' he says. 'But I wanted a different buzz for this record.' He's laughing but there's some truth in his excuse. He doesn't want this one to sound like the smack-sodden *Pills'N'Thrills*, he wants to hear music in a way he hasn't heard it before. There's so much ragga stuff going on here, he's really getting into it. Still, he promises Nathan he'll cut down. It's not a real problem yet."[19]

Within six weeks the band had laid down the instrumental tracks, but Ryder, who would spend hours sitting on the toilet, scribbling lyrics and smoking crack, hadn't recorded his vocals. Keyboard player Paul Davis was also smoking rocks, and Bez had broken his arm again. In desperation, McGough cancelled the rest of the session and flew the band home. The band began to fall out with each other, believing Ryder and Davis had let them down, and Ryder checked in to a £10,000-a-week rehab clinic in Chelsea. By the end of the summer, the album was finished, but although it cost around £250,000 to make, reportedly the most expensive indie album ever recorded, *Yes Please* sounded dull and flat, and sales were mediocre. "I just wasn't interested at the time," Ryder admitted later. "I wasn't writing, I didn't give a fuck. No one really gave a fuck."[20]

On November 23rd, 1992, Factory Records went into receivership with debts reported at around £2 million; the cost of the Mondays' record and the delay in releasing New Order's new album were quoted as contributory factors. Established in 1979 with £12,000 left from Tony Wilson's mother's will, the label had been important in countless ways: the building of the Haçienda, the elegant modernism of its design aesthetic, its demonstration of how to succeed without deferring to the capital, the fact that it had signed some of the most influential white rock bands of the eighties. Its problems had been building over the past few years. It wasn't simply overspending; there were also policy misjudgements: despite the fact that Factory ran the best-known dance club in Britain, it failed to sign any acts from the scene itself (instead it launched a classical label). The seminal *North* album, a compilation introducing Mancunian house to the world, released in December 1988 with contributions from Mike Pickering, A Guy Called Gerald, 808 State and other local machine dreamers, should in theory have emanated from Factory; instead it was released by Deconstruction, a label in which

Pickering was junior director and which would increasingly be identified with house in the north-west. Perhaps it was the perfect time for Factory to die, its mission complete and its vision exhausted, but it certainly contributed to the impression that Manchester was destroying itself piece by piece.

The following February, the Mondays were on the verge of signing a new deal with EMI, despite the fact that their internal conflicts had degenerated into enmity between the band's members. During a meeting with EMI A&R director Clive Black, Shaun Ryder walked out of the room, saying he wanted to get some Kentucky Fried Chicken. He never returned. The deal was off. The band was finished. "It was right that it ended then," said Ryder afterwards. "It was all over. Everyone had their heads up their arses. We had no respect for each other. It was just shite. It was all dough, dough, dough. The money had got to everyone. I really *did* go for a Kentucky, I didn't go for drugs. I was hungry."[21]

canal street

The transformation of "Madchester" into "Gunchester" – to use a glib phrase that was in vogue around 1993 – was a simplistic media construct, resented by many in the city who disliked its stereotyping as a lawless zone for gunmen and drug dealers, and the impression that the gangs were more organised and ubiquitous than they really were. However, the grim tag did embody a mood that was very real indeed, and the city's clubs began to experiment with a range of strategies to negotiate this monumental comedown and create spaces free from violence and intimidation.

The immediate reaction was a retreat from the egalitarian door policies of acid house – idealistically letting *anyone* in, people argued, had given the gangs access to the scene in the first place. Justin Robertson and Greg Fenton's Spice (and their later and more successful Most Excellent) was part of a nationwide move towards "Balearic" music, smaller clubs and smarter dress codes, an attempt to stand apart from the mass of the rave scene which had been initiated by London's *Boy's Own* fanzine in 1989. Robertson and Fenton's *Spice* fanzine echoed *Boy's Own*, proposing a "club for top bods to fuck off all the mental boys" and deriding "acid teds" in their "sweaty amyl nitrate soaked gaffs".[22] Ironically, in 1993 Most Excellent itself was stormed by a Salford crew and forced to shut.

Others chose to desert the city entirely: in order to escape the criminals' attention, Gary McClarnan set up Delight forty miles down the M6 at Shelleys Laserdome in Stoke-on-Trent, a club with a manic frenzy that would become legend and cement the reputation of its resident DJ, Alexander Coe, alias Sasha. A 1988-era Haçienda trouper who had made his name at the last and largest of the Blackburn raves, Sasha's impact came from his mastery of dynamics: the long, suspenseful introduction to a song dropping into a glittering shower of piano, the stratospheric cruise through the frequencies of euphoria. He soon ascended to the pantheon of the north-west's turntable deities alongside Mike Pickering and Graeme Park, his status confirmed when dance magazine *Mixmag* framed him in hyperbolic terms on its front cover, initially as "The First DJ Pin-Up", and later as "Son of God". "People were coming back from Shelleys and saying: 'There's guys queuing up to shake Sasha's hand, there's guys asking him to kiss their girlfriends.' It had never been seen before so we felt we had to write about it," explains *Mixmag* editor Dom Phillips. "Sasha locked in so well to the way people feel when they're on E, his music was so powerfully tailored to that. He was so much one of them as well."

Now Blackburn was over, there was nowhere to go when the club had finished but the mind was still racing. Instead, people would drive out to Knutsford or Charnock Richard service stations on the M6, Anderton on the M61 or Burtonwood on the M62, and turn the motorway cafeteria and car park into an impromptu rave, a sea of bobble hats, puffa jackets and hiking boots, cranking up the car stereo, changing sweaty clothes, skinning up and swapping stories with clubbers from Quadrant Park in Liverpool, Monroe's in Blackburn, Legends in Warrington or Oz in Blackpool. Sometimes the police would cordon off the motorway exits, turning sleepy businessmen and hungry lorry drivers away as well as the ravers, or the management would shut the coffee bar. The underlying problem was the licensing laws, and just as the authorities had bowed to the inevitable in the south-east, as mass gatherings of youth continued to assemble in the unlikeliest of places, a few clubs in the north-west began to be granted occasional licences to stay open past 2 a.m. Blackburn had left lasting effect.

In Manchester city centre, people retreated into the gay clubs in search of an atmosphere untainted by the macho bravado of the Cheetham Hill and Salford gangs that were now attempting to take over any new straight house venue. In a bid to capture a spirit of polysexual abandon, Paul Cons launched Flesh, the Haçienda's first gay night. One weekend a month, he filled the venue with transvestite extroverts, muscled disco boys, lipstick lesbians and dancing queens. The door policy was an emphatic "no straights" – if you appeared heterosexual, you had to prove good faith by tongue-kissing your friends – and the gangs didn't even attempt to come in. Flesh was an instant success, packing in more than a thousand from all over the north-west. It helped lay the foundations for Manchester to claim the crown of "gay capital of the north", with its thriving nightlife zone and "gay village" of clubs and bars centred around Canal Street, like the hedonist enclave around Old Compton Street in London's Soho. "It's not Madchester or Gunchester any more, it's *Gaychester*," Cons insisted. He even fantasised about launching his own band – a gay version of the Happy Mondays.

By the middle of the nineties, there was a creative renaissance under way in the city, as new Mancunian pop stars like Oasis shared the charts with former icons of acid house. When Mike

Pickering launched his new dance collective M People, whose second album won the record industry's prestigious Mercury Music Prize in 1994, he made great efforts to distance himself from destructive, repetitive patterns of drug use: "I played at a big rave in Scotland, about 7,000 people were there and every single one of them was out of it," he said. "I don't like the fact that you're excluded if you're not on anything. There's kids going: 'You on one, mate? No? What are you, a copper?' They think you're a copper if you're not on E. It's moronic."[23]

Gerald Simpson, A Guy Called Gerald, had been signed to the multinational label CBS in the wake of *Voodoo Ray*, then dropped and forgotten when he delivered strange techno mantras instead of potential chart hits. Simpson went on to develop a tense, claustrophobic strain of jungle that reflected the chaos and paranoia of living in Moss Side. The titles of his *28 Gun Bad Boy* and *Black Secret Technology* albums captured the tone. Gang warfare, gunplay and intimidation had become the stuff of everyday existence; the only thing he could do was attempt to exorcise it through music. "It's like fighting your way out of something," he suggested. "I've had people pull shooters in my face here in Manchester. They want to shoot you down if you're doing something for yourself, and that's what comes across in my music now."[24] As jungle emerged from the underground, Simpson rose with it.

Soon afterwards, Shaun Ryder's new project was unveiled, and those who had written him off as a dead-end smackhead were astonished: Black Grape, fronted by Bez, Ryder and his heroin buddy Kermit (Paul Leveridge, a former member of the Ruthless Rap Assassins, Manchester finest hip hop crew), were superb, hitching the Mondays' ruffian charm and elliptical narratives to fiery funk riffs. With killer irony, their debut album was titled *It's Great When You're Straight . . . Yeah*. The Mondays myth was instantly rewritten: not only the rehabilitation of Ryder, but the rise and fall and rise again of Manchester itself – although by this time both Ryder and Gerald Simpson had moved out of the city.

Three years after the demise of Factory and the end of the Happy Mondays, Manchester's nightlife was booming as never before due to the relaxation in licensing regulations. Over thirty new bars had opened and club capacity had doubled. New venues like Home, Sankey's Soap and the Paradise Factory testified to a tangible buzz in the city centre after dark. The idea, explained council leader Graham Stringer, was to capitalise on the nocturnal vitality of Manchester, and promote it as a cultural centre for the twenty-first century; a "twenty-four-hour city". Nightlife was no longer something to be seen as a problem to be policed and heavily regulated, but something to be celebrated, which could increase the city's international standing, attract visitors and pump up the local economy, an example that other cities like Leeds and Sheffield followed.

Ecstasy culture helped motivate this renaissance in Manchester's city centre, but optimistic free-market boosterism about the "night-time economy" tended to gloss over the fact that, all over the country, it was underpinned by criminality, something not so easily integrated with civic renaissance. The gang problem had not gone away after the Haçienda reopened in 1991. The Salford and Cheetham Hill gangs had first become involved in clubs through selling drugs, then began to take over control of venues' doors. By 1996, many had set themselves up as legitimate security firms and were getting paid to preserve a fragile peace.

It highlighted a perennial dilemma with the regeneration of any city through nightlife: club culture is a traditionally marginal economy, intimately bound up with the trade in illicit drugs, leaving it vulnerable to criminals and black-market operators. Although the re-entry from the fervid highs of the late eighties was destined to be a long and difficult one, Manchester was attempting to invent a new identity as a truly international metropolis – but the hard questions it posed about the changing nature of cities in the millennial decade had yet to be answered.

For some, the only feasible solution was to leave the past behind. By the end of 1996, the new vanguard of Manchester club culture had rejected the mass house scene that their predecessors had created in favour of micro-communities based around niche musics – jungle, techno, American garage – which they believed could disrupt the formulaic patterns into which mainstream house culture had degenerated, and point to new ways forward.

In June 1997, a few weeks after its fifteenth birthday party, the Haçienda closed its doors and went into liquidation. The club had debts of £500,000. Police officers had just completed another lengthy surveillance operation on the venue, and were demanding that magistrates revoke its entertainment licence after an attempted murder in the street outside: an eighteen-year-old man had incurred the wrath of a Salford gang which considered parts of the Haçienda its own territory. Police were reported as saying that the city would be a better place without the club. It was the end of a turbulent, fascinating era, and at that moment, the naive euphoria of 1988 and 1989 could not have seemed more distant.

6

techno travellers

**"Our generation is the best mass movement in history –
experimenting with anything in our search for love and peace.
Our temple is sound, we fight our battles with music, drums like
thunder, cymbals like lightning, banks of electronic equipment
like nuclear missiles of sound." Phil Russell, quoted in *A Series
of Shock Slogans and Mindless Token Tantrums***

This manifesto for the house generation was actually penned in
1974, by a man who would never live to see it implemented.
Phil Russell, one of the instigators of the first People's Free
Festival at Stonehenge, was writing in the aftermath of Woodstock, an event which inspired British hippies to establish their
own communal gatherings at the turn of the seventies. Russell,
as his alias Wally Hope suggests, was a dreamer by trade; he
believed that he could claim back an ancient, sacred monument
for the people from a government that had stolen it, and make
it a place for celebratory rites, music and dancing. The first
Stonehenge Festival lasted for nine weeks and the music was
supplied by a battered cassette recorder – hardly "drums like
thunder" – before the police served a legal notice to move the
hippies on, which they did: to the Windsor Free Festival, where
their revelries were forcibly ended with boots and truncheons.
A year later, sectioned in a psychiatric hospital, Russell's life, too,
would end tragically, but he had helped to re-establish

Stonehenge as a focus for spiritual activism, which it would remain for years to come.[1]

The travellers went through the doors opened by hippie culture. During the late seventies and early eighties, the numbers of disaffected middle-class dropouts choosing to live an itinerant existence in buses and caravans increased dramatically. They came to be known collectively as the Peace Convoy in 1982, when a group of travellers drove down to the anti-nuclear protest camp at Greenham Common air force base after the Stonehenge Festival. The travellers were not, at least at first, economic refugees, rather those who rejected city living, materialism and the trappings of a consumer society. Stonehenge was the high point of the travellers' year, and by June 1984, augmented by curious visitors from the cities, numbers attending had swelled to 50,000.

No one realised it at the time, but this was to be the golden era of Stonehenge, the final moment of post-hippie afterglow and freedom from legal sanctions: the last People's Free Festival at the ancient stone monument. Later that summer, police launched one of their first raids on a travellers' site at Nostell Priory, followed by a high-profile Army eviction of the Rainbow Village protest camp at Molesworth air base, led by flak-jacketed government minister Michael Heseltine.

The travellers had their own explanations for the severity of the crackdown: their numbers were doubling yearly, they said, they were pied pipers leading Thatcher's children out of the inner cities and into alternative lifestyles; their ideas of rural self-reliance were gaining ever greater mainstream acceptance. This was the era when the Campaign for Nuclear Disarmament had reached the peak of its renaissance, and the very name Peace Convoy, implying active links between nomadic dropouts and political activists, may have struck fear into sections of government that believed that the travellers' way of life involved a rejection of and threat to the system of property and land rights on which Britain is based.

On June 1st, 1985, a convoy of 140 vehicles crawling towards

Stonehenge was halted at a police roadblock and moved into a nearby field by a force of 1,000 officers. English Heritage, Stonehenge's administrators, had already taken out injunctions to prohibit this year's festival and erected razor wire around the monument: whatever the cost, Stonehenge must not go ahead. The Assistant Chief Constable of Wiltshire, Lionel Grundy, refused to negotiate an alternative festival site, and ordered his men to attack the convoy. As travellers scattered into a nearby beanfield, police with visored helmets and riot shields chased the buses, smashed their contents and beat their occupants.

"There were vehicles spinning in all directions," eyewitness Nick Davies recalled. "There were policemen trying to stop them by throwing anything they could lay their hands on – sticks, stones, even their own shields. There was glass breaking, people screaming, black smoke towering out of burning caravans – and everywhere there seemed to be people being bashed and flattened and pulled by the hair."[2] The destruction was followed by hundreds of arrests and a long summer of evictions, harassment, and vilification in the press; ITN footage of the carnage "disappeared" from its library and an impassioned TV report from the scene was replaced with a voiceover. The BBC screened the police's own video of events.[3]

The travellers, previously seen as quaint English eccentrics, throwbacks to a long-extinct sixties, or at worst as relatively harmless, pastoral anarchists, had become fully-fledged folk devils. Home Secretary Douglas Hurd described them as "a band of medieval brigands who have no respect for the law or the rights of others". Prime Minister Margaret Thatcher made her own distaste plain, promising that she was "only too delighted to do anything we can to make life difficult for such things as hippie convoys". It was a promise kept: the 1986 Public Order Act incorporated a section specifically aimed at preventing convoys from massing, the first of many attempts by government agencies over the following decade to make an itinerant existence impossible.

However, the police attention that accompanied the travellers' now well-established summer festival circuit did not prevent the movement's growth. The original idealists were increasingly being joined by a new generation: post-punk, urban squatters whose marginal city life had been emasculated by Conservative benefit restrictions. As the original punk scene fizzled out at the end of the 1970s, it was taken up by a number of bands who took the Sex Pistols' anarchist tenets literally. Foremost amongst these were Crass, who lived in a commune in Epping Forest and had helped Phil Russell organise the first Stonehenge festival in 1974 (although when the band played at the festival, they were bottled off stage by bikers offended by the arrival of punk rock). "When Johnny Rotten proclaimed that there was 'no future', we saw it as a challenge to our creativity," said Crass's Penny Rimbaud, "we knew that there was a future if we were prepared to work for it."[4]

Crass were crucial in drawing a large contingent of post-punks towards the idea of punk as a *way of life*, rather than a mere lifestyle: pro-squatting, nuclear disarmament, feminism and animal liberation. Following their inspiration, punks were taking on board sixties ideals, and slowly mutating into the hippie continuum. Many of them, dressed in raggedy black combat gear with haircuts that mixed and mismatched punk, Rasta and Native American styles – a look that would later be codified as "crustie" – began to join the travellers on the road. This influx from the cities not only changed the travellers, but brought new problems from wider society. After the Battle of the Beanfield, sections of a downcast and disillusioned travelling community started to seek oblivion through Special Brew superlager or even heroin as the hippie dream turned sour. Festivals had lost their shine, and were plagued by groups of marauding, sometimes violent drunks, the crustie punks of the "Brew Crew".

By the end of the eighties, many travellers were highly politi-cised. Their chosen path had already put them into conflict with the vested interests of landowners, and hence with the government and the police, yet they were also beset by internal conflict, struggling for survival. It was a perfect time for change.

brixton and camden

By 1989, house culture and its drug of choice had spread not only from small, exclusive clubs to huge outdoor raves, but also into the inner city squatlands of the capital, and its open-access concept was constantly being reinterpreted to suit the set and setting of new adherents. The moment that the words "acid" and "house" were joined together, it was inevitable that people with a long-standing interest in psychedelic drugs would be drawn towards dance culture. London already had a flourishing party scene catering for a loose alliance of latter-day hippies, mutant punk crusties, doleites, spliffheads and students. Foremost amongst these were the Mutoid Waste Company, who specialised in squatting derelict warehouses, filling them with outlandish scrap-metal salvage artworks then throwing huge parties, and Club Dog, who staged hippie dance nights in Finsbury Park's Sir George Robey pub with world music, jugglers and poets. Both thrived on the post-punk continuum which had been transformed through contact with anarchist bands like Crass, free festivals, and years inhabiting the capital's squatlands. Although neither was immediately converted to the house scene in 1988, both felt its influence.

Others had been scrawling manifestos in a vacuum, excluded by a pop culture that claimed to have killed the sixties in 1977. Fraser Clark, an impish Scot, took his first acid trip in Ibiza in 1965 and spent the rest of the decade on the hippie trail. He had been running an irregular magazine entitled *Encyclopaedia Psychedelica* since 1986, and scanning the cultural horizon for signs of a hippie resurgence. He got it when the magazine's graphic designers insisted that he accompany them to a club they had been enthusing about. "When I walked into Shoom, my first house club, I saw a hippie thing going on all over again. What else would make all these yuppie types dress down in colourful clothes? I thought: 'Thank God!' "

Clark, then forty-four, was sharp and media-savvy, and knew a good thing when he found it. He saw in acid house a technologically updated reflection of his own hippie idealism. "Before acid house, hippie was the most pejorative word you could use. Now here was the consciousness craze that I had been predicting, and the power of it was that we hadn't invented it: it wasn't some old hippie's plot to try and revive the hippie thing, it had spontaneously combusted among young people themselves. I got completely involved in it immediately." He perceived acid house as a *renaissance* rather than a new movement. "A new generation of over a million hippies has evolved overnight, more than there ever were in the sixties," he proclaimed breathlessly at the tail end of 1988. He labelled these new acid house "hippies" Zippies – "a combination of the sixties hippie and the late eighties techno person – a person who is using new technology for the good of the individual" – and renamed his magazine *Evolution* in a one-man mission to instil acid house with the hippie ethics he thought it deserved.

"I don't want to be a guru or a martyr," Clark insisted. "I've got far more exciting things to do. A guru is surrounded by yes-people who think everything he does is right; I'm certainly not right all the time." Nevertheless, he set out his stall as the man who would raise the consciousness of the E generation (or as Timothy Leary had once been called, a "cheerleader for change"). But taking drugs, in itself, was not enough; there had to be some way of ascending the evolutionary ladder, taking up where the sixties had left off. Psychedelics, Allen Ginsberg once said, would clean out all the garbage that society had dumped in your brain. Thirty years on, Clark echoed the beat poet: "The rave scene is the first step to awakening; you dance for hours to shamanic tribal drumming. That clears your head of all your conditioning and your mind is opened. Then you've got to re-programme it with a different philosophy."

Clark clearly saw himself as a re-programmer. He believed that the house scene was a contemporary version of the ancient dance-drug rituals of tribal shamans (perhaps his greatest success is that this idea has passed into popular currency and is endlessly repeated by those attempting to discern the "meaning" of house culture). This wasn't a new idea; in his book *Disco*, Albert Goldman claimed that the New York disco scene of the seventies reflected "an underground tradition of primitive tribal religious rites", a "quest for ecstasy and transcendence" through orgiastic dance mania.[5] Clark also had a romantic vision of a New Age Britain revitalised by the pagan energies generated by the fission between the house generation and the green movement, which he later summed up in a manifesto on the sleeve of *Evolution's Shamanarchy in the UK* compilation album: "As the depression in the dominator system deepens into final collapse, the co-oper-ative free festy/rave/squatter/new new age/techno tribal traveller cross-over counter-culture will grow unstoppably into the new dominant goddess-worshipping techno-tipi dwelling eco-culture that will inherit a cleansed planet." His project was nothing less than the psychedelicising of youth culture.

Interweaving fact and fantasy with boundless optimism, Clark believed he could *dream* situations into existence: if you will it hard enough, it might just happen. The *Shamanarchy* manifesto claimed that "in the nineties every High Street in the land of Britain boasts a club retailing shamanic dancing six nights a week" and suggested the house scene could revive "the noble Albion dream of a golden flowering of civilisation". Unbeliev-able? Try it and see! Clark gave – still gives – countless interviews, and tirelessly launched new projects based around the Zippie idea. In this sense he was more of an entrepreneur, a peddler of concepts, than a guru.

The Shamen, an indie rock band from Aberdeen whose music fused moody psychedelic riffs and left-wing politics – and whose lyrics had been reproduced in Clark's *Encyclopaedia Psychedelica* – were also drawn by the concept of acid house. The band had spent the eighties satirising war, religion and capitalism, and more recently had also begun toying with computer programming and electronic sequencers. Acid house not only confirmed that their chosen path was correct, but opened doors to new perceptions about where that path could lead. At RIP at Clink Street Studios in the summer of 1988, singer Colin Angus and bass player Will Sinnott, both former psychiatric nurses with an interest in LSD, Leary and, of course, shamanism, encountered something that would alter the course of not only their careers but also their lives. "It struck me as a technologically and musically updated Acid Test, but with more emphasis on sexuality and syncopation, and minus the 'verbal' (perhaps that should be 'intellectual') component," recalls Angus. "At the time, it seemed like a prescient glimpse of the entertainment-form of the future."

The Shamen played a few small shows with RIP DJ Eddie Richards spinning records around their set, but decided that it wasn't enough simply to play acid tracks before and after the main attraction, leaving the traditional rock gig format intact. They had to go further. As technology made the rest of the band obsolete, they pared down to a two-piece unit. In Colin Angus's Camden squat, he and Will Sinnott, their manager, lighting technician, sound engineer and Mixmaster Morris, sat down to discuss what could be done.

Morris, a pseudonymous DJ and musician with roots in punk, psychedelia and avant-garde electronics, had been thrilled by the potential he read into acid house. "Like every other trip-head in Britain," he says, "it gave me a lot of ideas."[6] In 1988, he had organised the first ever live house gig; Mad House, a melee of computer jamming to a half-filled hall at Brixton's Fridge – financed with his life savings – was untogether and overambitious, but again anticipated things to come: the idea of bands playing live in an acid house environment, not as a focus for the passive public's gaze but as an integral part of a total experience.

The Shamen took this on board. They drafted a manifesto declaring that the rock gig must be torn apart and remade, combining the human thrill of performance with the intensity of the house environment – "a cataclysmic culture clash on the cutting edge . . . indie bands on the dancefloor in communion with the house tribe . . . an entirely new kind of club where anything can happen". Will Sinnott dreamed that it could usurp the master–servant power relationship which underpinned rock'n'roll, and liberate its participants to define their experience on their own terms: "The political content of dance music is intrinsic," he insisted. "It stimulates ego-role behaviour reduction, offering the experience of unity and affinity with others. This experience invalidates liberal, individualistic ideology and creates true political opposition."[7]

Synergy was the logical name for the hybrid that emerged as a rolling revue of DJs like Morris, Eddie Richards and Paul Oakenfold, rapper Mr C from Clink Street, bands like The Shamen and another sublime electronic duo, Orbital, all seamlessly fused under a powerful light show reminiscent of 1989's biggest raves. Previous experiments with merging psychedelia, dance music and the rock gig had all been just that: experiments, imaginative but not wholly enjoyable. Synergy *worked*. Over the next year the tour crossed the country, seducing new converts from the indie rock constituency.

"When it started half of the audience would dance while the rest watched the band then went home to read the *NME*," recalls Mixmaster Morris. "Within a year everyone was dancing all night and it felt great because we were helping to drive a big stake through the heart of rock'n'roll. We were dancing on its grave."[8] Synergy was not happening in isolation; at the same time, both the Happy Mondays and Primal Scream were also asking questions about what rock'n'roll should mean in the digital era. Considered as a whole, the impact was immense. As far as the rock community was concerned, dance music had arrived.

Then tragedy struck. After finishing the video for The

Shamen's new single, *Move Any Mountain*, Will Sinnott stayed on in the Canary Islands with his girlfriend, taking with him, according to new Shamen member Mr C, "a dozen bottles of liquid E and some white doves". On May 22nd, 1991, he got into difficulties while swimming off the coast of Gomera and drowned. Ironically, *Move Any Mountain* became The Shamen's biggest hit yet. Even more ironically, in his last interview the week before his death, Sinnott had told an *NME* journalist: "Someone up there must like me. I must have good karma. I've been in a lot of situations on my motorbike where I should have ended up dead. I shouldn't have got away with it. I'm lucky to be alive."[9]

glastonbury

Manifestos alone weren't enough to spark a new counterculture; a major convergence of ideologies and lifestyles was necessary to finally make explicit the utopian undercurrents which were submerged deep within the house scene. Roger Beard, the former traveller who DJed at Spectrum, had tried to direct the traffic in both directions, planning (unsuccessfully) to take Shoomers down to Stonehenge for 1988's spring solstice, and bringing his travelling friends down from their sites to Future in March of that year. However, the first significant crossover between the house scene and the festival circuit took place at Glastonbury.

Since the Battle of the Beanfield, the increasingly businesslike Glastonbury Festival had become a more important stop-off on the travellers' annual round, a place for them to trade their wares and party. Initially, festival promoter Michael Eavis allowed the travellers to attend free of charge (though this would later change amidst much conflict). In 1989, the first sound systems, including east London's Hypnosis, trucked their rigs to the site.

"Everyone did one in 1990, but we did one in 1989," says

Hypnosis promoter Tim Strudwick. "We took a sound system in a humungous Mercedes van, all our security, lights and lasers and a 15K rig. We got down there before Glastonbury started and roped off a big area in one of the car parks on the top of a hill. We had this rig going for three days non-stop. We had punks, skinheads, travellers, ravers, and it was just one mental three-day orgy of music. A very good spirit as well; on one occasion we ran out of diesel and some travellers come up with twenty-five gallons of diesel. Incredible. You had hippies coming up and complaining about the noise. As far as I was concerned, the thing about Glastonbury was you do what you fucking like."

This had not gone unnoticed. In 1990, an alliance between travellers and ravers began to take shape. The travellers had the sites and the know-how to staff and run an event that would last for days rather than hours; the ravers had the electronic sounds and the seductive new synthetic, Ecstasy. It certainly seemed a lot better than what either the Brew Crew or the increasingly dated free festival rock stalwarts had to offer. And, although ideological and sartorial differences remained, both shared an interest in getting high and dancing all night.

Coming a month before Graham Bright's Bill outlawing unlicensed raves was passed, Glastonbury 1990 was perfectly placed to capitalise on the growing disaffection with what the "orbital" rave scene had become: commercialised, unreliable and seedy. Legal action against one section of the scene was having an effect, but not necessarily the intended one: the creative energy was breaking out elsewhere, infecting new people and pushing previously unconnected groups together.

At Glastonbury, sound systems proliferated, from London's Club Dog, who had begun to mix dance records with their offbeat world music, to Nottingham's DiY outfit and Tonka, a collective originating from Cambridge whose members had a heritage stretching from parties at Grantchester Meadows in 1969 through hip hop jams to London acid clubs and free raves on Brighton beach. Heavy acid rhythms pulsed as day broke over the dancers, who dug troughs into the sandy soil as their feet stomped in time for hours on end. Phone numbers were swapped, partnerships formed, and two generations of hippies appeared to join hands. When a traveller rode his horse around the dancefloor in the middle of the night, it seemed to herald the beginning of a new era.

Although many breathless accounts of 1989's outdoor raves read the superficial signs they displayed – the psychedelic drugs, the technicolour clothes, the argot of love and unity – and compared them to hippie festivals, this was a cosmetic analysis. A description of an all-night acid party in San Francisco in the mid-sixties could easily have been a snapshot of a contemporary rave: "A special kind of delirium took hold . . . a frenzy that bordered on the religious . . . a total assault on the senses: the electric sound washed in visceral waves over the dancers, unleashing intense psychic energies and driving the audience further and further towards public trance."[10] However, few people, except perhaps Fraser Clark, were under the illusion that the similarity was anything other than visual. Certainly not ideological.

"I don't think you can really liken the sixties to the eighties," insisted Tony Colston-Hayter at the time. "In some ways it was a throwback to the sixties but it was very much something else – it was totally non-political. It was the ultimate hedonistic leisure activity. It was about going out and having a good time. Fraser Clark was at the [Sunrise] Dance Music Festival we did, and he was saying that it was just like a big festival. Personally, it doesn't work for me. It's happened for a certain number of people, but to happen on a mass scale? There aren't enough people who are that bothered to take it to that sort of level, to change their whole lives around it. The difference is that people now don't want to live it."

Although the sixties and the nineties were both typified by thoroughgoing social changes, the people who devised the template for each drug culture could not be more different, socially, culturally or economically. The psychedelic scene of the sixties was born out of Harvard University, instigated by intellectuals, professors, poets, scientists, writers and artists, drawing on concepts from humanist psychology and Eastern mysticism, against the backdrop of the growing civil rights and anti-Vietnam War movements and the economic boom period and explosion of vitality following the end of the grey, sober, restrained fifties. The acid house scene was conceived in suburban, working-class south London by clubbers, blaggers, football casuals, DJs and a few bohemians, in an increasingly harsh economic and social environment with sweeping disaffection from politics.

Drug-taking in the eighties had lost the politicised, bohemian context it had in the sixties; it was more about hedonism, a holiday in an altered state, than it was about mind-expansion, and the adoption of hippie slogans by the original Shoomers was merely a reconstruction of received myths about the sixties in an attempt to put the Ecstasy experience in some kind of context rather than a desire to resurrect the hippie era wholesale. The way acid house developed reflected eighties Britain, not sixties America; it was strongly rooted in British youth cultural traditions – sampling liberally from the amphetamine-fuelled all-nighters of Northern Soul, the sound systems and illegal warehouse parties of the funk and reggae scenes, the DIY ethics of punk – not those of American counterculture.

However, what Tony Colston-Hayter didn't realise was that amongst his seething crowd there were people who *did* want to live it, and were disappointed when they touched the ideological void at the heart of his technologically enhanced leisure pursuit. Foremost among them were the DiY sound system, who became instrumental in taking the festival/rave crossover to its next stage. A collective of DJs that grew out of post-punk and hip hop circles in Nottingham, they had initially followed the open-air rave circuit before becoming disillusioned with driving round the countryside late at night, searching for a party that they had paid £20 each for but that would never take place. Their choice of name – Do it Yourself – referred not only to their punk lineage but to the ideals they believed the house scene should espouse. At Glastonbury in 1990, they linked up with a group of travellers from Salisbury who had similarly become disillusioned with the state of their own scene, specifically the drunken antics of the Brew Crew, and together began to throw free parties in the wide open spaces of Wiltshire and Somerset, where travellers and ravers danced a honeymoon rite together in King Arthur's country.

Initially there was a two-way exchange of knowledge and ideas. The house sound systems began to adopt the travellers' belief that parties should be free for all, and that charging for entry was not only materialist, exclusive and divisive, but destroyed some of the magic of communal celebration. When a DiY party in the south-west was raided later in 1990, the police, used to tales of orbital rave organisers making hundreds of thousands of pounds in one night, found it hard to understand why none of the instigators was carrying a suitcase full of notes. "When we were arrested, they couldn't believe it was free," says Rick. "They couldn't understand why we would want to come down from Nottingham to do something for nothing. They were convinced there was a Mr Big behind it making millions. We only had three quid between the four of us. They told us we were too scruffy to be acid house promoters." It was a stereotype that was soon to be updated.

stonehenge

"Me and my brother had been to the very first Stonehenge festivals when we were thirteen or fourteen, and had spent our childhood there, waiting for Hawkwind, who were the people with the illegal sound system and the stage and the music then. If they turned up, there was a festival; if they didn't, there wasn't. In those days we saw ourselves as freaks, we weren't hippies or punks. We had those roots, but from the age of sixteen or seventeen onwards I was a club person, and very affected by the whole acid house thing. In Manchester in 1988 I was down the Haçienda four nights a week. I remember one fateful Wednesday night the whole world changed, literally. It was an incredible jolt to the system, a very deep experience; a glimpse into this other dimension that up until that age I had no idea existed. I suppose it was something we were always chasing at the festivals but never really occurred."

From cultural flashpoints come new beginnings. Mark Harrison had experienced Stonehenge, the Haçienda at its peak, the outlaw raves of the late eighties, the Tonka sound system at Glastonbury. Now, living in a squatted house in London and working as a graphic designer, he and his brother Alexander, a tree surgeon, and friends Debbie Griffith and Simone Feeney, scraped together enough money to buy some sound equipment and threw a series of parties in a disused school building in Willesden.

"We were experimenting with the idea of free parties," says Harrison. "It seemed like a sensible thing to do – there were all these big commercial raves going on that had lost their mystery. Previous to that you'd had these huge illegal events that might have been quite expensive, but at least one got value for money: the biggest sound systems, the best light shows, the most amount of people, the loudest music, and lots of security with pitbulls, but you were paying for that and you didn't mind financing this very deep and dark mysterious pirate world. It was exhilarating, but it lost that magic."

Their first party at the Old School House in October 1990 was titled Detension. The black walls were covered with Harrison's Day-Glo artwork, a potent blend of Op Art, hieroglyphics and pagan imagery. He had found an ammonite fossil in the street and liked its graphic impact and its symbolism; now the sound system had a name: Spiral Tribe.

The Stonehenge People's Free Festival retained its title even though it hadn't been anywhere near the stones themselves since 1984. During 1991's summer solstice, it took place some twenty miles away, at Longstock. On June 21st, Spiral Tribe said goodbye to London's squatlands and rolled up in a van with a four-and-a-half kilowatt rig.

"It was on one of these ancient greenways, this old Roman or prehistoric road," Harrison recalls. "Up until that point I thought ley lines, solstices and all that mumbo-jumbo was just hot air, I had no belief in it. Suddenly that all changed. Something just clicked, we were on a groove and we knew who we were. We got an inkling of the gravity of what we were up to and what we were about. It was bigger than all of us! It wasn't just Spiral Tribe as organisers or co-ordinators, it was also the people around us. We would all be on that kind of buzz, realising that what we had here extended beyond each and every one of us and beyond the material thing of having a sound system. This is where the whole philosophy of the Spiral Tribe has its roots. But what was a great mystery and surprise – and still is – is that it was already within us. We hadn't actually been aware of that until it was up and running, and *it* showed *us*. It was spooky."

Longstock was the biggest festival for seven years, and the cornerstone not only of Spiral Tribe's spiritual awakening but also of their future influence. They looked different: uniform shaven heads, combat gear, black clothing. Their music sounded different: harder and faster than any other sound system. And they were in the right place at the right time, playing the loudest music to the largest number of people, many of whom were combining drugs and dance music for the first time.

The party over, Spiral Tribe didn't pack up and head back to London. Everything had changed; they had a purpose, a mission to accomplish. They had to travel, to do it twenty-four hours, seven days a week, to live on the groove, to *make some fucking noise*.

"We kept the sound system out and we never went home from that moment on. We stayed out and did the next weekend and the next weekend . . . After that was Stoney Cross, another amazing place. Every single venue that we gravitated towards had a very interesting history. During the war this area was where the authorities had camped all the gypsies because they were seen as undesirable and having dodgy ethnic origins. It was on this disused airfield; the year previously on the same spot there had been a similar incident to the Beanfield, the police had caned the festival and smashed up travellers' vehicles, so everyone was very nervous about coming down. We were totally ignorant and naive and that's the only reason we were there; we didn't know there was any threat of violence. We set up around these little raised banks which opened out in a perfect circle, switched on, and people started to arrive. So there we were, actually making the festival happen!"

They moved on, crossing Hampshire, Devon, Surrey and Gloucestershire, reaching the White Goddess festival, at Camelford in Cornwall, by August. Like Ken Kesey's Merry Pranksters on their historic bus trip across the States in the sixties, the Tribe grew constantly as it left a kaleidoscopic trail through the idyllic countryside of the south-west in its Luton van, attracting huge, multi-dimensional characters: Reggie the box man with his background in London's reggae scene; Hubert, alias MC Scallywag, with his clarion call of "we are not Spiral Tribe, you are all Spiral Tribe, it's you that makes the party happen"; Debby Staunton, a vibrant, idealistic mother of two in her thirties who ran their telephone information line; and Mark Harrison himself with his magnetic charisma, constantly smiling yet almost frighteningly intense (one journalist who interviewed him labelled him, not entirely joking, an "evil genius"). Local DJs would take turns on the decks and find themselves part of the Tribe.

"The Spiral Tribe euphoria was like the rebirth of the '88/ '89 acid house days," says Aztek, a DJ who enlisted at Camelford. "As the day progressed, the busier it became and the beats hardened up. The night returned and out came the fire eaters and jugglers. Whistles, horns and shouts from the overwhelming crowd could be heard echoing out over the moors, merging into the musical mayhem of hectic rhythms and wailing synths coming from the Spiral sound system. From that day forward I was hooked."[11]

At Camelford, people who were used to seeing bands thrashing on guitars and drums were riveted, then transformed. On one side of the arena was the rock stage, where the likes of Hawkwind were playing. On the other was Spiral Tribe. In front of the bands, a few drunks moshed frantically or sprawled woozily in the grass. Around the sound system, 2,000 people were jumping, prancing and smiling, suffused with the mania of revelation. The new rite was visibly eclipsing the old.

"It had total life-force – Spiral Tribe, all night, twenty-four hours, that was what it was about, that was why I'd been into rock'n'roll but it had become so fat and bloated and this was much more direct, a much purer form of expressing who you were." Simon Lee was a young festival-goer who immediately became involved in the free party scene after Camelford. "The festival was next to Brown Willie Tor on the moors, a really amazing place. At one point you could see the sun and the moon and Brown Willie at the same time. Everything was so flat you could see the horizon; it was like being in this huge cosmic tent. Everyone we went with ended up coming back and selling all their rock records – there was no need for them any more! It was immense, such a new sound."

The system played on and on and on, for fourteen long days and nights, from August into September, never slacking, never slowing, sleep deprivation driving the Tribe onwards to some sort of epiphany, a feeling that was almost religious. "To experience that, you experience a world you didn't know existed," explains Mark Harrison. "The sun goes down, the moon comes up and you see the world spinning. My record is nine days without sleep. It's a shamanic thing."[12]

Long periods without sleep inevitably alter your mental state. Add a few handfuls of magic mushrooms or some gaudy squares of LSD, then compound the feeling with the exhilaration of discovering new experiences and the intensity of living in close confinement with a small group of people for a long period of time. Out of this rigorous monastic existence came a powerful sense of identity, belief and purpose which seemed to take on physical shape, become an entity even larger than the sum of the Tribe members themselves:

"Within a few months it was totally out of our control. It manifested itself within everyone that got involved with Spiral Tribe – people shaved their heads, dressed in combats and dark clothes. All we did was build the system, the people that came put the energy into the system. Without wanting to sound Marxist, it really was the people's sound system and that's where its energy lay. That's what set it apart from anything else that was going on, because then there wasn't really anyone else providing that non-stop, and living it. The unspoken rule or initiation with Spiral Tribe was that you had to live it, twenty-four hours a day. There was this incredible amount of focus and concentration."

Whereas Tony Colston-Hayter had seen the English countryside as a green-field development site for his new leisure concept, the Spirals understood it as politically charged environment, a historic arena for a clash between rebels and oppressors. They were developing a romantic, purist philosophy, based on their background, the situations they found themselves in and the people they came into contact with while moving from festival to festival over the summer of 1991. They began to believe that techno was the new folk music, the voice of the culturally dispossessed, and for it to take proper physical and psychological effect it had to be played as loud and for as long as possible; that the Spiral Tribe were in some way connected to prehistoric tribes of nomads who had celebrated in music and dance thousands of years earlier in the same surroundings; that free parties were shamanic rites which, using the new musical technologies in combination with certain chemicals and long periods of dancing, preferably in settings with spiritual significance, could reconnect urban youth to the earth with which they had lost contact, thus averting imminent ecological crisis. And the only people capable of brokering this paradigm shift were the *real* hard core, the *rebel* hard core, the ones who would never back down or turn it down, who would *make some noise* until their voices were heard.

Although Mark Harrison says he was barely aware of Crass, there are some striking similarities between the eighties punk anarchists and the nineties techno rebels. Back in London for the winter of 1991, squatting on a filthy site in front of a dog food factory in Greenwich, the Tribe parked up their growing fleet of vehicles, huddled for warmth around fires built in an old sink unit and took stock of their evolving manifesto.

"There's a certain period of realisation where one's whole world is shaken upside down," Harrison explained at the time. "It isn't the way you were told, it's about seeing all the things you placed your security in, like wealth and status, are total shams. It's very important for people to realise that they've got to step out of the authorities' control. Even if it's just for a few minutes, that's all it takes . . . maybe that's why the parties are so popular. As legend would have it, there's a musical note that will free the people . . . there are rhythms that can induce trances and take you nearer to the spirit world . . .

"We don't care about money, ownership of property . . . it's our birthright to walk this earth, to drink clean water, to eat good food and to have some kind of shelter. It's not about squatting or sound systems, it's about society's way of life and how unacceptable it is."[13]

Harrison's complex, impassioned discourse eschews the reconstructed hippie platitudes of Ecstasy-inspired "peace and love". What seems to have had a far stronger effect on the development of Spiral Tribe, its belief system and its *modus operandi*, is a much more powerful drug than Ecstasy, one which turns minds inside out and worlds upside down, asking questions and demanding answers – LSD. Whereas Ecstasy evokes intense happiness and empathy, but doesn't necessarily force you to re-evaluate your way of life, the wild hallucinations brought on by a heroic dose of LSD can push the human ego to the brink of dissolution. Spiral Tribe wanted to tap the potential that was being filtered out by the central nervous system, to short-circuit years of conditioning. Their insistence was that pleasure in itself just wasn't enough. Ecstasy had been a useful tool, but now it seemed tame and domestic – happy little bunnies running round in ever-decreasing circles – and it was time to take things further.

"MDMA has its place, but once you've taken it a couple of times, its lessons are learned very quickly and it becomes unnecessary. It has a definite perimeter of experience, and, once tried and tested, it doesn't go beyond that. In habitual use, I don't know to what degree it leads to stagnant thinking. Culturally, I do not enjoy these parties where everyone is just fluffed up on MDMA, or whatever it might be in those pills, listening to very bland, inoffensive, passive music, with an attitude of just wanting to get out of it for no real reason, not even wanting to apply what's been learnt. From what I've seen, I don't think it has very much to show you, whereas I don't think you can go wrong with LSD and magic mushrooms. They are much more important, and non-toxic of course. LSD and magic mushrooms have a much more creative influence, not just on raves, but on life, on one's understanding of oneself and the world around."

Looking back at Harrison's account of the Tribe's spiritual awakening at the Longstock festival, it can easily been seen in the context of a revelatory, life-changing LSD experience; hence the Tribe's willingness to push itself further, beyond the bounds of both society and consciousness. Around the parties gravitated rarer and more exotic psychedelics – "the best substances, like ketamine and mescalin and stuff, that was part of the mystique as well," according to a fellow-traveller.

The Spirals' hallucinogenic trajectory synchronised with the marginal psychedelic discourses that were being factored into the small but industrious techno-hippie community back in London, which had found a focus in Fraser Clark's series of

Evolution lectures. In 1992, Clark invited a string of key figures within American counterculture to speak: Robert Anton Wilson, author of the ultimate conspiracy novel, *Illuminatus!*, Ecstasy chemist Alexander Shulgin, and, most influentially, Terence McKenna. McKenna was an ethno-botanist who had travelled widely in South America, collecting and sampling species of psychedelic mushroom. In his best-known book, *Food of the Gods*, he set out his theory that, from prehistoric times onwards, plants and humans have developed in symbiosis, with psyche-delic plants in particular playing a key role in the development of human mental capability. Thus, if such plants were reintegrated into society in contemporary shamanic rituals, they could avert the ecological crisis facing humanity by facilitating an evol-utionary leap to a higher level of consciousness.

McKenna invested his botanical history with an inventive zeal that verged on insanity, recounting how, after having smoked the plant psychedelic dimethyltryptamine (DMT), he found himself in an alien world listening to the musical chatter of jolly "machine elves of hyperspace" – and they seemed to be *trying to tell him something*. "If I'm not completely mad," he commented, "this is big news."[14] Both the sheer audacity of his arguments and the strangely hypnotic tone of his voice struck a chord with those who believed the human race was at a crossroads, headed either for a new age of enlightenment or a dark age of environmental destitution. The witty, bushy-bearded orator noted how his new audience had adapted their ideas of dance culture as shamanic ritual from his books, and tailored his words accordingly. "With electronic culture you can create shamans for the global planetary village," he said afterwards, clad in a fractal-patterned rave T-shirt and looking peculiarly like a hairy little mushroom, "and this to my mind is the function that rock'n'roll played in the sixties and house music should play in the nineties."[15]

One of the people at the *Evolution* lecture was Colin Angus of The Shamen, who found that McKenna encapsulated many of his thoughts about the transformative power of psychedelic drugs.

"Terence has revitalised the concept of psychedelics for the nineties and beyond, within the context of shamanism and concern for the future of the planet, a perspective notably lacking in the sixties," says Angus. "His idea that we should use the psychedelic tools to save humanity from itself, and in doing so 'save the world', has got to be worthy of consideration, however unrealistic this may seem in the cold light of day. Desperate problems require desperate solutions . . ."

McKenna's advocacy of natural psychedelics like psilocybin mushrooms and the fifteen-minute "rocket trip" of DMT, offered a route out of what Angus, like Mark Harrison, believed were the increasingly formulaic patterns of Ecstasy culture. On top of that, McKenna was a natural showman. Angus invited him to contribute to a track on the band's forthcoming concept album, *Boss Drum*, which was largely inspired by *Food of the Gods*. On *Re-evolution*, McKenna spelled out his vision of an "archaic revival", a reconnection with the planet's ancient energies – a concept familiar to anyone who had been listening to Spiral Tribe. "Through emphasis in house music and rave culture on physiologically compatible rhythms, that sound, properly under-stood, can actually change neurological states in large groups of people getting together," he droned mellifluously, "creating a telepathic community of bonding that hopefully would be strong enough that it would carry the vision out into the mainstream of society."

McKenna's philosophy seeped into the techno travellers' data bank. Like Colin Angus, the Spirals weren't interested in simply getting out of it. They wanted to change neurological states and break through to the other side, certainly, but then to return, carrying wisdom from the psychedelic dimension with them. "I read a very good description of it in the *Kabbalah*," says Mark Harrison. "You have people who want to leave this dimension and return to their source, and you have other people who want to manifest the source here in the material world. That is what we have always done."

Yet it couldn't be done with drugs alone. Earlier sound systems, like DiY and Tonka, specialised in a warmer, more sensuous and funky brand of house music, carrying on a tradition that stretched back to New York and Chicago in the eighties. The ones that spun off from Spiral Tribe, like Bedlam and Adrenalin, started by Tribe members who set their own rigs and lorries in motion, preferred full-on, no-compromise techno; a form that had been warped out of the shape given to it by its black creators in Detroit and invested with harsher edges and manic velocity. Mark Harrison insists that this soundtrack, too, was grounded in an ideological perspective: hard-core music for a hard-core world.

"Techno is the best theme music for this lifestyle. We're getting into the state of mind to be in this existence – breaking with the establishment, going off into the unknown and making it up as you go along. You not only make the emotional but the physical break with the reality that you know. This theme music has reinforced that break. I'm not interested in music that relies on tried and tested narratives. Techno is exploring the creative channels that the new technology gives us. Other music styles are all in the past – been there, seen it, done it – whereas techno is very futuristic."

Harrison's ideas again drew on the emergent techno-hippie continuum and its premise of using technology – chemical and computer – to create alternative realities. From 1989 onwards, there had been huge interest in the ideas flowing over the Atlantic from San Francisco's *Mondo 2000* magazine. *Mondo*, whose staff were a bunch of "reality hackers, nuts, flakes, entrepreneurs, trippers, con-men, students, artists, mad engineers", and whose ideas were later sampled, commodified and sold to the mainstream in the form of *Wired*, described a possible future at the interface between new technology and new age techniques: "cyberculture" or the "New Edge".[16] Using such tools as virtual reality, brain machines, bulletin boards, chaos theory and cognitive-enhancing "smart drinks", suggested science fiction author and *Mondo* fellow traveller Rudy Rucker, it was possible to hack the consciousness interface, to reprogramme your environment: "You can make your own literature, your own music, your own television, your own life, and – most important of all – your own reality."[17]

Never slow to catch the next wave and give it a snappy slogan, Timothy Leary weighed in with a book called *Chaos and Cyber Culture* which imagined a "new breed" of creative youth, into techno, psychedelics and computer networking. Leary saw computers, like acid, as a method to traverse the borders of human potential. "We wrestled the power of LSD away from the CIA, and now the power of computers away from IBM," he wrote.[18]

The growth of the Internet, the global computer network set up by the US military in the sixties to protect its communication systems from Communist attack but reappropriated by hackers and academics and infused with an ethos of hippie collectivism, synched neatly with the development of techno into a global network of scenes and contacts, equally vibrant in Berlin, San Francisco, Paris, Edinburgh, Tokyo, Frankfurt – or the English countryside. "In the sixties," suggested The Shamen's Mr C, picking up the Leary thread, "they didn't have the music, the technology or the information communication capabilities to carry it through, which we've got now: computers." Samplers, MIDI (musical instrument digital interface) recording equipment, mobile phones, video camcorders, e-mail: all could be reappropriated and repurposed, as the Xerox photocopier had been during punk, for the creation of an amorphous new techno counterculture.

Another key plank of Spiral Tribe's emerging doctrine surrounded the parties themselves. They *must* be free. To charge for entry would make them exclusive and élitist, a purely business operation, attracting only a certain kind of affluent raver (although, of course, a few sound systems will confidentially admit that they were funded by drug sales). The political implications of this were not lost on the Spirals. "Money is a discriminator; it discriminates between those who have it and those who don't," says Debby Staunton. "When it's free, it's truly open to everybody and egalitarian, and you get a completely different vibe. The government place a financial value on every goddamn thing that we have today, so yes, it is bucking the system if you decide that you don't need money."

Economic, social and spiritual issues were deeply intertwined, stresses Simon Lee, who immediately became involved in running squat parties in south London after returning from Camelford: "Clubs *sell* you a good night: all you do is turn up there and be a punter, whereas at a festival you are involved, your presence means something, there's a power to it. The government know it as well, that it's dangerous for a lot of like-minded people to come together in something which is totally opposite to their value system. Their value system is money, and ours is nothing to do with money, it's free. That's as opposite as you can get."

Other sound systems were not nearly so forceful in their ideological rigour. And other sound systems were not nearly so influential. After Longstock, Camelford and all the other festivals over the summer of 1991, Spiral Tribe were making an impact in the material world. The template they devised – a loose-knit collective of nomads driving buses and vans from site to site, blasting extreme, frenetic, raucous techno music for days on end – was immediately taken up by others. The Tribe set the pattern for the rest to follow because, believes Simon Lee, "they were in the right place at the right time with the right attitude. They were really good self-publicists, though being seen not to be publicity-seeking. They had such a strong identity – they all looked the same, they all dressed the same. They were a really easy thing to latch on to. They turned on so many people. They set the standards, they had the best parties. And they had all these really vibed-up girls with them." Within twelve months, Spiral Tribe had helped transform Ecstasy culture into an entirely new entity.

castlemorton

Little notice was taken of the new alliance between travellers and ravers in either the youth media or mainstream press. The police, however, were quicker to observe this cultural shift. They had been collecting information on travellers' movements at Devizes police station in Wiltshire since their Operation Solstice on the Stonehenge festival in the mid-eighties. Although they were informed, they weren't organised – yet. However, if the mobile sound systems were in any danger of completely severing their ties with consensus reality after a summer spent attempting to crack the frontiers of consciousness, they would be dragged forcibly to earth in the months to come.

While DiY had encountered the strong arm of the law – arrests, equipment smashed, records confiscated – until 1992, Spiral Tribe's dealings with police had largely been amicable. On April 20th, they installed their rig in a disused warehouse on Acton Lane, west London. According to a statement released later by the Tribe, a thousand people danced inside, oblivious of the fact that police in full riot gear had cordoned off the area. At 2.30 a.m. the police demolished the walls with sledgehammers and a JCB digger, and stormed the building, their identification numbers covered, flailing with long batons as panic erupted, beating and kicking the party-goers indiscriminately, causing hundreds of casualties, then vanishing, leaving a few uniformed coppers to direct the wounded away from the area.[19]

The same month, the Home Office floated the idea of legislating against free festivals, proposing new powers to turn back festival-goers on the roads, confiscate sound equipment, break up convoys and arrest those who refuse to leave a rave – tactics that police had already utilised without legal backing at Camelford the summer before, when motorists were ordered off the road up to forty miles away from the festival.[20]

As the pressure increased, paranoia set in. It felt, says Mark Harrison, like a dark, ominous cloud descending on Spiral Tribe's encampment. "It's the threat of violence which ultimately con-trols everybody in our society, which you don't know exists until you start tripping its trip-wires. 'Evil eye' is a good way of describing it, because the helicopters just *appear*. You're in this state of sleep deprivation and then *there it is!* You become very sensitive to the feeling that there you all are, in the middle of nowhere, travellers and ravers and all the undesirables of our society in a very isolated place, completely vulnerable and unde-fended, totally surrounded. After the Acton Lane thing happened, we were basically seen out of London by a police escort. We fled out into the countryside and went and hid up a mountain in a forest in Wales."

The Avon Free Festival was a well-established stopover on the travellers' annual circuit of rural England, vaguely scheduled for Whitsun bank holiday weekend. The venue wasn't fixed; like most festivals in the wake of the Beanfield it was an *ad hoc* gathering, taking place wherever significant numbers slipped the police net and coalesced out of the chaos. The year before, 2,000 had convened at Chipping Sodbury Common, where the fledgling Spiral Tribe were inspired to action by the driving house sounds of the DiY and Sweat systems.

By May 1992, the police were alert and waiting. The forces of Avon, Somerset and Gloucestershire combined in an attempt to prevent convoys of travellers' vehicles linking up and creating an unstoppable procession. Ten thousand had already descended on Lechlade in Gloucestershire over the May Day weekend. But the strategy backfired and they were caught unawares as a convoy of 400 vehicles started to converge on a square mile of land over the Worcestershire border, in West Mercia Police's territory. It was a beautiful setting; on the slopes of the Malvern Hills, lightly wooded with a clear water lake sparkling in the early summer sun. Simon Goose from Bedlam sound system was one of the first onto Castlemorton Common: "I just beat a five-mile convoy into the place and I watched it come in. There's a natural buzz when you watch a place fill up like that. You can't do nothing but smile, pulling that off and watching the police just standing by. There was nothing they could do."[21] Or rather, they chose to do nothing. According to a report on West Mercia Police operations, they had been planning their strategy for six months, and decided that there were "both tactical and strategic advantages in confining the site to one reasonably compact area". The Chief Constable ordered that "no turn-back operation would be implemented".[22]

The sound systems kept on rolling in. DiY. Spiral Tribe. Adrenalin. Circus Warp. Within a few hours, the Common was transformed into a fully functioning, independent state, under sole control of its inhabitants. A temporary autonomous zone in the English countryside with its own power, lighting, accommodation, catering and leisure facilities. All it needed was a bustling population, and when local residents went on national TV to bemoan their fate, any raver with a taste for outlaw parties was armed with directions to their weekend destination. It couldn't have been better advertised; cars began to pour onto the Common – Fiestas, Golfs, Escorts and 205s parking up alongside the travellers' venerable buses. And what a countercultural paradise! You could dance to the fierce beat of the systems as they raged on for well over 100 hours without pause; take in some more traditional festival entertainment, like street theatre or circus acts; eat at stand-up cafés; splash about in the lake; purchase and freely enjoy your drugs of choice, then rest awhile before starting afresh. Day and night lost their meaning in this twenty-four-hour city.

Published a few weeks after the Avon Free Festival at Castlemorton, the travellers' magazine *Festival Eye* was jubilant: "It is time to stop looking back to the Stonehenge festivals of the early eighties. The Golden Age is now! Watching things happen at Castlemorton was very reminiscent of Stonehenge – except Stonehenge never had such a range of musical entertainment."[23] More soberly, an editorial in the same issue warned that press reports were attempting to exacerbate tensions between travellers and ravers, divining that these were divide and rule tactics being employed by an establishment on the defensive. Certainly, many column inches were devoted to this fracture in the new alliance – the shit-shovel war. The story centred around the mess the ravers left behind them: more specifically, the turds they deposited in ditches and bushes. After years on the road with alfresco toilet facilities, the travellers had learned the advantage of burying their excrement. The ravers simply dropped their stinking faeces, then left it for the travellers to tread in.

There was a more complex problem. Although some travellers embraced the new festival format with glee and others enjoyed the economic gain of supplying party favours, significant numbers actively disliked house music and found the non-stop pulse of the sound systems deeply depressing. This was partly a generational divide: many older travellers were happy with their rock and folk stages; some had children who were kept awake all night by the thump of digital drums. Some resented the influx of "straight" clubbers from the cities, who came to dance all night and enjoy some illegal thrills, then drove home in their nice cars to their warm houses, leaving the people who lived the life full-time to face the wrath of the law. In a sense it was inevitable that festivals would be permanently altered by contact with the new dance technologies, and would come to reflect their time just as the original Stonehenge bashes reflected the afterglow of sixties counterculture. Some systems were aware of potential conflict and, as Castlemorton wound down, felt that enough was enough and turned their rigs off. Others carried on till the bitter end. Spiral Tribe refused to stop and, according to one observer, "there was almost a big punch-up".[24]

This was all in keeping with Tribe ethics, explained Mark Harrison a few months afterwards: "There are some people who moan and they do moan very loudly and they whine and they whinge, but as far as we know, free festivals are about playing music non-stop. Techno is folk music. Never before has folk music been so accessible or so loud. These people may have been travelling for years, but we've just come through hell and high water to bring them this sound system for nothing, and to keep it going. In that situation we're very polite, but no fucking way. We would never be there in the first place if we weren't there by popular demand. We play the people's music . . . Anyone who comes down there and asks us to turn it down, I'm sorry, we're not going to. Turn it up if anything. If you've got a voice, shout. Our attitude is, 'Make some fucking noise.' "[25]

The honeymoon period was most definitely over. As Castlemorton wound down, there were reports of vigilante groups of local residents arming themselves to burn out the encampment, incensed at police inaction (Castlemorton resulted in some 100 arrests, mainly for drugs). "You wonder at what stage it becomes reasonable to call in the Army, because there is an occupying force up there on the Common," said one. Nearby homeowners were freaking out: "There's something hypnotic about the continuous pounding beat of the music, and it's driving people living in the front line into a frenzy," warned another.[26] Tabloid reporters visited travellers' sites, ingratiated themselves, drank the nomads' tea, then wrote up lurid tales of dirty children running wild while their mothers sat stoned out of their gourds, plotting dole frauds. The Tory broadsheets bemoaned the fact that the State was giving benefits hand-outs to these ne'er-do-wells, and ministers promised they would take action.

As the travellers scattered over Hereford and Worcester, all under heavy surveillance, police tracked the Spiral Tribe convoy's progress. Then they moved in. "Everyone in the larger vehicles that had been identified from the helicopter was arrested," says Mark Harrison. "It just so happened that they arrested most of the people that were involved from the very beginning. Pure pot luck." Mark and Alexander Harrison, Debbie Griffith and Simone Feeney were amongst those held in the cells overnight, then released on bail. All the Tribe's vehicles were impounded, as well as their sound equipment, lights and personal possessions. They had nothing left. But they weren't about to skulk away quietly; that would not be hard core. Instead they began a sit-in picket outside Worcester police station that lasted over a week, bolstered by local sympathisers, who brought them food and bedding.

Within a month, the annual mobilisation over the summer solstice festivities and the battle for Stonehenge had begun again, but this year the stakes had been raised. The Home Office, as usual, imposed a four-mile exclusion zone around the monument. English Heritage, the National Trust and some local landowners took out an injunction against sixteen named people, preventing them from approaching the area. "Fourteen out of the sixteen named are ravers who are a new breed. The view has been taken that New Age travellers are taking a back seat, displaced by ravers," said their solicitor.[27]

The police's Operation Solstice shifted into gear. In Worthing, festival advice telephone operator Martin Bailey was arrested under the 1986 Public Order Act for refusing to close down his information line, and remanded in custody until after the solstice to keep him out of action. The Devizes police intelligence unit circulated its "family trees" of travellers and "rave tribes".[28] Devizes also summoned the assistance of Ken Tappenden, who from 1989 had run the Pay Party Unit in Gravesend and had years of experience dealing with rave organisers. After being outflanked at Castlemorton, the police were determined not to be caught out again. Stonehenge was closed. The A344 was closed. No travellers were to be allowed anywhere near the area. All quiet.

Meanwhile, Spiral Tribe were holed up near Watford. All they had was one lorry and a bender – a makeshift tent. Little in the way of possessions or privacy. People dossed down where they could. It was all getting very intense. Attempting to reach Stonehenge was out of the question – some members of the Tribe were covered by the English Heritage injunction, and they already had one charge hanging over their heads. But they had to celebrate the solstice which had meant so much to them since eye-opening Longstock last year. So what, then? How to reunite the techno-travellers, emphasise that Castlemorton wasn't just an isolated incident and show that despite the arrests they were far from beaten? The Tribe decided that they had to strike at the heart of their oppressors, undermine their power with one audacious, symbolic act.

In 1992, the priapic, pyramid-topped Canary Wharf tower in London's Docklands resembled a monetarist folly, a reflection of the ultimate failure of eighties values, starkly majestic yet faintly ridiculous. "Here, life is run as if designed by the Iron Lady herself," noted one observer. "Canary Wharf is a marble-clad ghetto for the representatives of upward-aspiring Enterprise Culture."[29] "Thatcher's dick", with its constantly flashing light at the pinnacle of the pyramid, was the tallest building in Britain, built in the eighties at a cost of £3 billion and intended as the country's new financial centre, but that year it was heading for receivership as property values crashed.

"Whenever I saw that fucking great big pyramid flashing across London, I got pangs of paranoia that we were moving into this new controlled world," says Mark Harrison. The Tribe put out the word that they would be celebrating the solstice by establishing a Sound System City somewhere in London. They hired a rig, no longer having one of their own, and brought it onto the Isle of Dogs in a forty-ton, curtain-sided articulated lorry. Some occultists have suggested that the park at Mudchute on the Isle of Dogs bears a remarkable resemblance to an ancient hill fort; that it is a spiritual centre – Omphalos – used for conjuring magic, on a ley line which runs through Greenwich Observatory and Canary Wharf. "It is more than likely that someone on the Spirals' team has at least a basic knowledge of witchcraft," one commentator within the scene has suggested; coincidentally or not, this was where Spiral Tribe set up their system.[30]

By 2 a.m. there were 1,000 people dancing under the tower's giant strobe. But the police were already sealing off roads around the Isle of Dogs, turning cars back, while those who tried to reach Mudchute from the south side of the river, through the Greenwich foot tunnel, or by scampering over the Docklands Light Railway's tracks, were blocked by private security firms. "That was the most intense crackdown I've seen on a party," says Simon Lee. "They totally surrounded it. There were millions of them and a helicopter with a spotlight. It was so extreme." Just over an hour after the party started, 300 police moved in and cleared the area.

What did Spiral Tribe gain from this spectacular dramatisation of their ideology, this foolhardy attempt to turn the voodoo on the establishment in its very heartland? Mark Harrison believes their options at the time were so limited, they either had to run and hide – which was never the Tribe's style – or stand and fight. "Even though it only lasted one hour, we had to do it, wisely or not. But I think it made its point. It was a victory for us because that pyramid doesn't work any more, it doesn't have that power."

By the end of June, the alliance of travellers and ravers was deeply embattled. Police drove travellers from a disused World War Two airfield at Smeatharpe, Devon, after 4,000 had partied through the weekend. At Kerry in Wales, another huge gathering, dancers were buzzed by Tornado jets. There was an uneasy stand-off between the protagonists after long battles to reach Hampshire's Torpedo Town festival (its title is a reference to the area's arms industry and the militarisation of the topography of the south-west). In 1991, numbers had swelled to 10,000 and police were determined to prevent a recurrence. Stones and bottles were thrown and twelve police injured; convoys drove through roadblocks; the National Farmers Union advised its members to dig ditches and spread slurry to stop vehicles. Some 2,500 managed to reach the site and the party went ahead, but the incident demonstrated how much the scene had changed, from relaxed hedonism to punch-ups with riot police.

The police did, however, succeed in quashing the White

Goddess Festival, which the previous August had helped establish Spiral Tribe as figureheads of the techno festival scene. This year, the Tribe didn't attempt to attend. They had just signed a record deal on the back of their new-found notoriety and were preparing their first release, a clarion call of defiance entitled *Breach the Peace*. They were also due in court in Malvern, to be charged with conspiracy to cause a public nuisance: conspiracy being the charge levelled at political undesirables from the emerging labour movement of the nineteenth century through 1960s anti-war activists and 1980s inner-city rioters right up to the present day.

During the hearing they were ordered to cover up the message on their T-shirts – "Make Some Fucking Noise". There was a small demonstration outside the court, and soon afterwards the Tribe left the country, bound for Paris. It looked like it was all over for them in Britain; nothing to come back to except court appearances, harassment and perhaps even prison. No way, after what they'd seen, could they slink back, defeated, into the mundane reality of nightclubs. "We felt from that point on that we wouldn't be able to operate," says Mark Harrison. "It was the right time for exile."

westminster

"New age travellers. Not in this age. Not in any age." John Major, 1992

This party conference speech by John Major, who had replaced Margaret Thatcher as Prime Minister in 1990, underlined the Conservatives' determination to finish the job they had started with the 1986 Public Order Act: to force travellers off the road and into houses, to reassert the property rights of landowners and to eradicate lifestyles they believed were unacceptable. The Home Office had been considering new measures aimed at ending the festival/rave convergence for over a year, and in March 1993, an amendment to the 1986 Act was suggested by Home Secretary Kenneth Clarke.

The police's Intelligence Units at Devizes, Wiltshire, and Penrith, Cumbria, were pooling reports from forces all over the country and planning a new computer system to log travellers and their vehicles, sound systems and drug dealers, and to track their movements. They were also liaising with the Country Landowners Association, the National Farmers Union and local authorities. Penrith officer Sergeant Peter Sharkey insisted: "We are now far better organised. Police forces will not be caught unawares as they were before." They then launched Operation Snapshot; over a period of forty-eight hours, police followed, stopped and questioned travellers – sometimes pursuing them in helicopters – took photographs and personal details and inputted them into their computer database, in an echo of the Pay Party Unit's activities during the raves of 1989, and at a cost of half a million pounds to the public.

The intent was clear: prevent large gatherings. No more Castlemortons. Harry from DiY suggested at the time that Castlemorton was "the first time the media and the government realised the size of the problem they were dealing with. Twenty-five thousand people under the age of thirty with a slightly different outlook on things were there. No information was printed, it was all word of mouth. We didn't even know about the site until twenty-four hours before it began. All these young people were able to group in one place, set up their own city, a police no-go zone. For a government whose reason for being is to control people, here was a very frightening example of people saying: 'We can and will do whatever we like.' "[31]

A year on, as if responding to these words, the police staged a show of force to prevent the 1993 Avon Free Festival taking place. In Operation Nomad, which cost an estimated £1 million (as *The Star* charitably put it, "£1 million wasted on scum"), 500 officers chased vehicles across Avon and Somerset, trying to stop a convoy gaining critical mass. The weekend culminated in an edgy showdown as scores of travellers, exhausted and frustrated, blockaded the M5, but although no arrests were made there was no festival either.

Within the loose structure of the festival/free-party alliance, there were differing opinions as to why the pressure was being applied so heavily. In 1993 the number of travellers was estimated at 40,000, and some, like Harry from DiY, pointed to the authorities' fear of *ad hoc* mobilisations of large groups of potentially subversive youths. Certainly, many newspapers at the time fretted about travellers with mobile phones and fax machines, the use of pirate radio and the monitoring of police frequencies. A government still in shock over the Poll Tax riot of 1990 – widespread disaffection with this key plank of Tory legislation led to its abrupt abandonment – understandably became nervous at the potential creation of a politicised underclass and an instant mass takeover of a rural area. Others believed it was part of a government strategy of increasing control on Britons' lifestyles which stretched back years, a gradual reduction of civil liberties, the first step on the road to fascism. This might sound like the conspiracy theory of a paranoid hippie, but to those at the sharp end of fourteen years of Conservative rule, and particularly those travellers who had lived through the Battle of the Beanfield and subsequent years of harassment, it was the only way it could be understood.

But some, including people within the free-party scene, blamed the likes of Spiral Tribe, saying that their confrontational attitude had forced the law to act. "Make some fuckin' noise is one thing but making so much noise that you piss everyone off – including the alternative community – is fuckin' stupid. A lot of sound systems have realised that keeping a low profile is the only way to keep in operation. Isn't it a bit of a damning indictment: the music's so crap, the only way to get people buzzing is to deafen them?" demanded alternative culture periodical *Pod*.[32] Mark Harrison had already responded to such criticism the previous year: "I know that some of our critics accuse us of bringing it on top and allowing the government to bring in legislation that they wouldn't have bothered with beforehand, but this is a catalyst. There are great injustices and great wrongs and we are standing up and being counted."[33]

The government had previously attempted to subdue the travellers with the 1986 Public Order Act, and was proposing further measures even before Castlemorton. While this historic jamboree may have spurred police towards greater organisation and steeled the government's resolve, Conservative politicians were aware that, whether as a result of their long-term policies of eliminating council housing and reducing housing benefit or not, the numbers of itinerants, squatters, dispossessed and disaffected were growing. The Poll Tax riot in Trafalgar Square in 1990 was proof enough of a trend they didn't wish to spread. They were also keen to offer encouragement to their voters in the south, the area most affected by festivals and free parties, who had time after time returned Conservative MPs even in the deepest recessions, yet were increasingly turning towards the Liberal Democrats. Conservative ministers, their standing falling in the opinion polls, attempted to rally support around the populist themes of law and order and "traditional moral values".

The strictures against unlicensed outdoor raves, festivals and travellers were ultimately bound up, with other proposed legislation to criminalise trespass and squatting, hobble hunt saboteurs and remove the right to silence after arrest, as the 1994 Criminal Justice and Public Order Bill. The underlying aims of the Bill, which lawyers described as ill-drafted, senior police called ill-advised and civil liberties groups branded oppressive, seemed to be to strengthen the property rights of landowners, to quell dissenters, to usher people back into licensed leisure patterns and to proscribe lifestyles that were anathema to the Tory vision of a compliant, consumerist country.

As with its policies on drugs, the government was using the criminal law to deal with social issues; Sir John Smith, president of the Association of Chief Police Officers, pointed out that the effect of the CJB would be "to increase the police's enforcement role by criminalising issues previously regarded as subject of civil law enforcement procedures or even matters of conscience".[34] The criminalisation of the act of trespassing on someone else's property had potentially huge repercussions for anyone who wished to register any sort of protest. The civil rights organisation Liberty damned it as "the most wide-ranging attack on human rights in the UK in recent years. It offends the basic principles of justice and is likely to increase discrimination against groups who are already marginalised, and to increase harassment and intimidation. Instead of tackling crime, it tries to outlaw diversity and dissent."

The Bill also defined and proposed to outlaw – when played in certain circumstances – a genre of music: house. It stated that " 'music' is defined as sounds wholly or predominantly characterised by the emission of a succession of repetitive beats", and for the first time the word "rave" appeared in British legislative language. Although other youth movements had inspired new legislation, never before, over years of post-war moral panics about the activities of teddy boys, mods, hippies and punks, had a government considered young people's music so subversive as to prohibit it. John Major's government, unlike many pop commentators, obviously didn't consider dance-drug culture to be either meaningless or apolitical.

In October 1993, some fifty people, mainly representatives of sound systems and particularly those connected with Spiral Tribe, gathered in a launderette in Kensal Rise, north-west London, to debate their response and attempt to forge a united front. Although initially frosty due to suspicions about motives, territorial rivalry and differences in outlook between systems, mutual fear of the impending Bill prevailed, and a plan of action was drawn up and an umbrella organisation formed: Advance Party. Its first move was a traditional one: lobbying Parliament alongside constitutional reform group Charter 88. "It was quite an experience," recalls Advance Party spokeswoman Michelle Poole, "all these people turning up with dogs on strings, the security gates were going berserk because everyone was going through with their metal body piercing; people were skinning up in the room at the back. It was a real laugh and it got a lot of press."

Meanwhile, out of the media spotlight, on January 10th, 1994, members of Spiral Tribe had returned to Britain to stand trial for "conspiracy to cause a public nuisance", alongside a couple who had sold pancakes at Castlemorton, a member of the Tecno Travellers crew, and a man who ran a cycle-powered gyroscope, all caught in the net when the police swooped. The judge promised the thirteen defendants prison if convicted, talking in terms of four years' jail, although in theory the sentence could have been anything from an absolute discharge to life imprisonment. This bolstered police confidence. "The Castlemorton court case at Wolverhampton Crown Court is going well," gloated an internal document produced by the Southern Intelligence Unit. "There is no support for the defendants at the court, they are all on their own. Ah!!" Simone Feeney, who had recently had a child, pleaded guilty, wanting no more part of it all.

The prosecution called around fifty witnesses with the intention of proving that Spiral Tribe were the ringleaders who had provided the entertainment and therefore caused the gathering. But at the committal stage much of their expert evidence had been thrown out, and, says the Tribe's solicitor Peter Silver, "None of their evidence was specific or to the point, it was a grapeshot approach: something must stick. It was very poorly prepared, a lot of evidence but very little substance." The case demonstrated an almost farcical misunderstanding of how such events operate; it was as inept as the failed prosecution of Centre Force in 1989. None of the witnesses from the public could identify the defendants as the troublemakers they had seen on site, and the Tribe were impressive in the box. "They were highly articulate and intelligent people," says Silver. "The prosecutor had his work cut out for him to cross-examine them, because they had an answer for everything. These people fought back, they had intelligence and, the jury obviously thought, a certain amount of integrity as well."

The defence called four witnesses. Three told how they had heard about Castlemorton on the news, and that, not some shadowy conspiracy, had caused them to attend. The other witness was Willy X, the real organiser of the Avon Free Festival who, according to Silver, told the court: "With the greatest respect to Spiral Tribe, nice people and all the rest, when it comes to organising a festival they are absolute amateurs. I'm the man."

It became clear that the defendants accused of masterminding what Judge Gibbs and Crown Prosecutor Alister McCreath called this "nuisance by numbers" could not be held wholly or even partly responsible. Spiral Tribe weren't even the first sound system to reach the Common. The police had admitted that they allowed Castlemorton to go ahead; Superintendent Clift, head of police operations on the Common, added that "a small group of local residents contributed to their own misfortune by inciting/encouraging the TV and press to go to the site and giving interviews, etc. Many 'ravers' attended the site as a direct result of the publicity generated."[35] Then there was the question of organisation; was this a planned event, or had it simply gelled out of the chaos surrounding the police crackdown on the original site at Chipping Sodbury Common? Nothing could be proved.

After ten weeks, all defendants were acquitted of the conspiracy charges, even Simone Feeney, who was allowed to re-enter her plea. Peter Silver estimates that the whole scenario had cost some £4 million, an enormous waste of public money conducted entirely for ulterior, political motives. He believes that the Home Office was still in the process of formulating the Criminal Justice Bill at the time, and that this was a test case to find out whether public nuisance charges would be adequate to stop free parties, or whether they needed something tougher. "It was clear from what was going on that lots of strings were being pulled," he says. "It's very difficult to give instances but you just got the feeling that no matter how you tried to reason with the prosecution, what they were telling us between the lines was: 'You're probably right, but we've been told we've got to do this.'" The Tribe, meanwhile, headed back to Europe, where they had already established a new base.

twyford down

"Fifty years from now, Britain will still be the country of long shadows on county grounds, warm beer, invincible green suburbs, dog lovers and pools fillers and, as George Orwell once said, 'old maids bicycling to Holy Communion through the morning mist' . . . Britain will remain unamendable in all essentials." John Major, 1993

After fifteen years of Conservative rule, British political culture had changed beyond recognition. As the government sought to construct a hegemony over all aspects of the political sphere, increasing its control on the civil service and abolishing sectors of local government, hundreds of thousands of voters became disenfranchised, not registering to vote through fear of being hounded for Poll Tax payments. There was a pervasive disillusionment with a political system that seemed to have failed. Conservative promises to go "back to basics" and return to "family values" sounded like threats rather than enticements to many young people, and in the 1992 general election, around 40 per cent of eighteen to twenty-five year olds did not vote. It wasn't so much that they had rejected politics but politics had rejected them.

This formed the background, if not the direct cause, of the rise of a new era of political protest based around *ad hoc* organisations fighting campaigns around largely environmental issues. These organisations – roads protesters, squatters, self-help groups, alternative news services – proffered no manifestos or left-wing party politics, preferring strategies of direct action and mutual collaboration, and displaying a keen sense of how to make protest dramatic, newsworthy and, above all, fun. In their hands, fears about ecological damage became transmuted into an amorphous cultural movement as concerned with values and responsibility as saving the whales or the rainforests.

Some trace the roots of what became known as the "New Protest" or "DIY Culture" back to the Battle of the Beanfield. Their role model was the traveller: a free spirit, living outside the confines of suffocating urban society, rejecting the destructive greed of consumerism and claiming a spiritual heritage encompassing centuries of anarchistic itinerants back to the dawn of British history. Others see the "New Protest" era as beginning with the anti-nuclear peace camps at Greenham Common in the eighties or the Poll Tax riots of 1990, when the government was stunned by the massing of a new alliance of protesters. But at the same time the vigorous energy of DIY Culture, like the rave scene, was another unforeseen manifestation of Thatcherite self-reliance and entrepreneurialism.

The catalyst for this fusion of party and politics was a "tribe" of protesters called the Dongas. As contractors moved in to build a motorway link through an "Area of Outstanding Natural Beauty" at Twyford Down near Winchester in 1992, they were met by an eclectic band of opponents: environmental activists from Friends of the Earth and Earth First!, concerned middle-class locals, and the Dongas themselves, who lived rough on the Down and had links to the travellers' circuit. Their protests resembled free festivals, celebrations as well as demonstrations. Although they did not prevent the motorway being built, they did put the issue of the social and ecological consequences of Thatcher's "great car economy" on the national agenda, held up proceedings to a cost of £1.7 million, and contributed to a rethink of the Conservative road-building programme.

The Dongas' inspired, theatrical direct actions sparked a

renaissance of environmental politics. In the early months of 1994, the anti-CJB movement gathered momentum. Protest groups mushroomed at an amazing rate: a year after Twyford Down, there were around 200. The Freedom Network, an umbrella organisation based at Cool Tan Arts, a squatted Brixton dole office where Prime Minister John Major had once signed on, was set up to unite the various activist strands. Within twelve months it had ninety branches around the country; the Criminal Justice Bill had forged links between disparate groups that were bound together by its scattershot clauses, and gave them a common identity. "The CJB actually unified this generation," says Freedom Network's Camilla Berens. "People were just waiting for a common threat to bring them together, and [Home Secretary] Michael Howard did it for us. It couldn't have been better really."

It's easy to see how Spiral Tribe's ideas of "reconnecting with the earth" dovetail with environmental protesters' concerns about cars' and roads' unsustainable impact on the ecosystem. The protesters, too, had picked up some strategic guile from the rave scene's mass mobilisations, and employed mobile phones, video cameras and the Internet as well as low-tech media like telephone trees, fanzines and leaflets.

Yet the increasing politicisation of the free-party network increased its distance from the club scene, which was becoming ever more mainstream and institutionalised. This process had been ongoing since the Bright Bill, and since 1990 the majority of clubbers had been ensconced in legal venues and focused on drugs, music and fashion, with little common ideology other than hedonism. Although many clubbers perceived the CJB as an attack on their own culture and generation, others felt it was aimed at outlawing parties they never went to and lifestyles they had no intention of following. DIY Culture was also criticised for escaping into woolly utopianism and prioritising trees and fields above issues of poverty and health.

One free party system, Luton's Exodus, did attempt to tap

into wider political issues like unemployment and housing, channelling rave proceeds into self-help projects, squatting local buildings and turning them into informal community centres and housing co-operatives. Their motto, "Peace, Love, Unity, Struggle", reflected this more robust ideological edge, although it led to harassment by local police, raids by riot squads, eviction from squatted properties and repeated arrests – around fifty in total, sparking a local council enquiry. After the first bout of arrests in 1993, 4,000 Luton ravers demonstrated for their release outside the police station where they were held. Exodus's story demonstrates how any political manifestations of Ecstasy culture were taken very seriously indeed, and dealt with ruthlessly. Radical politics and drug culture was still an explosive combination.

A predominantly working-class, multi-racial outfit, Exodus resembled anarchist punk activists Crass even more than Spiral Tribe did. Their Luton commune, HAZ (Housing Action Zone) Manor, like Crass's Epping Forest retreat, had been squatted and completely rebuilt by the sound system, whose ranks numbered former roofers, plasterers, engineers, construction workers, factory hands, estate agents, students, soldiers and jailbirds. Exodus had a kind of communal charisma that drew people in, a mystic magnetism that claimed roots in socialist traditions (their lorry was decorated with red stars), yet bordered on the religious. "We are taking back God's land and applying God's law," insisted Exodus spokesman Glenn Jenkins, a former train driver and union shop steward. "We see ourselves as freedom fighters . . . It's a way of life that has clear values – *life* has sanctity, not property."[36] Their dream was to turn the temporary autonomous zone into a permanent revolution.

This synergy of rave and politics, explained Jenkins, was a concrete manifestation of the house scene's rhetoric of unity and community: "Direct action seems the best way forward. The idea is not to wait for others but to change your own environment. There are forty-five of us. We raise money via raves, take over derelict buildings, repair them and open the doors to the homeless. Meaningful work is a distant memory for many young people now. Many don't stand a chance. So it's best to start your own society, start creating things for yourself. It's happening through a collective of people regenerating things, showing that dreams can come true. Out of this darkness comes self-esteem."[37]

The Advance Party's first mass march against the Criminal Justice Bill on May Day brought between 6,000 (according to police) and 20,000 (organisers' estimate) party-goers and politicos together for the first time. In Trafalgar Square, the mood was joyful, as the Desert Storm sound system pumped house rhythms from speakers mounted on an armoured car and revellers danced in the fountains as if it were New Year's Eve. The second, in July, attracted 20–60,000, but as the march passed Downing Street, a knot of anarchists peeled off and scaled the gates, attempting to break them down. Following the time-honoured rituals of confrontations between police and demonstrators, ragged missile-throwing was followed by a horseback charge.

By October, things were looking grim. John Major had chosen to ignore the views of senior policemen who feared that the CJB would make the police force a political tool of government, and Labour's Tony Blair had decided that his party should abstain from voting on the Bill, effectively removing any serious opposition to it within Parliament (although some forty Labour MPs disregarded his dictum and voted against). Left-wing lawyer Michael Mansfield raged that the Opposition leader had "allowed a fascistic piece of legislation almost certainly to become law". Blair preferred to concentrate on attempts to amend elements of the legislation, and recalled with delight how Home Secretary Michael Howard's jaw "dropped about six inches" when he announced his intention.[38] His reasoning was that it would undermine the opportunity for the Conservatives to declare Labour "soft on crime", although his strategy only compounded the prevailing view that politicians on all sides saw neither civil liberties nor the concerns of young people as vote-winners.

On October 9th, the Advance Party and their allies mounted one last show of strength, marshalling what they estimated as 100,000 supporters in central London. Once again, the atmosphere was good-humoured, if a little resigned to impending defeat. But as the rally approached its end, a sound system crawled up Park Lane followed by over a thousand dancing bodies and attempted to enter Hyde Park, contravening a previous agreement with police. As the dancers were confronted by riot police who also effectively trapped demonstrators attempting to go home, the mood darkened and missiles were thrown. "At times the atmosphere was almost surreal," reported *Guardian* correspondent Duncan Campbell. "A fire-eater and a unicyclist entertained crowds in the middle of one of Britain's most prestigious avenues while riot police stood at one side and rave music blared out on the other."[39]

Eventually the police charged, then charged again, beating everyone in their path as panic broke out and people scattered in all directions. Mounted police moved in, and the missiles started flying in earnest. At around 9 p.m., officers in body armour, many with identification numbers removed, launched a pincer movement to disperse the 1,500 remaining demonstrators, pushing them down Park Lane. Scores fled into McDonald's in fear of injury as ugly clashes raged outside, while others ran down Oxford Street smashing shop windows, chased by police who felled some of them with truncheon blows. Police chiefs claimed the violence was caused by the same hard core who had led the Poll Tax riot in Trafalgar Square five years earlier, while some of the organisers blamed left-wing or anarchist instigators, and suggested that this kind of police response was what dissenters could expect if the Bill became law.

On November 3rd, Home Secretary Michael Howard attempted to quell what he called "exaggerated fears" about the potential impact of the legislation: "It is not going to ban all raves," he insisted. "It is only going to ban unlicensed raves, and it's going to be perfectly possible for people to get licences to hold raves when it is not going to interfere with other people's peace and quiet. It will not interfere with people's right to demonstrate. The principle is that people should be allowed to behave as they wish, as long as they don't interfere with the rights of others."[40]

On the same day, royal assent was given, and the Criminal Justice and Public Order Act 1994 became law.

Then nothing. No mass arrests, no wholesale evictions, no internment of undesirables, no crying in the street. Yet even though the CJA was now on the statute book, the protests continued. A few hours after it was passed, five protesters dodged the House of Commons' closed-circuit TV and shinned up drainpipes to its roof, unfurled banners reading "Defy the CJA" and settled down to build a spliff. This was followed by a march on John Major's prime ministerial retreat at Chequers, Buckinghamshire, then a mass trespass at Windsor Castle, in the Queen's back garden.

However, differences were showing in the fragile unity of the free-party scene. At a meeting of Advance Party directly following the passing of the CJA, a number of key people announced their intention to defect from the organisation and set up another campaigning body, United Systems. They argued that now the CJA was law, Advance Party had served its purpose. Rather than a fluid, proactive, devolved entity, it had become bureaucratic and unwieldy, and was occupying itself with issues outside its original remit. United Systems would concentrate purely on supporting free parties and sound systems in their struggle to stay operational in the wake of the new law. "Free parties will not be saved by political campaigns, by TV chat shows, by magazine articles, by speech makers or celebrity appearances. Nor by flyers, newsletters, posters or stickers," stated its inaugural bulletin. "Only free parties can save free parties!"[41] It would be marvellously amorphous, a true adhocracy, a name that could be used as a cloak or banner by any sound system that wished to do so, and would offer hard, practical advice on how to put illegal raves in motion.

The mobile divisions of United Systems included the ranks of sound systems which had sprung up in the wake of Castlemorton and taken up the hard-core banner after both Spiral Tribe and Bedlam had left the country, operating in the many and various deserted buildings of London's squatlands, sink areas of the inner city where the Mutoid Waste Company, The Shamen, Spiral Tribe, Club Dog and so many others had risen from. Again the focus was Brixton and Hackney, where new squat crews like Ooops, Jiba, Vox Populi and Virus catered for a community who felt excluded by the suburban materialism, aspirational dress codes, high door prices and "commercial music" of what they defined as the "mainstream" house scene – the Saturday night fever of mass Ecstasy culture. The squat systems' raucous acid and techno was intended, like Spiral Tribe's, as a scream of defiance, although, of course, they had their own unwritten dress codes and hierarchies.

"It's a choice thing," suggested Aaron from Liberator, another acid crew. "I don't dis what other people do. They wanna dress up, they wanna go somewhere nice that they feel appreciated at. If they come to our parties they definitely won't. 'Cos their nice new shoes they bought will get scuffed, their nice new shirt will get beer down it. We get the misfits, the ugly cheap crew, and that's what I love about it because that's what we all are."[42]

These sound systems were another manifestation of a British techno-hippie phenomenon that had been evolving since the first interventions of psychedelic adepts like Fraser Clark, Mixmaster Morris and The Shamen in the late eighties. This was not a defined scene, rather an amorphous, constantly changing continuum of concepts, another interpretation of the possibilities enabled by an interface of drugs and technology. Its pick-and-mix philosophy – drawing on acid house hedonism, the post-punk, inner-city squat scene, travelling sound systems and road protesters, the psychedelic trance-dance movement that had been imported from the shores of Goa in India, the "New Edge" cyberculture of *Mondo 2000* and sampled fragments from philosophers like McKenna and Leary – marked out new territory for the psychedelic tradition, confirming that the hippie ethic was in renaissance, and that it was not simply a pale simulacrum of the sixties, but something entirely new.

europe

The new police powers under the Criminal Justice Act were largely discretionary. Forces could choose whether to use the Act to stop outdoor parties or rely on the means they had employed previously. By the spring of 1995, it appeared that most were favouring a softly-softly approach, whether in fear of engendering mass protest or simply because they didn't want or need the Act. Ten years after the Battle of the Beanfield, over May Day bank holiday, while part of the country was celebrating the anniversary of VE Day, United Systems were involved in weekend-long parties in Woodbridge, Suffolk, and Bangor, north Wales. Local police appeared sanguine, allowing both to proceed unhindered until Monday afternoon, when their attitude changed unexpectedly and the sites were unceremoniously cleared and rigs confiscated. Although the CJA wasn't used, United Systems imagined they could see the dark hand of the Home Office at work. "In the case of Bangor, the police were turning up saying: 'Sorry lads, we don't want to do this but we've had orders from on high,' " says Debby Staunton, who ran United Systems' phone lines.

Although the Act was already being used to arrest hunt saboteurs, animal rights and roads protesters, in its early months it was the *threat* of prosecution that was having the most impact, creating a climate of fear and paranoia. Police operations over the previous two years had almost extinguished the free festival circuit, which travellers relied on not only for their social life, but also for their economic subsistence. At festivals, travellers could sell their wares or put on shows to bring in cash to fund their lifestyle. Now, the free festival all but dead, not only was their income and entertainment gone, but they dared not congregate together for fear of eviction and harassment. Isolated and depressed, many either moved into houses, parking their buses in the inner cities, or left the country altogether, seeking a less stressful life in Ireland, France, Spain or Portugal. Ten years after the Battle of the Beanfield, it appeared that the government had finally defeated the travellers.

The free-party scene, however, continued to flourish in remote locations and inner-city warehouses, the number of sound systems and illegal events increasing as the nineties progressed despite petty hassles and low-level interference from the law. "If the party's smaller than 500 people, the police don't give a shit really," suggested Rick from DiY at the time. "If they get loads of complaints they'll come over, to appease the neighbours really." But for those systems whose actions were defined by outlaw ideology, business as usual wasn't enough. The Criminal Justice Act must be shown to be unworkable, not just oppressive but a complete farce.

Earlier in the year, a group of people connected with systems in the south-east had met and decided to stage an event on the scale of Castlemorton, a huge gathering of the clans which would undermine the Act, humiliate the police and pour scorn on the government. The date was set for July and word was spread across the informal networks: something big would be happening on the "seventh of the seventh". The plan was that different groups would organise in their own way and in their own area, but all would link up in one place at the same time for a high-profile show of strength. A press conference would be called on site and, in front of the world's media, the Act forever damned. Then the united tribes of the disaffected would celebrate by dancing on its grave.

The problem was that if everybody knew the date, so would

the police, whose intelligence gathering was far more sophisticated than it had been in 1992. Furthermore, Castlemorton wasn't strictly planned, but spontaneous. It was hoped that if there was no central organisation or definitive plan of action, no one could be hauled up on conspiracy charges afterwards, like Spiral Tribe had been. But if there was no conspiracy, how could secrecy be maintained? The week before the festival, which was nicknamed "The Mother", a meeting was held in a disused factory in south London and the location was chosen: a huge, secluded farmland site near Corby, Northamptonshire. Maps were distributed, memorised and destroyed. But there were immediate disagreements as one faction insisted that they wanted to use a disused airfield at Smeatharpe, Devon. The united front was shattered; now there were to be two festivals.

Well before dawn on July 7th, sound systems began to arrive at the Corby site, parking their vehicles in a circle for protection with sound systems concealed. But within an hour a police van and helicopter were on the scene. Ambiguous messages about the festival had been disseminated via free-party information lines for a number of weeks, and police had been monitoring key activists' telephones and knew what was planned. At 6.30 a.m. – the classic dawn raid – police kicked down Debby Staunton's front door in Burnt Oak, Middlesex, rummaged through the house and arrested her and her boyfriend Jim, a United Systems DJ, for conspiracy to cause a public nuisance. Simultaneously, Northamptonshire police threw up roadblocks around the Corby site, and arrested three members of Buxton's Black Moon sound system under the Criminal Justice Act – the first time anyone had been detained under its anti-rave provisions. The remainder of the people on site were ordered to leave the county, and crawled towards Cambridgeshire in a convoy over a mile long. Back in London, Michelle Poole of Advance Party returned to her Kentish Town flat to find the door hanging off its hinges and policemen preparing to leave having taken her phone, fax machine, maps, posters, address books, even her dog. She and her boyfriend Andy were also arrested for conspiracy to cause a public nuisance.

When sound systems reached the Smeatharpe site, police had already set up roadblocks. DiY and Virus's rigs were confiscated. One cunning policeman lured ravers into his clutches by playing rave music from his riot van. Over the weekend, small impromptu parties went ahead in Devon, Cambridgeshire and Lincolnshire but the mass convergence, The Mother, never happened. The police's intelligence was too good and the festival's organisation was flawed and inadequate. Some sound systems had travelled miles from the Midlands to the south-west, unaware that a party was planned for their area. Others had made the journey in the other direction. While the police hadn't proved that the CJA could stop free parties, they had shown that it was almost imposs-ible to stage a huge event like Castlemorton, and that if any attempt was made, they would spare no resources in crushing it.

Over the following weeks, police made more arrests and con-fiscated more address books, compounding the mood of paranoia. Telephones, whether land lines or analogue mobiles, could be tapped, and it was rumoured that police were monitoring Internet newsgroups used for discussion of free parties. Some suspected that informers, even *agents provocateurs*, were being employed. Debby Staunton, awaiting committal, was uncon-cerned, insisting that the police, however detailed the information they were gathering, didn't have a clue what was really going on; their frame of reference was so wrong-headed that whatever action they could take would almost be irrelevant as the free-party movement was fuelled by a higher, *spiritual* power.

"Although it might sound like airy-fairy cosmic stuff, that is our secret weapon. If you believe in the Gaia theory and you think that society is its own self-regulatory mechanism, then what we do is a product of society trying to redress the imbalances that have been created by certain power-crazed people. They can tap my phone, that's fine, but what we're doing is the right thing."

All the conspiracy charges were subsequently dropped, but on February 27th, 1996, the three members of the Black Moon system were convicted under the CJA at Corby Magistrates' Court, fined and forced to forfeit £6,000 of sound equipment; the first rave crew to be convicted under the Act. "We have not let this so-called British justice put us off, and we are desperate to return to playing free parties and free festivals as soon as we can replace our rig," they stated defiantly afterwards. "We can't get depressed about it. It has been a kick in the guts but we'll get over it. If they get you down, that means they've won."

The police strategy of targeting the networking of information, rather than parties themselves, appeared sound. They had stopped The Mother, and it didn't appear feasible to stage another large-scale event without a genuine, clandestine conspiracy, which would lay people open to serious charges and the potential of long prison terms. The only effective party protests were the Reclaim the Streets events. These meticulously timed anti-roads actions took over key traffic junctions in Camden, Islington and Greenwich in the summer of 1995, and a year later occupied and dug up a section of the M41 motorway in west London using pneumatic drills hidden under stilt-walkers' skirts, planting trees where the tarmac once was. Part rave, part festival, part street theatre and part demonstration, Reclaim the Streets featured pumping music played from a sound system mounted on an armoured car, colourful banners and kiddies' playgrounds, all organised with the secrecy and precision of a successful military coup.

Reclaim the Streets was the most coherent manifestation of dance culture's politicised vanguard. "RTS is a direct action network committed to ending the rule of the car," stated its manifesto. "We are FOR walking, cycling and cheap (free!) public transport, and AGAINST cars, roads and the vested interests they serve." Although the numbers it attracted to its demonstrations – hundreds, sometimes thousands – were relatively small, Reclaim the Streets managed to sustain the convergence between ecology and hedonism. Its street raves dramatised the colonisation of public space by the car by staging impromptu carnivals in zones that were forbidden to pedestrians: humanising the motorised cityscape. "The sound system is such a powerful focus of attention," explained an anonymous representative of the nebulous "non-organisation". "It turns a static demonstration into a jubilant celebration."[43]

Behind the green slogans and techno music lay a wider anti-capitalist agenda. "The struggle for car-free space must not be separated from the struggle against global capitalism – for in truth the former is encapsulated in the latter," RTS stated. "For Reclaim the Streets, the car is a focus – the insanity of its system clearly visible – that leads to questioning both the myth of 'the market' and its corporate and institutional enforcers."[44] These urban Castlemortons had specific intent – to satirise and undermine consumerism and its trappings.

RTS staged one of the most audacious political stunts of the decade just before the 1997 general election. At around midday on April 12th, thousands of demonstrators – a rainbow coalition of striking dockworkers from Liverpool, green campaigners, revolutionary socialists and ravers – gathered in Kennington Park, south London, to join a "March for Social Justice" to Trafalgar Square. On their way along Whitehall, a few anarchists began causing chaos, firing distress flares over Downing Street and breaking into the Foreign Office. By the time the speeches had finished in Trafalgar Square, a mood of anticipation was rising. Most people knew that something was about to happen – but what, exactly, they weren't sure. At 3.45pm, a white Ford truck containing Immersion's sound system, travelling at forty miles per hour, forced its way through the police lines which had cordoned off the square and took up position outside the National Gallery. A banner was raised: "Never mind the ballots, reclaim the streets." The truck's side panels swung open and DJ

Gizelle cued up Chuck Roberts' incendiary invocation, *This is My House*. As Roberts' voice urged people to dance, drum loops pounded and echoed around the picture-postcard vista, and 7,000 people erupted into motion.

After the party concluded four hours later, fighting broke out when hundreds of police, some in riot gear, attempted to disperse the crowd. The drivers of the sound-system truck were arrested and charged with attempted murder; this was what made the headlines: "Riot frenzy: anarchist thugs bring terror to London," declared the *Evening Standard*. After media interest died down, the attempted murder charges were dropped. RTS were triumphant; they had successfully transformed Britain's most famous public space into a full-on rave. "Trafalgar Square was for a mass of disillusioned people who are ignored by mainstream politics," a spokesman said later, restating the contemporary direct-action imperative: "Politics is not representative. We have to represent ourselves."[45]

A year and a half after the passing of the Criminal Justice Act, it was estimated that over a thousand people had been arrested under its provisions. A considerable number of these arrests were for anti-roadbuilding protests, which reached fever pitch during demonstrations against a new bypass in Newbury in 1996, but very few of them were for outdoor parties. Even though the CJA had not quelled dissent – the huge festival/raves were extinguished long before it was passed, the smaller free parties continued and, if anything, the Act had boosted the determination of the post-Twyford Down eco-activist movement – nonetheless, it remained a symbol of a generation gap in understanding and outlook, a schism between the Tory dream of an industrious, obedient Britain and the reality that the younger generation inhabited. And if the CJA's impact was relatively minimal when compared to the wide-ranging fears that preceded it, its statement of intent was still evident: that Britain must remain Grey.

Meanwhile, across the Channel, Spiral Tribe had helped set

off a fresh chain of events. Their self-imposed exile had begun
in the autumn of 1992 when, in the climate of uncertainty and
depression following their arrest after Castlemorton, they had
fled to the squatlands of Paris and established a new operational
base with the little equipment they could scrape together. In July
1993, they staged the first Teknival, another break with the past:
old-style festivals were dead, they reasoned, and the new free
festivals were bouts of frenetic techno which lasted for days on
end – so call them Teknivals.

Soon, as in Britain, they began to gather ranks of acolytes
around them, all shaving their heads, dressing in combat fatigues,
and setting up their own rigs. Later in 1993, the Tribe moved
on to Berlin, spending six months squatting in the no-man's-
land of Potsdamer Platz, the former site of the Wall, once believed
to be home to Hitler's bunker, another site of intense psychogeo-
graphical significance. Potsdamer Platz was soon to become the
most sought-after piece of real estate in western Europe, where
multinationals like Sony and Daimler-Benz constructed their
headquarters in preparation for Berlin's ascendance to the full
status of capital city in 1998.

Already on the site were the Mutoid Waste Company, the
salvage-sculpture artists cum post-apocalypse travellers who had
themselves fled Britain in 1989. The Mutoids had built a spectacular, Day-Glo-painted Stonehenge there out of
decommissioned Eastern Bloc tanks, and had planted MIG
fighter jets in the ground like bizarre techno flowers. Soon the
two units were staging shows together at Tacheles, the labyrinthine squat art centre in Oranienburgerstrasse, and collecting the
kind of cast-off military hardware that was so easy to obtain in
the impoverished East, repurposing war machines as technologies
of pleasure. "You can't resist it, they're just lying around!" smiled
Mark Harrison gleefully. "Some of the most amazing vehicles
you've seen in your life are going for almost nothing. We had a
huge convoy, two MIG fighters on tank transporters, huge circus
trailers and massive six-wheel-drive amphibious vehicles. It was

like being musclebound, we couldn't move for the tonnage of steel that we had on the road."

The convoy rolled on through the Czech Republic, Austria and Italy, then back to France, where the twelfth Teknival took place on the Atlantic coast in August 1995. The Spiral system raged non-stop, twenty-four hours, and thousands of locals descended each night for twelve days. The Tribe were augmented by ten French systems, all blasting full-on, hard-core noise. Despite the threat of eviction by armed police, the Teknival powered on and on regardless. Far from its origins in both time and space, the virus was mutating again, and another chapter was beginning.

7

urban blues

"Now hear this! Feel the rush London Town, let's get hyper! Going out to all the bad boys, all the red eyes, all the liberty takers, the nutters . . . oh my bloody God! Come alive! Come alive!" Pirate radio MC, 1992

If its vitality were gauged in newspaper column inches, the rave scene seemed to have simply evaporated some time towards the end of 1990 after Graham Bright's Entertainments (Increased Penalties) Act had undermined illegal promoters and raves began to shift into licenced venues. This was an illusion of circumstance, for the exact opposite was true: although the media focus had shifted elsewhere, the phenomenon was actually growing more rapidly than ever. As the pirate entrepreneurs of 1989 moved on, others stepped in to take their place, the emphasis began to shift, and new leaders emerged who would explore new frontiers.

Fabio (Fitzroy Heslop) and Grooverider (Ray Bingham) were the rave heroes of 1989, their names appearing on flyers six or eight times every Saturday night, whether or not they were booked to appear. While most DJs are just that − disc jockeys, people who play records − a few, by picking up on specific musical elements and exaggerating them in the mix, create something that is more than the sum of the vinyl itself, forcing genres into new shapes. Some have actively instigated musical advances, and few as distinctively as this pseudonymous duo from Brixton whose mesmeric, percussive style had something tangibly special about it.

Fabio was a former insurance agent, Grooverider had been a computer operator and accounts clerk; both were in their early twenties and had roots in the soul and funk enclaves of south London. They met whilst DJing on a local pirate station, Phase 1, graduated from The Trip and Spectrum, and subsequently helped bring acid house south of the river to illegal drinking dens and warehouses like Mendoza's in Brixton and Carwash at Elephant and Castle. At the time, they were among the very few black house DJs. "I don't know what attracted me to acid house, to tell the truth," says Grooverider. "I didn't know anybody that liked it apart from myself and a couple of others. They used to think it was 'faggot music', didn't they? I was a lone ranger really."

Their personalities seemed to complement each other: Fabio was laid-back, introspective; Grooverider fiery and militant. Their weekly club, Rage, was a laboratory dedicated to intensified sound manipulation. Like reggae sound system DJs, they consciously sought to transform the very nature of the music they played, part of a long black futurist lineage dating back through Detroit techno and Jamaican dub, Jimi Hendrix and the cosmic big bands of Sun Ra. "We were always looking for this certain type of sound and no one was making it," explains Fabio. "It was subconscious, we knew it was coming." At the height of the Sunrise era, they dreamed of stringing together seamless blends of uptempo jazz-funk, techno and house to create a new hybrid genre – one that would eventually emerge five years later; jungle.

Rage had opened in October 1988 as an acid house club, and initially the duo were confined to the upstairs bar. A few months later they were offered a one-off session in the main arena, and the hysterical response ensured that they remained there until the club closed in 1993; shadowy silhouettes high above the throng, chasing the digital voodoo down amidst a cacophony of airhorns and whistles and a torrent of sweat and flailing limbs. Like Spectrum before it, Rage was at Heaven in Charing Cross, with its devastating sound and laser rig, and just as young ravers had stared, bewitched, at Paul Oakenfold, Fabio and Grooverider's devotees would press their noses against the cage outside the DJ booth, dreaming of emulating them. One even amassed a collection of Fabio's discarded water bottles.

"Rage was magical," recalls Storm, one half of the female DJ duo Kemistry and Storm, two of the many DJs and producers whose careers started on Rage's dancefloor. "It was a really awesome vibe, spine-tingling, the hairs on the back of your neck would stand up – it was really emotional. It was one of the most innovative clubs; Fabio and Grooverider would have the new music every week and that would be really exciting. At the end everybody would be talking about what they'd played. When we got home we would switch on pirate radio and dance all night in Kemi's kitchen then go to work in the morning. We were devastated when it finally closed."

During 1989, a series of house records emerged that employed breakbeats – the looped segments of solo drums that formed the basis for hip hop – or subsonic, depth-charge basslines, most notably Frankie Bones' *Bonesbreaks* series, Renegade Soundwave's *The Phantom* and Unique 3's seminal piece of bleeping, Yorkshire steel cybernetics, *The Theme*. The breaks and bass boosts seemed to energise a British dance crowd that had grown to love hip hop in the eighties, and would be the building blocks on which a new music was built. Using whatever technology was available, in the sonic-hacker tradition of Frankie Knuckles and Ron Hardy or early hip hop innovators like Kool DJ Herc and Grandmaster Flash, Fabio and Grooverider would take beat loops from the flipsides of house records and play them at double speed, or switch the pitch control on a techno track from 33 to 45 to achieve the desired effect: amplified energy and power.

To the unaccustomed, it sounded like a demonic cacophony. House DJ Sasha recalls hearing their style for the first time at a rave in Blackpool in 1989: "It did my head in. They were playing breakbeat after breakbeat – it sounded so weird and different." Britons were now remixing the very essence of house, and the genre would never again be the sole prerogative of Chicago, Detroit or New York: the torch had been passed to another place, another time, another generation, and, after the raves of 1989 propagandised Ecstasy to the entire country, house culture began to diversify. There would never again be one single defined "scene", but scores of interlocking subgenres, sub-subcultures, split along fault lines of class, culture, area, musical preference and drugs of choice.

East End duo Shut Up and Dance crystallised a direction for the breakbeat house of 1989 and 1990, turning it into a recognisable genre all of its own: raw, urgent and noisy. They produced hip hop tracks, informed by their background in reggae sound systems in the dancehalls of Hackney, which tampered with the conventions of the American genre, speeding up the breakbeat for a more edgy, aggressive feel that embodied east London's panorama of struggle and deprivation. In 1989, their single *5678* became a rave anthem, much to their bewilderment, as it hadn't been intended for this purpose. They had never been to a rave, and believed that the scene's professed ethics were a drug-induced illusion. "If you ask us what positive aspects have come out of raves, we'd have to answer, absolutely nothing," said Smiley (Carl Hyman). "People always argue that raves have successfully united blacks and whites, but in reality that argument's bollocks. Everyone at raves is on a fucking E. If you took the drugs out of the raves and everyone was just on spliff and drink, you know what would happen? There'd be fights. In fact, if you did take Es out of the rave scene it wouldn't even exist in the first place."[1]

Steeped in blag culture and street-level self-help ethics, Shut Up and Dance brought ironic commentary (their second single *£10 to Get In* and its remix *£20 to Get In* satirised rave profiteers), social awareness (dissections of cocaine economics and drug-dealing in Hackney pubs) and narratives from reggae and soul traditions to their productions. They prided themselves on their independence from the music industry, and believed in owning their own means of production, being in thrall to nobody.

"They were really important – speeding up the breaks, talking about what was really going on," says Jumping Jack Frost, another pseudonymous DJ who emerged from acid house, part of the same south London set as Fabio and Grooverider. "I don't think they even knew how important they were." Somehow they locked into the mood of young ravers who were moving away from house towards a sound and scene that reflected an inner-city working-class set and setting. Beneath the restless fingers of Fabio, Grooverider and their acolytes, house music's throbbing heartbeat was warp factored upwards. Faster. Harder. "You know the score!" the rave MCs would holler over the DJ's mix, ident-ifying the name it would adopt: "HARDCORE!!"

The Ibiza veterans felt that hardcore was a final desecration of their sunshine positivism; they found rave flyers, which had replaced hearts and flowers with dystopian horrorshow graphics and psychotic cartoons, nightmarish and inexplicable. Many had become deeply embittered with the way Ecstasy culture was developing. They believed they had glimpsed a kind of paradise, only to have it snatched away from them, diluted by sheep-like followers: the acid teds; the identikit masses of hardcore; drugged-out, spotty, scruffy, clueless teens. "Better dead than an acid ted," a *Boy's Own* flyer snarled vitriolically during the summer of 1988.

"They thought we were going in the wrong direction, making it commercialised," says Jumping Jack Frost. "I saw it as a fear thing – people felt threatened about their positions, intimidated about this whole new thing happening that they had no control over. Before it was a very controlled clique, and that all seemed to be falling apart." The reaction of the Ibiza crowd was to rally around their own banner – *Balearic* – a catch-all tag loosely defining a series of music, fashion and club door policies: melodic house, smart dress, exclusivity. "It's basically everything that

Shoom stood against," explained Terry Farley of *Boy's Own*, "but when you've got millions of kids running around with hooded tops and lilac bottoms, there's got to be a reaction."[2] "Balearic" referred to Ibiza, but more specifically to the Ibiza of 1987 and the honeymoon period of early 1988; the "original spirit", the pre-ted idyll before acid house took hold. It was the blueprint for what would, by the mid-nineties, become the pre-eminent leisure concept amongst British youth; but for hardcore, there was no turning back.

leicestershire and hampshire

"A girl chatting to Prince Charles at an unemployment training centre confided in HRH about the friendliness of 'raves'. She told him, if he was interested, that everyone puts their arms around each other. To which the prince replied: 'Ah, one does not have to be introduced.'" *The Independent*, **1993**

The legacy of the open-air raves and the Entertainments (Increased Penalties) Act was that by the end of 1990 some clubs were able to open later and raves began to be licensed. "It's been a funny old year," noted *Time Out* club correspondent Dave Swindells. "1990 began with the spectre of Graham Bright's Bill hanging over the future of house raves and ends with Islington Council promoting a huge rave on New Year's Eve."[3] Although Sunrise had quit the game, a second wave of rave organisers like Raindance, Amnesia House, Rezerection, Fantazia, Living Dream and Perception – amongst literally hundreds of others – moved in to organise large-scale raves in legal venues: big nightclubs, exhibition centres, sports halls and leisure complexes. This new leniency, coupled with the growth of interest spawned by the events of 1989 and attendant media coverage, meant that 1991 was another golden year for rave culture.

As the Balearic scene sought to distance itself from the term "rave" and all its connotations, bringing in door policies and dress codes to attract the "right" crowd and establishing an economic power base within the youth media and the record industry, hardcore was left voiceless, undocumented, ignored. At times it almost felt as though a cultural war was being fought for the soul of house culture: the élitists versus the populists, clubbers versus ravers. The Balearic DJs had better media contacts, particularly with editors at the major youth magazines with whom they shared a common social outlook, which meant that their scene was always reported more frequently and in more glowing terms than any other strand of house culture. Rave releases got little coverage in the dance press; if they did, they were generally dismissed as, at best, derivative, at worst, moronic. Record companies preferred to sign house tracks rather than hardcore records which, although they enjoyed strong sales and chart placings, were released almost exclusively through independent labels, creating a firm network that would nurture a fierce sense of its own self-sufficiency in isolation: an outsider subculture. "That's why the scene has become so strong, because we've fought against everything," says Storm. "Rave was very anti-establishment, it was like the working classes coming through, saying: 'This is our thing, you're not taking it off us.' We felt very militant about it."

Marginalised, the hardcore rave scene went underground, almost totally unreported and all but invisible for three years after it severed its links to the body of house culture. Its only media was internal: pirate radio, flyers, and a single publication, *Ravescene Magazeen*, an A5, black-and-white, 20,000-run freesheet launched in October 1991 and "dedicated only to the headstrong, hardcore raver". In the youth press, raves were typified as "commercial", downmarket, scuzzy, strictly for underclass adolescents – inner-city youth who had missed the Big Bang of 1988 – and were now dubbed *cheesy quavers*. When one dance magazine sent a journalist to Labrynth, Joe Wieczorek and Sue Barnes's club in Dalston, east London, she returned with a striking article that typified the reporting of the hardcore era, laced with unease, incomprehension and plain fear of this freakish phenomenon that had somehow taken life in the shadows:

"The breakbeats seem to be getting faster, the faces bonier and uglier, the eyes expanding like they're about to explode . . . I'm alone in hardcore hell, being jostled by skinny lads who are jogging on the spot. Everywhere I look I see *The Scream*. The phrase 'loved up' could never apply to these hardcore gurning children. The grinning ones look like mass murderers; the aggressive dancers resemble skinhead thugs and the ones with vacant stares look like the scary schizophrenics you meet in shopping centres. Somebody grabs my arm and I actually scream."[4]

Not that any of this bothered the young initiates; they were hitting the peak of the rush, embarking on the same innocent voyage of discovery that their detractors had enjoyed a couple of years previously. Turning in on itself, the rave scene produced some bizarre sartorial manifestations, just as Shoom had done in 1988; the wearing of white gloves to reflect LSD-enhanced lights and lasers; a kid's dummy to suck and gnaw on as the E buzz wobbled the jawbone; glowing lightsticks to fool about with; industrial face masks; bare chests and necks smeared with Vicks VapoRub decongestant, which cleared the lungs and was thought to intensify the MDMA hit.

"The Vicks and white gloves were just to fuck up your senses," says Eddie Otchere, then a sixteen-year-old south London raver, later to author a book about the scene. "With lasers, lights, dancers, the whole big circus, it was all about being lost in some netherworld where you never grew up." The popularity of Vicks – some ravers would walk around with an inhaler permanently inserted in each nostril – was such that its manufacturers Proctor and Gamble felt the need to make a public statement denigrating its "misuse". As 1989's ravers had been "mental", the class of 1991 declared themselves "nutty"; not in the sense of being insane, more in celebration of juvenile fun and games, a kind of drug-induced playfulness. Again the rave was fulfilling the role of fantasy theatre, a place where people could become the magical characters that their everyday lives would not allow.

The rave hits of 1991 and 1992 reflected both this state of wonder and its tougher urban environment. On one hand there were the abrasive, stomping riffs of Belgian hardbeat (or "heavy metal techno", as it was derided) and the dark Detroit techno of Underground Resistance and Kevin Saunderson; on the other were the cartoon kiddie anthems, *nutty* tunes. "Hardcore was a delinquent music," says Eddie Otchere. "It sounded like a giggle, a laugh. It was silly, quirky and off the wall. I think that's why people could never appreciate it, because it never took itself too seriously. It was like childhood all over again. We were all one big happy family and everything was wonderful."

In pop chart terms, the biggest hits were The Prodigy's *Charly*, which featured a sample of a mewling cat from a 1970s public information broadcast over crushing polyrhythms, *Sesame's Treet* by Smart Es, a novelty record that set the theme from the American children's show to a hardcore beat, and Altern-8's *Activ-8*, its comical, druggy refrain recited by a three-year-old: "Nice one, top one, get sorted!" Hardcore was pushing its own limits, going ever further *out there*: the helium babble of double-speed disco divas, accelerated piano riffs and breakneck drum loops formed a homology with an increase in amphetamine use and a perceived decrease in the quality of Ecstasy. By this time, "Ecstasy" no longer simply meant MDMA, but was a common name for a range of substances that might include MDMA, the heavier MDA or the more speedy MDEA. "The music was getting faster because the drugs were getting faster," commented Chris Simon of hardcore record label Ibiza. "They pushed the tempo further to see how high they could take the music."[5] Or perhaps it was simple overindulgence, binge dosages inducing an almost uncomfortable, nervy state. Either way, it was all about *speed*, both musical and chemical.

Simon Reynolds, one of the few music journalists to celebrate hardcore in print, suggested that "the vibe has changed (from trance-dance to mental-manic) as Ecstasy has become adulterated with amphetamine, or simply replaced – by pseudo-E concoctions of speed, LSD and who knows what. The subculture's metabolism has been chemically altered, till the beats-per-minute soar in sync with pulse rates and blood pressure levels. Speedy E has changed the whole vibe of rave culture, from celebration to a sort of aggressive euphoria. Dancers' faces are contorted with weird expressions midway between snarl and smile."[6]

On the Scottish hardcore scene, stories abounded of young ravers mixing prescription sedatives like Temazepam with Buckfast tonic wine, Es and speed. As the music got faster, the exertion more frenzied and strenuous, it was perhaps no coincidence that the hardcore honeymoon period of 1991 saw the highest yet number of Ecstasy-related deaths, just as the first Ecstasy fatalities in Holland followed the development of the hyperspeed Lowlands hardcore known as *gabber* a few years later. The employment of paramedics at many hardcore venues was another grim indication that the ravers just wanted to burn, burn, burn, to "stay up forever" (as a techno record label would later title itself), to speed not just out of their minds, but out of their bodies as well.

"Perhaps there's a submerged political resonance in there too," Simon Reynolds suggested. "Amidst the socio-economic deterioration of a Britain well into its second decade of one-party rule, where alternatives seem unimaginable, horizons grow ever narrower, and there's no constructive outlet for anger, what is there left but to zone out, to go with the flow, to *disappear*? There's also an inchoate fury in the music that comes out in an urge for total release from constraints, a lust for explosive exhilaration. 'Ardkore frenzy is where the somnambulist youth of Britain snap out of the living death of the nineties to grasp at a few moments of fugitive bliss. 'Ardkore seethes with a RAGE TO LIVE, to cram all the intensity absent from a week of drudgery into a few hours of fervour. It's a quest to reach escape velocity."[7]

Dance as escape, Saturday night fever – the idea could be

applied to any section of the house scene. But in a country experiencing ever-increasing economic polarisation, and in 1991, the year of the deepest post-war recession, the end of Thatcherite ideological certainties and generalised fear about the consequences for Britain of the outbreak of war in the Gulf and the Balkans, this analysis had powerful resonance. The use of the stylised 'ardkore emphasises how hardcore was seen at the time, in class terms; as a uneducated, brutal mutation. "We were working class," says Storm, "so we were nobody." The idea of ravers as lumpen proletariat on E is undoubtedly oversimplification, although it does contain an element of truth.

There are also powerful echoes of another, earlier British dance scene: Northern Soul. Manchester DJ Mike Pickering had been calling house "the new Northern Soul" since 1987, and the similarities are endless: the frenzied, sweaty dancing to high-velocity, uplifting sounds, the DJs as scene-makers spinning obscure imported records and bootlegs, the devotional dancers travelling miles across country to cavernous venues in towns throughout the North and Midlands, the arcane fashion codes – and the chemicals.

Northern Soul and hardcore shared the same speedfreak intensity, and both cultures emerged in tune with changing drugs of choice. In the late sixties, when mods started taking more black bombers, French blues and "green and clears", prescription pills stolen in bulk from chemists' shops, the music's tempo rose and Motown and Stax transmuted into the pounding, emotionally charged rhythms of Northern Soul. As Steve Dixon, a Yorkshire musician and writer whose clubbing career spans the late sixties and the early nineties, recalls: "When the amphetamines hit, the music got faster. Northern Soul came in and the stompers started taking over; the bass and drums were brought up, the beat hardened – a faster, amphetamine-driven thing. I can see that now with the hardcore."

The premier Northern Soul venue, the Wigan Casino, was alcohol-free and only opened after midnight, enabling a drug-induced communality which sublimated aggression beneath euphoria. "That dancefloor was something special. The epicentre of a special underground scene," remembers Pete McKenna in his keynote account of the era, *Nightshift*. "You had to make sure you could keep up with the best of them on the night. Get your gear down your neck. Wait for it to bring you up, and then get out there in that seething mass of amphetamined humanity. The floor would be pulsing. Alive with the weight of people on it, and you would find yourself a space and just glide into it with the music, and that would be that." After its giddy peak in the early seventies, Northern Soul endured a harsh comedown, fatigued by tabloid excoriation and police raids, its casualties strung out and exhausted after too many pills and powders. "Everything was becoming really crazy," says McKenna. "The drug scene was over the moon in the out of control stakes. It just couldn't go on."[8]

Harder, faster; harder, faster. Looking back, the hardcore scene which grew out of the raves of 1989 probably reached its peak some time in the summer of 1992. This was when two of the biggest raves Britain had ever seen took place. The first, Fantazia at Castle Donington, Leicestershire, a site better known for its annual heavy rock festival, attracted a crowd of 25,000; the second, Vision at Popham Airfield, Hampshire, claimed an incredible 38,000. But these raves won't only be remembered for their size, but also for the unpleasantness that highlighted some of the perennial problems with mass illegal drug culture: criminality, adulteration and a sweeping ignorance about the effects of drugs, especially amongst younger ravers. At Fantazia, drug squad officers seized hundreds of Es, but 97 per cent of them were fakes – hay fever capsules, vitamin pills or paracetamol. It was open season for exploitation and deception. Two hours after Vision finished, a seventeen-year-old soldier, Robert Jeffery from Southend, was found dying by the side of the A303, miles from the party. He expired from dehydration after taking Ecstasy. Had hardcore's lust for speed come up against the final barrier of human physicality? How much faster, how much harder could it get?

hackney and brixton

"Ragga Tekno, Jungle Techno, Ragga Jungle, Hardcore, Darkcore, The Dark Stuff, Ambient Jungle. All just labels to try and describe a feeling that transcends labels. More than the sum of its myriad parts. It is the lifeblood of a city, an attitude, a way of life, a people. Jungle is and always will be a multi-cultural thing, but it is also about a black identity, black attitude, style, outlook. It's about giving a voice to the urban generation left to rot in council estates, ghettoised, and neighbourhoods and schools that ain't providing an education for shit. Jungle kickin' ass and taking names. It run things, seen." Two Fingers and James T Kirk, *Junglist*, 1995

Jumping Jack Frost: "We were on our own . . ."
DJ Ron: "In the jungle . . ."
Rebel MC: "In the wilderness . . ."
Jumping Jack Frost: "As far as the magazines and record companies were concerned, we didn't even exist. We were on our own. So what did we do?"
Rebel MC: "We built our own foundation from the street."
Mixmag, July 1994

On the hardcore rave scene, the winter period linking 1992 to 1993 was *dark*. Nights closing in, pills deteriorating in quality, and music changing to fit the crepuscular mood. As *Ravescene* eloquently described it: "The strong summer sunshine bleached the scene to a pale reflection of its former glory, and then the nights of autumn '92 became darker and so did the music."[9] This period in hardcore – which the DJs also called "dark" – was typified by horror movie samples, evil noises, queasy sound effects and metallic breakbeats, mirroring the ravers' collective mental state. The techno DJs who had once been part of the rave scene now rejected it, heading off to start their own "pure techno" clubs. The drugs seemed to have turned to poison: the pill of the moment was the "Snowball", a huge blob of MDA, an enormous dose of MDMA's stronger, longer-lasting analogue, part of a batch of millions produced by a former Soviet factory in Riga, Latvia, which was like a knock-out punch, leaving many incapacitated in heaps at the corner of the dancefloor; *cabbaged*.

In December 1992, *Ravescene* warned, its message coming through despite its pharmacological inaccuracy: "Don't take Es. These days if you buy a Snowball you are buying a hideous mixture of maybe PCP, synthetic opiates and hallucinogens, plus other cheap crap such as smack, amphetamine, toilet cleaner etc. Every time you take one you are playing Russian Roulette with your life. You know it's true as you've all seen the monged effect they have."[10]

People were murmuring about stabbings and muggings, racial divides on the dancefloor, nightmares at the edges of the rave, underlining the prevailing atmosphere; one of post-honeymoon comedown from the highs of 1991 and yearning for paradise lost. As one clubber told *Mixmag:* "All the raves, they feel different, like everything's gone wrong. People have got to get back to the original feeling again."[11]

It was at this point, sometime in early 1992, that the term "jungle" began to be employed to describe what the music was becoming: ragamuffin techno. The first record to use the phrase was a white label entitled *Jungle Techno* on the Ibiza label. Ibiza, run by soul veteran Paul Chambers (who had never been to the Balearic island), had roots reaching back to 1989, when Chambers had staged huge warehouse parties in King's Cross, one of the few black promoters of the era, who consequently encountered problems with both police and white football firms. Chambers says he adapted the record's title from James Brown's album *Jungle Groove*, although the word was already part of the vernacular of rave MCs like Rat Pack. The origins of the term are controversial: Shut Up and Dance damned it as racist – "anybody who uses that phrase in front of me, I'll punch them in the head," raged Philip Johnson – while others insisted it was simply a word that conjured a mood, one that had been applied to tribal house sounds in the late eighties and now fitted this new music.[12]

Like Chambers's records, jungle was incorporating samples from Jamaican imports, ragamuffin invective and gunshot volleys, and the deep sub-bassline which had been around since 1989 was taking on a reggae flavour. "The term 'jungle techno' described it perfectly because it was a mixture of European and sound system traditions," says Kemistry. "That mixture became the British sound." By the beginning of 1992, London's Sunday Roast club, which blended the frenetic euphoria of early acid house with a reggae blues party atmosphere, and the Hackney-based pirate station Kool FM, whose ruffian sorcery updated the East End outlaw tradition of Centre Force, had consolidated this development. "As jungle got bigger and it became a black thing, it just drew all the raggas," says Chambers. "They were hearing their favourite artists like Buju Banton and Ninja Man in it and it drew them in, so you had this new breed of crowd. Everyone was amazed by it. And no Es – pure weed smoking. Sunday Roast set the trend and everyone followed."

One of the key narratives within what would become the jungle scene is of black youth reasserting control over what was originally the black music of Chicago, New York and Detroit. This, again, is over-simplification; the people producing jungle were multi-racial, as Jumping Jack Frost is quick to stress; the product of a generation of British black and white youth growing up together in the inner city, bonded by shared concerns and values, set and setting: "Some of the most important records weren't made by black people. This is a multi-cultural society, and this music is a product of that multi-cultural society. If it was a black thing alone, I don't think it would be what it is now.

We took the inspiration and the vibe from the acid scene and modernised it. If it had an ID tag, it would just say 'UK' on it."

But nevertheless jungle spoke to a black British identity. Jungle raves began to attract a black inner-city crowd who might have been interested in hip hop or ragga, but would never have considered going to a house club. "When it first came over here, a lot of people thought house music was poof music, white people's music, and a lot of black people wouldn't go to raves," explains jungle DJ Kenny Ken. In turn, they helped mould the environment to accommodate their own needs. "As more black people started going to the raves," says DJ Ron, "the black influence showed up in the music."

One turning point was a devastating track called *Terminator* by Metalheads, alias Goldie, with its shredded, snake-like drum loop that contorted and writhed around the speakers. Goldie was a hyperactive character with an apocalyptic turn of phrase – another of those charismatic individuals who brought new dimensions to the dance scene – and whose life embodied the entwined histories and cultural miscegenation that birthed jungle. Born in the West Midlands in 1965, the son of an English mother and an absent Jamaican father, Clifford Price had been brought up in council children's homes and with foster parents, a runaway and petty criminal, brooding over the feeling that he never really fitted in anywhere.

"I would look at the colour of my skin and think: 'I'm not black, I'm not white, I'm not anybody, who am I?' I was half-caste in a school that was almost all white. They used to say: 'Goldie, you're a fucking Paki', or 'you're a nigger'. I had it for years." In the early eighties he was enthused by the emergence of hip hop, breakdancing and graffiti, and became one of Britain's primary exponents of aerosol art. He then moved to Miami, where he manufactured customised gold teeth caps, the kind rappers would wear, engraved with Playboy bunnies or Mercedes logos. His own mouthful of gold incisors gave him his nickname.

On returning to Britain, he met Kemistry and Storm, who

introduced him to Rage, and a new chapter in his remarkable life – although it took him eight attempts to finally gain entry to the club. Taking Ecstasy for the first time, the breakbeats seared through his consciousness. He was mesmerised by Fabio and Grooverider and spent his nights dreaming of giving them a "forty-foot graffiti masterpiece", a darkside epic, assembled from beats morphed out of those he recalled from his breakdancing days. He achieved it with *Terminator*, repurposing the technology of the recording studio to deliver a unique sound. "I started fucking around with this equipment and realised I could change the music, I could take a breakbeat, make it seem like it was speeding up and changing tone but it was actually still at the same speed," he says. "I finished the project and EQ'd it on three Es. And you know what Es do to you, you start hearing shit that no one else is hearing, and I really used it as an artist. I pushed myself to the limits artistically."

Goldie and his colleagues Dego MacFarlane and Mark Mac of the seminal hardcore duo 4 Hero would spend endless weekends cloistered in their attic studio in Willesden, not recording tracks but researching digital sound, building up processed data banks of looped and twisted noise, tools that they could later use to access new domains of sonic experience – "trying to make the unimaginable real", as MacFarlane put it.[13]

Hardcore's cartoon phase was over, and its roots in house were years away. Nowhere was this better evidenced than in *Junglist*, a remarkable work of pulp fiction written by a pair of black twenty-one year olds, Two Fingers (Andrew Green) and James T Kirk (Eddie Otchere). In one of its most striking passages, the authors compare jungle to its musical progenitor. In an echo of the schism between the escapism of disco and the urban realism of hip hop in the late seventies, they describe house as a false consciousness, a denial of reality, beloved of people who seek "that false high, that false hope. That false love when you're EEEEing off your face and then tripping off your nut . . . When you love everyone and everyone's your soulmate, the closest person to you in the entire universe."[14] This compounded the realisation that jungle was qualitatively different, a break with the past and a break with Ecstasy; it had begun to tell a very different story. A letter to *Mixmag* declared: "It's recession music, it prepares you for life in the nineties, not hands in the air, way-hey we're all such wonderful people, we're not. We're just off our heads."[15]

By 1993, the hardcore scene was splintering. Jungle had turned it upside down. It was labelled as dark, evil, a portent of doom framed in almost Biblical terms. Anguished missives flooded into *Ravescene* bemoaning "moody vibes", "moody people" and "moody music": "My worry is that the hardcore rave scene is slowly withering away," fretted one. "I think the problem lies with the DJs. The music they play is so depressing, it could never in a million years make people ecstatic, joyous, carefree and loving. In fact it is more likely to make them frightened."[16]

Jungle was invariably linked to violence and crack cocaine: bad behaviour and even worse drugs, the antithesis of rave's purported ideals. Junglists – and by implication black people – were moody, aggressive, violent. "I don't take it personal," mused the *Junglist* of Andrew Green and Eddie Otchere's novel, "it's just what they've been socialised into thinking; one black person might be alright but a mass dance and all that dark, depressing, dangerous black music? No way, not this boy . . . Anything that involves more than one black person, that is aimed at other black people, is inherently dangerous. Because it hasn't been reconstructed and regurgitated for the white mass culture."[17]

It came down to fear. Fear of the new crowd, the new music, the new atmosphere; fear of change, fear of losing control, fear of the Other. Some of the fears were very real: the rave was no longer a safe playground for E babies. "A lot of criminals and dealers got involved in the scene because it was easy pickings," remembers Kemistry unhappily. "They could go in there, mug a few punters, get their drugs and their money and people couldn't do much about it because they were off their face. By the end of the evening they could have a pocketful of drugs and loads of money and get away with it. It did attract a lot of undesirables because it was such an easy vibe, they didn't have major searches for weapons then, nobody had heard of bringing a weapon to a rave. It was a shame because it did have a nasty effect on the scene and of course that brought bad press – the press loved it because they could say: 'I told you so.' "

Allegations of widespread crack use were further symptoms of this fear. Cocaine seizures had been rising throughout the nineties – the National Criminal Intelligence Service reported that twenty-five times more was being seized in 1994 than in the mid-eighties – and the substance, in both powder and rock form, was increasingly a part of nightclub culture. However, crack, like heroin, was considered by ravers to be the last Devil Drug. Jungle's primary stimulants of choice were weed and champagne, although the heavy, bittersweet fumes of burning rocks had been detected on dancefloors as early as 1991. Rock smoking remained a taboo subject, alluded to in various anti-crack jungle records but never openly discussed, whether out of political correctness or to protect the scene's public image.

Undoubtedly, jungle was no longer defined by Ecstasy and was losing both the empathetic textures of rave and its stylistic flavour. The junglists wore pricey casualwear, the flashy designer excesses of Versace and Moschino – symbols of conspicuous consumption reappropriated – the girls in flesh-revealing lace, lycra and gold; they would flash cigarette lighters to applaud a favourite record or even set fire to butane gas canisters, spurting jets of flame towards the ceiling. It was a ragga-influenced style with a cool demeanour that contrasted sharply with the carefree, "nutty" rave garb.

It wasn't long before the scene cleaved in two, leaving the predominantly white ravers with their pills, their white gloves, face masks and lightsticks, and a music full of cheery piano riffs, preposterous samples and vocal shrills – named, almost in defiance, *happy* hardcore – which bathed in nostalgia for the euphoria of 1991 and shamelessly celebrated the pure state of Ecstasy: weekender hedonism taken to the borders of oblivion. "The mainly 16–22 crowd revel in their altered state," one observer noted. "They show off their rictus grins, massive pupils and empathic over-friendliness as badges of pride."[18]

The reaction to the rise of jungle was a stark dramatisation of attitudes to race in nineties Britain. Right through the narrative of post-war pop culture, from rock'n'roll, R&B, soul and funk to house and techno, black music has soundtracked white youth's leisure activities and provided the basis for white pop, particularly within dance clubs. When large numbers of black people start turning up to these clubs, however, the majority begins to feel uneasy. Black men are often barred from city-centre nightspots for spurious reasons; black and white may have danced together at raves, but generally on white terms, with whites in the majority, and whites taking the proceeds. The panic about jungle commenced when black people ceased to be a minority and were visibly in control of the scene. Institutionalised racism reaches into all corners of British society, and house culture, for all its rhetoric of unity, was no exception. "All too often, the dislike of jungle translates into fear of the rudeboy from the council estate who's supposedly spoilt the peace-and-love vibe and the dream of trans-tribal unity," suggested pop theorist Kodwo Eshun. "Jungle, so this racist myth goes, is what turned every raver's little Woodstock into an Altamont with bass bins."[19]

The initial response to jungle from the music industry was reminiscent of its early dismissiveness towards hip hop and house. Like hip hop in the seventies, it was left out of the commodification loop and thus allowed to develop, grow roots and forge a coherent ideology relatively free from commercial pressure to deliver sales and chart hits. Marginalised, jungle's media were autonomous by necessity: independent record labels and pirate radio. Before 1994, the only legal show in England giving regular airtime to hardcore was Stu Allen's slot on Key 103 in Manchester. The music had no other voice; it was consigned to illegality.

Between 1992 and 1994, there was a remarkable acceleration in its musical development. It was one of those weird flashpoints in pop culture, a genre taking flight and completely reinventing itself. Utilising the entire sonic spectrum, jungle redefined the parameters of dance music at a metabolic level to create an immersive womb of sound. Drums and bass became the lead instruments, complex webs of percussion rather than the stark four-to-the-floor pulse of house. While The Prodigy, with a thrilling live show and virtuoso programming skills, were turning their apocalyptic hardcore into a radical strain of electronic rock'n'roll – *Music For the Jilted Generation*, as their second album was titled – jungle producers were refining breakbeats into a polyrhythmic blend of influences from house, hardcore, reggae, hip hop, soul, jazz, ambient music and techno; a melting pot of urban signals and styles that Fabio and Grooverider had envisaged five years previously.

In pop terms, jungle was a historic sound: the first truly *British* black music – or, to be more accurate, multi-cultural music. Many of its practices were adapted directly from reggae sound system traditions, like the MCs' microphone banter and the use of "dub plates", one-off exclusive editions of recordings on acetate rather than vinyl, circulated only to opinion leaders like Fabio and Grooverider, the endless "versions", remixes and re-remixes, and the endlessly shifting *ad hoc* alliances of producers and DJs: a mode of production a world away from marketing-driven, CD-formatted rock economics. Jungle pirate stations like Kool FM conjured up a surreal world, a menagerie of ghetto glossolalia, hissing cymbals and rhythmic mania that captured a moment in time – the confused, chaotic middle nineties – as well as pop music ever could.

"Anywhere I go in the world, if I look at a travel brochure about London, I know what I'm going to see: Buckingham

Palace and red buses," says Jumping Jack Frost. "But there's always another story – the untold story." Just like hip hop in America, jungle articulated the repressed desires and fears of a disenfranchised underclass – "*all the bad boys, all the red eyes, all the liberty takers, the nutters*" – although through sheer sonic texture rather than lyrics. It was a virulent denial of despair, a flash of positivity and hope against all odds: *Shining in the Darkness*, as a key track from 1993 was titled.

Goldie explained it as a kind of urban realist blues that encapsulated basic truths about the way many young people lived. "In my music," he says, "is everything I've learned, everyone I've met, everything I've experienced, and a lot of other pressures that are going on socially, like girls having kids young, guy's left them, no money, guy's doing drugs, no way out of it, the whole pressure you're living with in that inner-city situation. Jungle isn't black or white, it's everybody below a certain level that has socially been fucked by drugs or living in the inner city."

Jungle was another example of how black youth subcultures are initially feared and demonised before ultimately being packaged and commercially exploited by the white mainstream. It's a process repeated again and again throughout pop history. In 1994, as happened a decade previously with hip hop, there was an explosion of interest in the form, beginning in the youth press, spreading to the record companies and, within a year, to national radio and television. This about-face was received with anything from scepticism to outright derision within the jungle fraternity, which had developed a distinctive hierarchy and remarkably close-knit, cellular structure based on its exclusion from the youth culture industry. "The press hasn't done us any favours," growled Grooverider. "Now they want to come in and we don't need them. We don't need anybody any more because we do it all ourselves. We don't have to talk to anybody. When we needed help, nobody wanted to give it to us." The DJs despised the labels they felt were thrust upon them by the pop press, as if journalists were trying to take control of their language, divide and rule them, even steal their soul by trapping it in phraseology.

The urge to retain control was exaggerated as the economics of the scene began to change during 1994 and 1995, when a number of key producers were offered album deals with dance subsidiaries of major record labels, beginning with Goldie, who went on to sell 100,000 copies of his debut album, *Timeless*, and become an international star. London radio station Kiss FM instituted regular jungle shows, followed by BBC Radio One. At one point a circle of leading DJs even set up a Jungle Committee to defend their collective doctrine against interlopers and potential exploiters. However, jungle, unlike the absolutist decrees of punk, concerned itself little with the concept of "selling out" to major labels – it was, after all, born out of the grey fringes of the enterprise economy – its worry was of losing its cultural identity. Creative independence was considered far more significant than commercial independence, as evidenced by the fact that some producers negotiated contracts with not one but many different labels, while still running their own independent operations and doing remixes for those of their colleagues. It was about circumventing and getting what you wanted from the establishment rather than struggling to destroy it.

While some hit paydirt, those who remained outside the commodification loop, unsigned and unreported, could still rely on the self-supporting infrastructure that jungle had established in its wilderness years, a marginal economy of small-run white-label releases, pirate radio stations and specialist record shops that had enabled its survival. "It's an underground mafia," insisted Goldie. "We've got ranks. We know what's running, we know what ain't running. This is a genre that *we* control. It's on *our* fucking terms."

The network of personal intercommunication forged outside the public eye, plus this sense of purpose – Goldie and others would speak of it in almost religious terms, eulogising about "the brotherhood" and "defending the faith" – again summoned images from American hip hop and its tenets of "respect", "representing" and "coming correct". Such notions of unity and self-help, driven by necessity, became jungle's central creed. The utopian vision of a self-sufficient community, a creative adhocracy that could help the DJs and producers negotiate their way through the perils of commerce, the threats of commodification and assimilation into mass culture, became more focused as jungle – or "drum and bass", as it was increasingly known – filtered into the mainstream during 1996, deployed in advertising jingles and kids' television shows and imitated in other dance genres. Wherever it went next, jungle's culture of entrepreneurial pragmatism and mythic resistance had provided an illustration of how, in a fleeting moment of meritocratic autonomy, real or imagined, the acid house ethic could still be an empowering force; a way of hacking out space in which to dream.

8

the chemical generation

Fifteen years after the first Britons were introduced to MDMA on hedonistic excursions into New York nightlife and a decade after house music emerged from the black gay clubs of Chicago, the synthesis of the two had produced the largest youth cultural phenomenon that Britain had ever seen. Ecstasy culture had become the primary leisure activity for British youth, seamlessly integrated into the fabric of the weekend ritual. From 1990 onwards, as the fall-out from acid house germinated across the country, its sounds, signs, symbols and slang had become all-pervasive, part of the everyday landscape.

It was a highly lucrative business for operators on both sides of the law. In 1993, the British dance scene was assessed by market analysts at the Henley Centre to be worth £1.8 billion a year, similar in size to the book or newspaper industry; a wild estimate, perhaps, but indicative of the stakes for which club promoters, record companies, radio stations, DJs and drug dealers were vying, and confirmation, if any was needed, of its ascendance into the popular mainstream. The continual expansion of London listings magazine *Time Out*'s club section demonstrated how rewarding the profession of club promotion had become: on New Year's Eve 1985, twenty parties were listed, with a typical ticket price of £10; ten years later, there were over 100, and the cost had risen to £25. The market place had grown more than fivefold in a decade, while the gross financial proceeds had multiplied well over ten times.

The best-known DJs – top-ranking names like Sasha, Paul Oakenfold and Danny Rampling – were able to command ever-increasing fees in line with their crowd-pulling potential. By the middle of the nineties, some could demand, and receive without comment, upwards of £1,000 for two hours' work, four times what they might have been paid in 1989. A favourite scene conviction held that DJs were contemporary shamans, leading their intoxicated congregations on a trip into the unknown; now the top mixers appeared to have become a wealthy priest class. On New Year's Eve 1995, it was rumoured that the populist showman DJ Jeremy Healy played at four clubs during the night, earning £5,000 from each and chartering a private plane to transport him between venues. True or not, it demonstrated how much cash was sloshing through this nocturnal economy.

As the scene expanded, its constantly evolving strands and specialist cells – house, techno, jungle, ambient, trance, garage, plus innumerable subdivisions and regional variations of these styles – became ever more diverse. Perhaps because a definitive set of musical and cultural rules had never been established, instead of stagnating into self-parody, as British youth cultures had traditionally done after brief years of vitality, it remained in constant creative flux, regenerating itself year by year with fresh blood and influences. Yet although many options still remained open, Ecstasy culture's central core, its apolitical, hedonist heart, was slowly assimilated into the British leisure industry.

This process began in earnest at the turn of the nineties, following the split between the populist rave movement and the "Balearic" descendants of the original Ibiza fraternity, who, disgusted with the rave circuses of Sunrise, began to stake out their own territory using the exclusive door policies they had once rebelled against. Both sides prospered; alongside the techno-hippies, they would define the primary strands of the acid house diaspora over the next five years.

By 1991, the legal, licensed hardcore raves that followed in the wake of Graham Bright's Entertainments (Increased Penalties)

Act had swollen to gargantuan proportions, preparing the ground for the rise of jungle; simultaneously, most of Britain's larger cities could boast a Balearic venue that took its ideology from *Boy's Own* fanzine and a clientele that, although it still took Ecstasy, differentiated itself with an immaculate designer chic. Aspirational fashion, rejected for the dressed-to-sweat dungarees and bandannas of acid house, was also back.

The interconnected tribe of DJs and promoters that ran Balearic clubs like Flying in London, Most Excellent in Manchester and Venus in Nottingham – what was tagged the "Balearic Network" – was instrumental in developing a national infrastructure for house culture. They were tireless entrepreneurs, creating self-employment out of their nocturnal economy, opening shops and record labels, establishing agencies to represent their DJs, who travelled from town to town, spreading the word and building the market. But it was the third wave of British house promoters that emerged in 1992 and 1993 who, although they built their empires on the infrastructure the Balearic Network had created, began to employ more sophisticated marketing techniques, giving house culture a formal business foundation. "Club promotion is now a career," noted Jon Hill, promoter of Golden in Stoke-on-Trent. "House music's taken over the mainstream. It's getting bigger and bigger. And promoters are getting more and more professional."[1]

Those at the vanguard of that new professionalism, the ones booking the celebrity DJs and staging the most opulent parties, adopted expansionist strategies to consolidate their success. "Superclubs" like Liverpool's Cream, London's Ministry of Sound and Renaissance in the Midlands took the marketing process yet further, diversifying into ancillary services, starting their own labels to release DJ mix CDs (a legal extension of the illicit bootleg mix tapes that proliferated in specialist shops), launching merchandise and clothing ranges, opening bars and shops, promoting nationwide club "tours" and package holidays to destinations like Ibiza (where the British began to take over the

Balearic isle's summer season, usurping the sexually ambiguous cosmopolitanism that had once constituted its special magic). Across the country, hundreds of other club promoters strove to duplicate their commercial triumphs.

Within four years of its launch, the Ministry of Sound, financed by James Palumbo, former City dealer and son of Lord Palumbo, the multi-millionaire property developer and retired chairman of the Arts Council, had become the world's biggest club fashion and merchandising company, with an estimated turnover of over £10 million. It had launched its own syndicated radio show and lifestyle magazine, and was striving to become a force in the record business. Clubland had always boasted its share of maverick entrepreneurs, but none with the old money, aristocratic credentials of Palumbo.

The Ministry refined the idea of club culture as pure product, and the nightclub as a marketing tool. "We are very ambitious," explained Ministry managing director Mark Rodol. "We want to become a global brand. We need to exploit the brand beyond the 5,000 people we entertain at weekends."[2] The club linked up with brands like Pepsi and Sony for sponsorship deals, following the example of Germany's techno scene, where rave flyers resembled Formula One motor racing cars, spattered with brand-name logos, the graphics of Camel or Philip Morris competing for space with DJ line-ups. Renaissance was backed by Silk Cut cigarettes, the Haçienda by Boddingtons beer, as sponsors bought in to subcultural credibility. While in the early nineties club flyers had mimicked corporate logos, twisting their graphics into cheeky drug references, now many clubs had established their own instantly recognisable logos to be capitalised upon via T-shirts, jackets, record bags and CDs.

What was originally intended as an alternative to the "mainstream" nature of raves had generated a new mainstream; a High Street dance-drug culture. Leisure opportunities for young people outside the capital had altered fundamentally since the eighties and pleasures that were previously only available to a bohemian élite were now open to all. It was hedonism distilled to its purest essence. The lack of any ideology bar the ceaseless pursuit of sheer pleasure made it even more accessible, and there were no jarring extremes of incomprehensible "mental" or "nutty" behaviour. The Saturday night dance session – and house music itself – was no longer considered in any way subversive or extraordinary, merely the natural thing to do if you thought yourself hip. Drug use excluded, there was no leap of faith involved, no huge commitment necessary. Mainstream house clubbing, with its closed-circuit security cameras, registered door supervisors and council-imposed procedural guidelines, had become the regulated opposite of its illicit origins.

In 1996, the British Tourist Authority launched its first campaign to target the 18–30 age group since the sixties. It printed a magazine, *UK Guide*, that aped the youth press and focused on what were considered to be two of Britain's main tourist attractions – Leeds club culture and the rock band Oasis, with a guide to Oasis-speak lifted straight from club dancefloors that included drug-inspired slang like "sorted", "bangin' " and "mad for it". Foreign journalists were flown to Leeds, Manchester, Liverpool and London, and shown around nightclubs. House, the brochure intimated, had finally been made safe for tourists and casual consumers.

In the realm of music production and distribution, acid house had also left lasting impact. Since the late eighties, a self-supporting, *ad hoc* production network had developed around dance music, based on small-run white-label records, home studios using cheap technology and a distribution system hooked together by a web of mobile phones. It was an independent alternative based on the same ethic of autonomy that punk rock had once propagated, but with a reach far wider than punk ideologues had ever dared to envisage, and one that catalysed an enormous, relentless output of recordings.

This dance boom forced the established record industry to find new ways of packaging and selling music in a rapidly fragmenting marketplace. The major labels – Bertelsmann Music Group, MCA, Polygram, Sony, EMI and Time Warner, the six multi-nationals that controlled the worldwide distribution of the majority of pop music – sought to exploit the febrile urgency and vital cash drift of the swelling independent sector, just as they had assimilated profitable elements of the hippie and punk movements in previous decades. They launched subsidiary dance operations headed by scene heroes such as Paul Oakenfold, bought out or affiliated themselves with cutting-edge indepen-dent labels, issued mix compilations, marketed DJs as celebrities, and used the remix phenomenon to bolster product sales and longevity. While some of the music was thrilling and adven-turous, and many of the premier electronic *auteurs* received just recognition and reward, much seemed cynically manufactured to throw E-heads into Pavlovian raptures.

In its early stages, house music was unconcerned with the rock mythologies of authenticity, career development, the musician as Artist and the staples of rock commodification: the live gig and the album. However, the rise of recognisable and marketable (often white) techno and ambient "bands" who played live gigs and worked in the record industry's format of choice, the compact disc album, rather than anonymous (often black) recording-studio avatars whose primary mode of production was the relatively unprofitable 12-inch vinyl single, made dance music comprehensible in both business and rock press terms.

The scene became comprehensively mediated. In 1988, apart from sporadic articles in *i-D* and *The Face*, no one had really got to grips with acid house. Its nuances were hidden, undocu-mented, subterranean. By the middle nineties there had been an explosion in media coverage as a new generation of pop writers emerged who had entered the profession in the wake of acid house, from the brace of home-produced, do-it-yourself fanzines that followed in the wake of *Boy's Own* to monthly specialist magazines like *Mixmag*, *DJ*, *M8*, *Jockey Slut*, *Eternity* and *Muzik* – all buoyed up by revenue from the nationwide club network's advertising. Here the latest news on drug research featured along-side reviews of dance tracks; *Eternity* even had its own medical correspondent.

There were dance pages in the weekly music press, club reviews in the newspapers, dance resources on the Internet and new, legal dance radio stations like Kiss FM. Once pirates were the only people playing the music and thus defining a communal ethos, but now Britain's national pop station, BBC Radio One, began to recruit ex-pirate broadcasters for its evening shows, just as it had poached DJs like John Peel from the offshore rock pirates of the sixties.

Radio One's initial reaction to acid house had been to censor it. Six years on, in 1994, with its listenership falling by millions and its output sounding tired and middle-aged, it recruited former Shoom and Kiss DJ Danny Rampling to host a new Saturday night show as part of a strategy to reposition itself as a credible wavelength for the late nineties. The arrival of a pre-senter who was "one of the founders of the drug-ridden acid house craze" was heralded by *The Star* as "an outrage".[3] The fact that no one picked up the baton of moral umbrage that the tabloid proffered was another indication of how deeply Ecstasy culture had permeated the collective consciousness of the nation.

Rampling attracted 2 million listeners for his *Lovegroove* show, whereas he had only claimed 100,000 on Kiss FM – a further democratisation of what had once been the music of metropolitan cognoscenti. By the end of 1997, Radio 1 was playing a total of 34 hours of dance music each week. The balance of power had shifted, from rogue traders in the East End to the BBC broad-casting establishment from flyers and fanzines to publishing houses.

This pervasive mediation meant that it was difficult for any club phenomenon to develop without being instantly reported and commodified. The dance scene had become transformed into a dance *industry*. Its secret codes had been cracked and nothing could remain "underground" for long. The graphical attitude and design values of house and rave also infected the collective image-consciousness, picked up on by businessmen and marketeers and flashed back at the constituency that invented them. From junk food like Pot Noodle to soft drinks like Tango, from Regal cigarettes to Fila footwear, scores of youth-oriented advertising campaigns used hedonistic, irreverent and psychedelic imagery, just as, at the end of the sixties, the agencies had cashed in on the sounds and slang of the hippies. In 1967, Jefferson Airplane had revamped the psychedelic classic *White Rabbit* as *White Levis* for an advertising campaign – over a quarter of a century later the same denim company would employ techno tricks and tripped-out iconography to sell its jeans. The trend was confirmed by a report from the European Union's drugs monitoring unit, which accused companies of cynically marketing products with Ecstasy-related imagery and hence promoting drug use: "Much of this marketing is implicitly or explicitly drug-related," it stated. "International corporations appear to have become increasingly blasé about ads with explicit drug imagery. Rapidly they have become directly aware of rave culture and indirectly aware of Ecstasy use, aided by astute marketing."[4]

Part of the impulse came from younger creative planners in the ad agencies who had been involved in the scene themselves and whose work had been affected by Ecstasy. One, coming down in his kitchen after a dance session, found himself munching breakfast cereal at 4 a.m.; his experience, so the story goes, was then translated into an advertisement aimed at post-club consumers. Marketeers attempted to cut through the media overload and engage the interest of increasingly aware, media-literate youth, generating the bizarre spectacle of a cider brand, Drum, compiling club CDs, or a beer company, Fosters, financing white labels for bedroom producers, projecting themselves as facilitators to a dance-drug culture.

While most clubbers were too busy enjoying themselves to care about the economics of pleasure, a few railed against what they derisively labelled "corporate clubbing", where every aspect of the experience was defined by business interests. Had the spontaneity, they demanded, been quantified and regulated? In the book *Highflyers*, journalist Stephen Kingston lamented that house was comprehensively packaged and neutered like rock had been at end of the sixties. Clubbers had become a huge market-place to be "farmed" by corporate concerns, following the classic trajectory: revolt into style, rebellion into money; the outlaws becoming the new establishment. The dream was finally over, Kingston insisted, its fragile spirit extinguished: "The house movement has been herded into a capitalist kraal. Club culture used to talk a lot about 'freedom'. It's turning out to be the freedom to be farmed."[5] Many in the pop culture vanguard agreed with him. Innovation comes from the margins, not the mainstream, they argued, and house had become a bloated, conservative mainstream, formulaic and predictable, dominated by a self-satisfied, self-serving élite.

In 1997, the debate finally went public as people began to sift through the psychic debris of a decade of euphoria, questioning whether the grand equation that underpinned the scene – *Ecstasy plus house music equals mass euphoria* – had finally lost its trans-formative power. This could have been seen as a necessary period of reassessment, but the term that many commentators within the scene preferred was "comedown". It was not a mood measured in hard science or statistics, but in empirical evidence: most agreed that the "vibe" had shifted perceptibly.

"What goes up must come down," declared music journalist Bethan Cole. "Clubbers have begun to wonder how long the party can last, and what will happen to those who have dropped through the supposedly life-affirming communal net created by Ecstasy, or found the dream shatters and have to re-enter reality."[6] The psychological, physical, legal, cultural and commercial side-effects of Ecstasy culture were weighed up in banner headlines in the youth press, all asking questions that indicated a collective loss of confidence: "Are Drugs Driving You Mad?", "Has the

Chemical Generation Lost the Plot?", "Is This the End of E Culture?" Only a few years previously – when records still fervently celebrated the state of Ecstasy intoxication – it would have been unthinkable.

Although many older players had become warped by greed or twisted with cynicism, this was not the perennial cry of "it's not as good as it used to be" uttered by those sidelined by the pace of change. It was something deeper: as dance culture became part of the pop mainstream, some of its unique mystery – the special secret – had been lost forever as it entered the public domain. Those who desired creative space in the margins were moving on. The emergence of post-Ecstasy dance forms – Goa trance, Big Beat, speed garage, music that was not predicated on the ingestion of MDMA – demonstrated an enduring fertility, but also a desire to break with the old certainties of the Ecstasy equation.

A decade on, the key words did seem to have changed, from love and peace to investment and promotion, from music to marketing. Was club culture profiting by the infrastructure it had established for itself and creating valid alternative employment, or was big business reasserting its dominance, moving in to clean up after the comedown? The answer depended on vested interests, on set and setting, as writer Nigel Fountain once noted of the transformation of sixties psychedelic exploration into a lucrative rock industry: "For some it was the fulfilment of the dreams of 1967, the growth of an organism serving and being served by the young, the dissident, independent of the mainstream metropolis. For others it was hip capitalism, the wooing of the virtuous into the antechamber of the old gang."[7]

Behind the ideological divisions, the reality was more complex. Ecstasy culture had always thrived through the trading of commodities. The arguments over creeping commercialisation laid bare the central, often conflicting impulses – entrepreneurial, hedonistic and utopian – that both drove and divided the scene. But although statutes like the Entertainments (Increased

Penalties) Act and the Criminal Justice Act had disrupted the dreaming of house's dissident fringes, they also had the opposite of their intended effect: by driving it towards the mainstream, they brought the dance-drug virus to a wider community of willing hosts. Furthermore, the sense of communality engendered by MDMA's pharmacology still had the potential to create resonance beyond the confines of the dancefloor, as alternative cells spun off from the mainstream in unpredictable directions, from political rave collectives like Exodus to the technological rhapsodies of jungle, from the nomadic hardcore Teknivals to the electro-paganism of psychedelic trance. If this was a new establishment, it was an unstable one that constantly questioned its own certainties, and could never shed its anarchic edges completely because it was still bound up with mind-altering, illegal drugs that hadn't been slotted into legal, formal strictures.

Beyond Britain's borders, Ecstasy's influence was also being felt. From 1988 onwards, as the acid house formula was exported overseas, it began to assume local characteristics and cultural influences. Germany, with a rich electronic music tradition stretching back through the *Neue Deutsche Welle* synthesiser pop of the eighties to Kraftwerk, the *kosmische musik* of the seventies, Tangerine Dream and Stockhausen, became a techno stronghold. The fall of the Wall in 1989 established Berlin as a European club capital, with techno as the soundtrack uniting post-communist East and capitalist West in extraordinary parties that occupied disused GDR bunkers, power stations and factories. Holland, Belgium, France, Spain, Italy, Japan, Australia; all adapted the music into novel forms, while long-haul destinations like Thailand and Goa became techno tourist spots. Ecstasy culture was also reimported into its country of origin, the United States, but not as part of the gay disco scene that inspired it; this remained subterranean and marginalised. Instead it was young, white Americans who appropriated elements of 1989's orbital extravaganzas to create their own rave circuit, embracing acid house's hippie trappings without irony. The result was a global dance network covering every region that possessed the First World wealth to sustain its decadence, but one that, in each country, bore ever-diminishing resemblance to the British blueprint: new mutations, new possibilities.

In the UK, Ecstasy culture had reshaped the leisure market, and no one in the business of youth entertainment could afford to ignore it. The brewers and distillers – like the record companies, who had at first seemed threatened by autonomous independents and bedroom-studio self-producers – looked like they had the most to lose. If a generation forsook alcohol for Ecstasy and pubs for raves, what might that mean for the profit margins of tomorrow? At the turn of the nineties, with economic recession at its height, many brewers began to worry that the shift might be irrevocable: a nascent nation of teetotallers fuelled by pills, powders and puff, drinking only Lucozade and Evian water. "Youngsters can get Ecstasy for £10 or £12 and get a much better buzz than they can from alcohol," said an anxious Richard Carr, chairman of Allied Leisure, the entertainment arm of the beer and spirits conglomerate Allied-Tetley-Lyons, in 1992. "It is a major threat to alcohol-led business."[8]

According to official statistics published the year afterwards, as drug offences rose, alcohol consumption fell. Pub attendances were also slowly diminishing. For an industry generating £25 billion a year, this was serious news. Evangelical E-heads looked down on "beer monsters" as lumbering, clumsy, unenlightened, potentially violent and likely to drunkenly harass women on the dancefloor, and regarded the traditional British pub as stultifyingly dull. The idea that alcohol intoxication had become unfashionable – coming from a generation that loved to quote the fact that while less than 100 people had died after taking Ecstasy in a decade, almost 30,000 people died from alcohol each year – scared the hell out of some brewers. Frazer Thompson, strategic development director at Whitbread, stated: "The young seem less prepared to sip beer for four hours. Culturally, they like short, sharp fixes."[9]

However, brewers weren't about to sit back and let customers slip away as club culture changed the nature of the youth market. Strategic planners applied their imagination to a whole range of new initiatives to woo back the crucial 18–24 age group, from "style bars" aimed at clubbers, playing house music and selling hip imported beers, to sponsorships of dance events and premium-strength lagers that could deliver that "short, sharp fix". Carlsberg-Tetley even contacted drug agencies about Amsterdam-style cannabis cafés in case of a change in the drug laws.

Three years after the first fears about a move to abstinence, Bass produced the "alcoholic lemonade" Hooch, the brand leader in the lucrative new "alco-pops" market – sweet, high-alcohol sodas aimed at those who hadn't gained the taste for beer or spirits. The packaging for some of the thirty brands on sale (marketed by a whole range of companies) was unashamedly appropriated from the dance scene: one was called Ravers; another, the alcoholic water DNA, had a glow-in-the-dark label which its manufacturers stated was "to enhance its fun value in nightclubs".

It appeared that some strategic planners had studied Ecstasy culture well, and were now packaging certain products *as drugs*: potent, instant stimuli, a hedonist kick. And as the honeymoon period faded, many were returning to the tried and tested legal drug – alcohol. Brewers had not lost a generation after all. The difference was that many clubbers now regarded beer and spirits as they would Ecstasy or cannabis, as another option in the polydrug pharmacoepia, one buzz among many. And the most insightful thinkers in the alcohol trade realised this. "People now treat alcohol as part of a repertoire of things that they're able to do rather than the only way of getting out of it," explained Whitbread's Frazer Thompson. "Five years ago there were less alternatives for getting high and getting a buzz. The challenge for the industry is to make alcohol part of that choice."

Alongside coffee, tea and cigarettes, alcohol is Britain's favourite drug, and the alcohol industry is one of the most powerful economic forces, and therefore political lobbies, in the country. As such, it became a target for radicals within the dance community who suggested that it colluded with Conservative government, to whose coffers some of its major players contributed, to secure the victory of its own legal intoxicant over dance drugs. Speculative conspiracy theories were regularly aired about brewers exerting their financial muscle on the Conservative Party to bring in anti-rave laws. Glenn Jenkins of Luton's Exodus sound system believes that lobbying from the alcohol industry contributed to Graham Bright's Entertainments (Increased Penalties) Act outlawing unlicensed raves in 1990, seeking to funnel customers away from alcohol-free events and back into licensed premises, and that deaths from Ecstasy-related heatstroke are a logical outcome of this legislation, as ravers were forced back into overheated clubs. "Dehydration is a British phenomenon because Britain passed the Entertainments law," he insists. "Who spiked the dancefloor? Was it the Es or was it the breweries?"

In 1995, the government raised the recommended limits of weekly alcohol consumption against the advice of the medical profession; World Health Organisation medical officer Maristella Monteiro accused it of "being in the pocket of the drinks industry".[10] A year later, new Home Office measures proposed a clampdown on dance clubs involving the closure of venues where drugs were available. The legal drug killed tens of thousands annually; the illegal drug hadn't yet killed a hundred (although the numbers using it were far fewer) — but did the perceived contradiction in attitudes constitute a coherent campaign, what counterculture periodical *Squall* called a "war for recreational drug control"?[11]

The last sector of the leisure industry to catch on to the financial potential of club culture was the book trade. But as the nineties progressed, Ecstasy tracts began to flood the market: from pulp-fiction drugsploitation and reverent profiles of DJs to self-published, independent works which were knocked out quickly and cheaply, like do-it-yourself white labels from bedroom house producers.

The most celebrated independent was an unlikely hero. In the early seventies, Nicholas Saunders had authored *Alternative London*, a guide to fringe pursuits in the capital. Now he was an earnest, balding gent on the far side of fifty, hardly a typical house-head; rather, as one commentator noted, "a trendy vicar on E, closer to that recognisable national type, the harmless English eccentric".[9] Saunders had fallen in love with MDMA in the eighties, and was distressed when what he considered a tonic for the soul was demonised by the press. In August 1992, he called a meeting in London's Covent Garden under the banner "Positive Aspects of MDMA", and began obsessively collating every bit of medical and scientific data he could find, publishing the results in book form from his desk-top design studio.

Saunders' trilogy – *E for Ecstasy, Ecstasy and the Dance Culture* and *Ecstasy Reconsidered* – became an underground success story. But although his mission was to combat misinformation while advancing his own belief that MDMA could be beneficial, particularly in spiritual and therapeutic contexts, Saunders was no Tim Leary. Like the American psychonauts he admired, he offered no wild slogans, simply statistics, reports and gentle persuasion delivered in an understated tone tinged with enthusiasm for the drug's virtues.

Saunders positioned himself as a kind of MDMA consultant to the dance scene, publishing monthly tests of Ecstasy pills' chemical constituencies on his World-Wide Web site, visiting drug researchers worldwide and reporting back on their progress via the Internet or in dance magazine *Eternity*. The reverence in which some clubbers held this tireless networker (he was even afforded a free supply of MDMA by one admirer) was another indication of how much people yearned for knowledge of a drug about which they were so well informed yet, paradoxically, knew so little.

But the extraordinary literary phenomenon of Ecstasy culture was an Edinburgh author called Irvine Welsh. Brought up in the cheerless Muirhouse housing scheme, Welsh had drifted through the fringes of the post-punk milieu, in and out of heroin addiction. In 1993, aged thirty-five, he delivered his masterwork, *Trainspotting*, a narrative of incandescent brilliance tracking the blind hopes and crazy dreams of a group of Edinburgh youths: junkies, people with AIDS, ravers, brawlers, boozers and losers. Within three years, around half a million copies of the book had been sold, and its film treatment had become one of most successful British movies of the decade.

Trainspotting was *the* cult text of the nineties not just because of Welsh's literary talent, but because it struck a deep chord with anyone who had been immersed in drug culture. A narrative alchemist with the kind of mastery of inner dialogue and dialect that characterised older Scottish writers like James Kelman, Welsh was more than a "rave author", but his surreal, often grim yet conversely life-affirming prose expertly delineated the hedonist's headspace. With the books that followed *Trainspotting*, he explored the social and emotional outlines of the club scene, becoming its icon and its bard. "One pill," he noted of his own transformation, "and nothing was ever the same again."

These two chroniclers of the chemical generation reflected some of the conflicting ideological strands that had characterised the culture since the entrepreneurial/recreational Texas Group of MDMA dealers had split from the therapeutic/spiritual Boston Group in the early eighties. "Is it a big shattering New Age thing?" asked Welsh. "Or is it just a more sophisticated way to get off your tits and have a good time?"[13] Those evangelising the gentle spiritual power of MDMA believed that it was some kind of sacrament and, if taken in the right circumstances, harmless.

They found it hard to understand why people would hammer four or five pills a night, topped up with wraps of speed, gulps of booze, snorts of amyl nitrate and lines of cocaine. Those with a grounding in street drug use retorted that the middle classes were insisting that their drug-taking was educated and superior, that what amounted to their own version of Ecstasy parties were somehow more meaningful than sweaty ravers getting "off their tits" in clubs.

If Saunders translated the concerns of the American neuroconsciousness movement – before he died in a car crash in 1998, he had started work on a book about "the use of psychoactive drugs for spiritual purposes" – Welsh dissected a tradition of proletarian hedonism that was handed down to Ecstasy culture from Northern Soul freaks, sharp mods and label-conscious football casuals who had lived for clothes, music, intoxicants and weekend lunacy. His characters were neither bohemians nor entirely conformist, but embodied the dissonance and contradictions between materialism and collectivism, between licit and illicit, that underpinned the nineties. In a country where the economic and social certainties of the past had evaporated, Welsh's voices mused, where politics had failed and the chasm between dreams and reality was widening, what better than to dress up and go crazy on a Saturday night? They were simply employing a logic that fitted their set and setting: turning in on themselves, retreating into the only world they could control – their own mental landscape and physical sensation. As one character in his fourth book, *Ecstasy*, suggested, it was almost their *duty* to party – to prove that, despite everything, they were still truly *alive*.

london and manchester

"Whoever it was that brought house music and Ecstasy and amphetamines together is a total genius and I want to shake that man's hand." Anonymous, *The Face*, November 1991

"I was taking five times as much as everyone else. Because everyone used to take Es as tablets, we'd snort it. We wanted to experiment more. I was an addict, definitely. It was the wonder drug. I just took as many as possible. I was getting into sort of a coma, being sick, paranoia ... disorientation, anxiety, confusion ... it was an alarm bell. It all built up to a point where everything fell apart ... it was like being on the crest of a wave and falling ... If I had carried on for a further six months, I don't think I would have survived. I would have lost it totally ... lost my mind. Ecstasy is really good to break down barriers but it can also destroy. It destroyed a lot of confidence in myself, my self-respect ... I abused the drug so it abused me in the end." Gary McClarnan, *Young People Now*, April 1992

In the nineties, recreational drug use in Britain underwent a process of democratisation that mirrored the evolution of dance culture. The Home Office graph of drug seizures had remained almost horizontal in the years leading up to the birth of acid house. Then it dipped slightly, as if it was drawing breath, and just as it nosed its way into 1988 it went completely berserk, charging upwards relentlessly. In the seven years that followed, the value of the drug economy grew by over 500 per cent – particularly the amounts of Ecstasy, amphetamines, cannabis and LSD. A causative link is impossible to prove, but the year that acid house turned Ecstasy into a dance drug, drug consumption exploded.

One of the central dynamics of Ecstasy culture is the attempt to recreate the initial euphoria. This opened out new vistas of creative potential, as initiates explored fresh directions according to their own perception of that primal experience. In terms of drug use, however, the attempt to relive the exhilarating high, to chase the thrill of the rush, produced a recreational drug culture on a scale that eclipsed anything that has existed in Britain at any time this century. It is difficult to overstate the impact that Ecstasy had on young people's perception of drug-taking. It was, many believed, not only an alternative to alcohol and tobacco, but a *less harmful* alternative, an axiom that was then extended to justify drug consumption across the board.

To the thousands of people who had never taken illicit substances, Ecstasy's innocuous appearance was the opposite of everything they had ever been told about drugs. There were no hypodermic needles involved, no grim paraphernalia or ritualistic preparation. It was, literally, an easy pill to swallow, and it came packaged, not as a drug cult, but as the ultimate entertainment concept, with its own music, clubs, dress codes – and to many it was the euphoric peak of a lifetime. In the eighties, government drug campaigns had hectored young people with images of addicts resembling pox-ridden anorexics, but these were far removed from their own experiences of Ecstasy. Thousands of sunny smiles, the chatter of positivity, embracing total strangers – little wonder that Ecstasy's overriding impact was to give people an overwhelmingly positive experience of illegal drug use. Armed with belief in what appeared to be an unassailable logic and glowing with the euphoria of MDMA, the "chemical generation" passed through the doors of perception into a world where drugs were not only acceptable, but all-consumingly glorious.

By 1991, things were changing, both culturally and chemically, as the initial innocence began to fade. The year was characterised by vicious recession, the outbreak of war and heightened economic uncertainty; the perfect time for excess and escape. Dance culture unconsciously reflected this. Acid house had elevated hedonism to the status of dogma; now many seemed to believe that pleasure was their *right*, and as increased Ecstasy ingestion led to diminishing returns and the music accelerated in velocity, some began to searched for a higher buzz, *beyond* MDMA. They started to explore a range of psychoactive stimulants, taking them in any and every combination – from alcohol to amphetamines, cocaine, LSD, amyl nitrate, cannabis, ketamine, "natural highs" such as the caffeine-like Guarana, the growth hormone stimulant-cum-psychedelic GHB – anything to heighten the intoxication, to get further *out there*.

By this time Ecstasy culture was no longer driven by MDMA alone. Although amphetamines, LSD and cannabis had always been and continued to be more popular than MDMA, they had never defined the prevailing mood; now, however, the culture had become what drug experts call a "polydrug" scene. The Californian MDMA advocates had believed that the drug had no abuse potential – but they were taking occasional doses in controlled, comfortable settings with specific therapeutic goals. Hedonists had redefined their spiritual "tool". But were they now chasing unrealistic expectations?

"Ecstasy is such a pleasurable experience that you want to repeat it. And you want to repeat it as often as possible. In retrospect, I'd say I became completely addicted. I took thirty-eight Es one week – I used to start as soon as I got up." By 1991, this rock journalist had become a renowned character on the London Balearic scene; like countless others, he was "serving up" in clubs to finance his own prodigious drug consumption. One night, without knowing, he sold a batch of capsules containing the anaesthetic ketamine, a "dissociative" drug that detaches the mind from the body – hence its efficacy in battlefield amputations and veterinary operations, and its sometimes frightening impact in nightclubs. "I thought it was E," he says. "Somebody gave it to me, clear plastic pills full of white powder. I said: 'What is it?' He said: 'It's like Ecstasy, but better.' I said: 'Is it Ecstasy?' He said: 'I'm not really sure, but it does the trick.' I actually dealt the whole lot that night – it caused absolute fucking chaos. One woman was lying on the ground, crying. *But lots of people kept coming back!*"

Although this was an extreme example, it was nonetheless representative of a significant minority. As the forty-eight-hour weekenders pushed the envelope, the language also altered. People no longer talked about "getting on one", but "getting off my face". While some cut down or dropped out of the scene, the chemical extremists cranked up the buzz, wolfing down more pills, speed or cocaine, and they soon found that palliatives were necessary to return from orbit and manage the crushing comedown. Some did it with booze and spliffs, others with prescription tranquillisers like Temazepam, a few with heroin. People became expert manipulators of mood, choosing exactly what to take in each situation to produce specific psychopharma-ceutical responses, applying sophisticated cost–benefit analyses to each substance. They had turned into drug adepts.

It was also in 1991 that many began to realise that Ecstasy was not the miracle pill they had once believed it to be. People were ending up in hospital after long nights on the dancefloor. A few were dying, and dying horribly, with blood pouring from every hole in their body. The numbers were minuscule, but the percep-tion of Ecstasy as a safe recreational drug was being seriously questioned for the first time.

The sporadic fatalities that had occurred in 1988 and 1989, which had been viewed as freak accidents and largely dismissed by clubbers who wanted to believe that "their" drug was inno-cent, now seemed to form some kind of emerging pattern. Talk in clubs was about mouth ulcers, blackouts, confusion and depression, projectile vomit, creaking joints, aching guts and unusual bowel movements. The finger was pointed at dealers and manufacturers, who were accused of cutting pills with every-thing from heroin to rat poison. While it was undoubtedly true that Ecstasy was being adulterated with what later transpired were harmless substances, it was also in 1991 that MDA began to reappear on the nocturnal marketplace. Compared to its chemical cousin MDMA, it was a heavy-duty experience – clubbers called it "smacky", erroneously believing that its exaggerated impact derived from some kind of heroin concoction – and could some-times incapacitate the body. The influx of MDA "Snowballs" resulted in squatting rows of cabbaged clubbers clinging desper-ately onto walls: *monged out*. "Es are not as good as they used to be," was the collective moan that echoed around the dancehalls.

The first journalist to take stock of the changing mood was Mandi James, who had witnessed Ecstasy turning to excess, nights out evolving into sleepless, psychotropic weekends of what could only be called abuse, in her hometown of Manchester. In *The Face* in November 1991, she attempted to gather the sum knowledge on the health risks of Ecstasy use in Britain at the time. It didn't amount to much. "Never before have there been so many people going to clubs, so many people consuming drugs about which we really know very little," she wrote.[14] It was the first time that any youth magazine had uttered what had previously been considered a heresy in club circles – that Ecstasy could be detrimental to health – but apart from common-sense information about scoring from reliable sources and replacing body fluids that had been sweated out in hot club environments, all James was able to conclude was: *slow down*.

The year before, Manchester drug agency Lifeline had issued the first edition of its drug-awareness comic *E by Gum!*, featuring cartoon hero Peanut Pete, a pop-eyed scally perennially buzzing off his nut, pulling on a spliff and simultaneously dispensing no-nonsense advice. Lifeline coupled cutting-edge drug knowledge with a harsh realist outlook untainted by romanticism about "counterculture" or "consciousness expansion". Within a few years, it would become as much a part of the fabric of club culture as DJs, and its propagation of self-preservation rituals through the dance media would undoubtedly save lives.

The idea for *E by Gum!* had come out of *Smack in the Eye*, a comic for heroin users that Lifeline had produced in 1987. The strip was designed as a *Furry Freak Brothers*-style underground comic and employed the black humour and street vernacular of the user to get information across without sermonising. At the time, its explicitness was a radical departure. "We were interviewed by the Director of Public Prosecutions twice and several other drugs agencies wrote to the Department of Health trying to get our funding stopped," recalls its designer Mike Linnell. "We expected the flak to come from the media, but all the criticism came from the professionals." Lifeline's philosophy was "harm reduction": accepting that people were going to take drugs whatever they were told, and that the only reasonable response was to minimise the risks. Initially this meant needle exchange schemes and methadone maintenance prescriptions to minimise the spread of AIDS among heroin injectors.

When the first reports about acid house began to filter through to the drug agencies, they hadn't known how to respond. In the eighties, the key issue was heroin addiction and HIV, and Ecstasy was a qualitatively different drug than they had experienced, used by a group of people they had never come into contact with. Their initial response, if any, was to view it in terms of HIV risk, to hand out condoms and advise people to practise safe sex; Ecstasy, they had heard, was a love drug. Still focused on opiate dependency, the only additional information they could offer was legal – the reminder that this was a Class A substance, and possession could mean prison. Now Lifeline and others had begun to apply harm-reduction thinking to Ecstasy users, yet, for all its success, *E by Gum!* had next to nothing to say about the drug itself. "One of the most interesting things about Ecstasy," the text shrugged, "is how little we know about it."[15]

There had been moral panics over MDMA when the scene first took hold in 1988 and 1989, but since then, the newspapers seemed to have forgotten about Ecstasy and its culture altogether, or perhaps believed that it had been neutered when the illegal raves were contained in legitimate venues after the Entertainments (Increased Penalties) Act. In June 1991, the multi-million-selling right-wing tabloid, *The Sun*, had even declared that "rave is all the fave", publishing a four-page pull-out guide to the "hot dance craze", which instructed, at the height of hardcore mania: "Forget the shock and horror of acid house. Raving is about good, clean fun . . . Drugs of any kind are considered to be very uncool."[16]

The first wave of harm-reduction leaflets, compounded by Mandi James's article, reactivated the panic, throwing the tabloids into a frenzy of scare stories, vilification and abuse directed at Ecstasy users and harm-reduction advocates alike, ranting and screaming about a nation's youth, as one headline put it, "In the Grip of E". Coroners' reports were unearthed and galleries of dead Ecstasy users' portraits paraded, the drug agencies excoriated for "telling kids it's OK to use the killer drug".[17] Ultimately, questions were tabled in Parliament. Conservative MP Gerald Howarth demanded that the Home Secretary withdraw funding from Release, which had published a leaflet on harm reduction, "until such time as it sends a clear message to young people about drugs – namely 'no, no, no'."[18]

The alarm was redoubled in the summer of 1992, when a doctor at the National Poisons Unit, John Henry, published two papers in medical journals, one of which was sensationally titled *Ecstasy and the Dance of Death*. Henry and his colleagues had been inspired to investigate after a "striking increase" in inquiries about the drug to the Poisons Unit during 1991.[19] His analysis of seven MDMA fatalities armed the tabloids with a cornucopia of toxic reactions to the drug: extreme temperatures, convulsions, blood clotting disorders, muscle breakdown, kidney failure, liver problems, jaundice. "Ecstasy is widely misrepresented as being safe," he noted, going on to warn that the deaths, however small in number, might be an indication of a far worse catastrophe in the future.[20] "These few people who have died are tragic, but the critical factor is the possibility of long-term damage. What we have going on at the moment is a massive experiment, and we will only know the full answers in years to come."

Henry's theory, which was immediately accepted by all but a minority, was that people dancing all night in hot, crowded environments, sweating out body fluids and not replenishing them, were in danger of overheating and death; the symptoms of heatstroke. The picture of a grey-suited, stern uncle, Henry delivered the catchphrase that he would repeat again and again over the coming years: "Taking Ecstasy is like playing Russian roulette."[21] However, even though dance magazine *Mixmag* felt concerned enough to question, "Has the nightmare finally begun?", Ecstasy-equals-death was not a message that clubbers wanted to hear.[22] It was generally rejected as anti-drug propaganda: unthinkable, impossible, another con trick from an establishment whose drug policy made no distinction between heroin and MDMA (while embracing alcohol and nicotine) and the summit of whose reasoning was "just say no" – not to mention a tabloid press whose currency was misinformation and lies. Ecstasy would breed a generation of cabbages – wasn't that what they had said about LSD in the sixties? They should try some themselves, that would chill them out a bit, it was often said. Then they'd know the score.

Whatever his agenda, John Henry had offered the first coherent explanation for Ecstasy deaths. At last there was a proper medical syndrome – heatstroke – and clubbers could ease their fears with the reassurance that the dangers of overdoing it could be avoided. Liaising with the Poisons Unit, the drug agencies had already started to offer guidelines for minimising the risk of dehydration, including the advice to drink "about a pint of water every hour". Keep cool, don't overexert yourself and you'll be OK, was the message.

Armed with the first hard medical information about Ecstasy use in the UK, the agencies began to target the clubs themselves. Leeds City Council had already introduced special conditions for clubs that included a supply of free tap water, and in January 1993, with the backing of Manchester City Council, Lifeline launched its Safer Dancing Campaign. The Campaign's code of conduct included the monitoring of temperature and air quality, chill-out areas, cold water taps and the provision of drug risk information. For clubbers long used to venues that resembled overpopulated greenhouses with only expensive bottled water for relief, such guidelines were a long overdue triumph for common sense. Finally, chorused agencies and clubbers in unison, something was being achieved: safer environments for Ecstasy use. And with the message hitting home, concern shifted to the drug itself.

In October 1993, *Time Out* ran a feature that articulated the predominant preoccupation of that year – the fact that what was being sold as Ecstasy was rarely MDMA. "Thousands of lives are at risk as spiked Ecstasy tablets flood the capital," warned the magazine.[23] By this time there was as much MDA and MDEA on the market as MDMA. Concern was raised about whether either drug might be more dangerous, but the central anxiety surrounded the issue of "dodgy gear". "Drug agency workers believe that adulteration with heroin, LSD and even crushed glass and rat poison will eventually force casual users to shun the drug because of horrific side-effects," suggested *Time Out*.[24] The crushed glass scare story proved to be based on an unreliable anecdote, and the heroin information was only half right: heroin had never been found in tablets that contained MDMA; it had, however, been found in a handful of pills designed to simulate Ecstasy that included other substances such as ephedrine. The article touched on the clubland paranoia of the time, reinforcing the commonly held beliefs of Ecstasy users themselves – that contaminated pills, not MDMA itself, were dangerous.

It took three deaths at the Ayr club Hangar 13 the following year for this belief to be brought into doubt. These were the first Ecstasy-related fatalities in Scotland, and they shocked clubbers and drug agencies into a panic of speculation. Rogue batches of Ecstasy cut with ketamine and other impurities, the ingestion of GHB, the suggestion that MDA was some kind of "killer Ecstasy"; all were cited as possible causes. Some sensationalist reports blamed it on the "macho" Scottish rave scene, painting the club as a kind of disco death camp where bare-chested teenage schemies necked handfuls of Es on top of wraps of speed, Temazepam "jellies" and bottles of cheap, strong Buckfast tonic wine, inflaming themselves to the borders of oblivion with a brutal techno din. There was a collective refusal to believe that Ecstasy, the miracle drug, the innocent empathogen of Californian dream and acid house Summers of Love, could have been the cause of death. And yet at the subsequent inquiry into the deaths, it was revealed that all three dead youths had taken MDMA.

The truth was that received wisdom about Ecstasy was little more than a collage of unproven suppositions, prejudices, vested interests and misinformation, often amplified by journalists who recycled fallacies and oversimplifications from each other's articles as if they were gospel. The intricate nuances and grey areas of scientific debate hardly made for definitive and thrilling news copy, as one British doctor noted: "Most people want an answer. I've talked to a lot of people in the media, and they want to know, is it safe or is it not safe? Is it safer than alcohol, or is alcohol more dangerous? Is it safer than tobacco? And these are questions which we simply can't answer. Science isn't black and white."

Could Ecstasy really kill, or was heatstroke to blame? Did it cause some kind of irrevocable brain damage? No one could even agree on how many people had died through Ecstasy use. Some, gleaning their information from press cuttings and coroners' reports, suggested it was around sixty in ten years, and that the chance of death, if it was assumed that half a million pills were consumed per week, was one in millions. Others, like John Henry, insisted the fatalities ran at nearly fifty *per year*; it was just that many were not reported. Others disputed the amount of Es consumed; the figure was less, they insisted, or more. And what about the people who were physically damaged but didn't die? How did they figure in the calculations? Nobody really had a clue.

There was more consensus on the question of why exactly people died after taking MDMA. Of the Ecstasy-related deaths in Britain, most had displayed the same heatstroke-like symptoms: fits, loss of consciousness, unusually high body temperatures, muscle disintegration, sometimes liver damage and kidney failure, and what is known as "disseminated introvascular coagulation", when the blood loses its ability to clot and the victim suffers uncontrollable internal bleeding, blood filling the body and pouring out of every orifice, including the eyes: a complete system breakdown. The second explanation was an idiosyncratic reaction – that some people might have a susceptibility to the drug, and that one person's normal dose was their overdose. Water intoxication, or "dilutional hyponatremia", was a third, additional explanation, advanced after three Ecstasy casualties were found to have drunk large amounts of fluid, diluting the blood, swelling the brain and thus causing death. This hypothesis caused drug agencies to swiftly rethink their advice about drinking a pint of water per hour; it appeared that some clubbers, like twenty-year-old Andrew Naylor from Derby, who drank twenty-six pints of water before expiring, were taking their advice a little too seriously. "Water is an antidote to heatstroke, not Ecstasy," became Lifeline's new slogan.

Despite the folk myths that resounded through clubland, there was, however, no evidence that anyone had died as a result of taking contaminated Ecstasy. Although, by the mid-nineties, only about 40 per cent of the pills in circulation were actually MDMA (the rest were mainly MDA or MDEA, plus a few ketamine/ ephedrine/amphetamine fakes), no toxic disasters had been unearthed, confirmed the police forensic laboratory at Aldermaston. Nevertheless, words like "contamination" and "adulteration" were still bandied about, both by clubbers who felt that "real E" couldn't kill and by anti-drugs propagandists who believed the scare would put people off taking Ecstasy.

But if no one really knew what Ecstasy did to the body, how could they quantify its effects on the mind? This was, after all, a chemical that had been popular among therapists for its ability to break down psychological barriers. What would happen when huge numbers of people took huge amounts of it for years on end – would those defences crumble for ever? Each successive generation of initiates developed its own oral history of mental deterioration, of Ecstasy casualties "losing it", having nervous breakdowns, being institutionalised, even committing suicide. Were these just people who were halfway to insanity already, and the long sleepless weekends had simply pushed them over the line? Was the drug itself to blame? Or was it just a way to explain away the inexplicable?

In 1991, the first reports of paranoid psychosis and depression began to appear in British medical journals. While these featured a handful of individual cases, mainly people who were already psychotic and bingeing to excess, drug agencies also began to take calls from clubbers reporting moodiness and weird psychological states. Dr Karl Jansen of London's Maudsley Hospital, a specialist in drug-related psychiatric problems, suggested that "everybody who takes a lot of E is going to punch holes in the wall between consciousness and unconsciousness because of the nature of the drug. If you take a drug that is an emotional releaser, and do that repeatedly, then you are going to bring about some psychological changes."

Jansen compared the current situation with MDMA to that of amphetamines – once a popular prescription drug – in previous decades. "It was not until the late 1960s that it was officially accepted that amphetamines were addictive and that amphet-amine-induced paranoid psychosis was relatively common among heavy users. This picture took decades to form. With respect to Ecstasy, deleterious effects upon serotonin were found in 1985, and it is really the 1990s which have seen an increasing frequency of reported psychiatric complications . . . Our understanding of the actual relative risk from this drug is at an early stage."[25]

And yet, he qualified, mental hospitals were not full of Ecstasy casualties. Check the wards for yourself, he invited. "It's not a big problem compared to the number of people with alcohol-induced hallucinosis, who are psychotic with the DTs, suicidal when drunk. It is nothing compared to the effect of alcohol on your mental health."

There was a big gap between the hopeless grey mood of the midweek comedown, the Ecstasy hangover that most clubbers learned how to deal with, and Dr John Henry's bleak prediction that Ecstasy might create a future generation of manic depressives. Once again, tangible facts were hard to come by.

Even in America, where genuine research into the effects of MDMA was continuing, albeit on a tiny scale, there were more questions than answers, and the more results that were published, the more confused the big picture became. When Ecstasy was made illegal in America in 1985, the reason given was that scientists had shown that it might cause brain damage in humans. The evidence was based on animal experiments, and one of the neurologists involved, Dr George Ricaurte of Baltimore, had been on a mission ever since to conclude the case. What he discovered in the ten years following criminalisation was that in some animals, levels of serotonin – a neurotransmitter in the brain that affects mood – failed to return to normal levels for up to eighteen months after being given MDMA. Low levels of serotonin, some experts believed, were linked to depression, aggressive behaviour and suicide, but exactly how was unclear.

However, the injections that Ricaurte gave his rats and monkeys were many times greater than typical human doses, and he admitted not only that "we did not set out to mimic human MDMA use", but that, in another study he carried out on long-term human users, hostile and impulsive behaviour seemed to be reduced, not exaggerated. How relevant was the research, people demanded? Ricaurte responded: "I think it is important to recognise that, particularly in the rave situation, there are individuals who are taking six, eight or ten tablets over a twenty-four to forty-eight-hour period. So some of the more recent patterns of human MDMA use in the rave setting are beginning to mimic the regimen of drug administration that we employed in our monkeys." What did Ricaurte believe he had proved? "The message should be that MDMA has neurotoxic potential." That Ecstasy *could* cause brain damage in *some* animals. Maybe.

The debate continued: could his results be extrapolated from animals to humans? And did serotonin depletion actually constitute "brain damage"? Ricaurte thought that there was some connection (one that the British media was perennially quoting and exaggerating), but, again, he was not exactly sure what it was: "It's important to underscore that we don't fully understand the functional role of serotonin in the human brain," he said. Another American scientist, Dr James O'Callaghan of the National Institute for Occupational Safety and Health, also studied neurotoxicity, again giving MDMA to animals. He found serotonin depletion in some species but, confusingly, not in others, and concluded that while serotonin depletion might be unwelcome, it was not the same thing as brain damage.

A crucial turning point in American MDMA research came in 1994, when, on May 18th, Dr Charles Grob of the Harbor-UCLA Medical Centre in California became the first American doctor to legally give MDMA to a human being since criminalisation – another advance for the neuroconsciousness movement led by the indefatigable Rick Doblin's Multidisciplinary Association for Psychedelic Studies, which now felt confident enough to talk of some kind of worldwide "psychedelic renaissance". Would such research have been allowed to continue if the brain damage argument had been conclusively won, they asked? The results of Grob's programme of tests stressed two key points: that MDMA caused a small increase in core body temperature, despite the fact that his patients were lying immobile in a hospital bed, not waving their hands in the air on a humid dancefloor – which seemed to suggest that the drug itself did contribute to heatstroke – and that there was a mild but persistent elevation of blood pressure, making MDMA potentially problematic to people with heart conditions.

Grob was studying the effects of occasional Ecstasy use in a therapeutic setting with a view to the potential treatment of terminal cancer patients, not its use in sweaty nightclubs. "We're at the very early stages," he commented cautiously, "because before, research like this was not permitted. I think the most important thing we've accomplished is that research on humans can be done." It was a beginning, but its relevance to dance-drug culture was limited. There was no indication as to what might happen if a subject was to ingest a cocktail of, say, Ecstasy, speed, alcohol and cigarettes, then dance for four hours. Indeed, there had been no scientific studies on the synergistic effects of the kind of polydrug use that was common in Britain.

The American MDMA research was characterised by contra-dictions and uncertainties. All that some of the scientists had in common were phrases like "I'm not sure", "we don't know", "there is insufficient data" and "sometimes we have problems replicating these results". There was little agreement and no love lost between researchers with different ideological agendas; some funded by the National Institute for Drug Abuse, whose vested interest was in deterring drug use, and others linked to the neuroconsciousness movement, which was lobbying for prescrip-tion use of MDMA. Unsurprisingly, the lack of concrete information that characterised British thinking on Ecstasy was a reflection of the situation across the Atlantic.

No one could pinpoint exactly how MDMA produced its unique empathetic high, other than that it was linked to the release of neurotransmitters like serotonin and dopamine. On top of that, knowledge of the workings of the brain itself was strictly limited. There was heated debate over MDMA's effects and whether they were harmful, and no one could confirm exactly how or why it could kill. The only certainty was that, since 1988, in Britain, an unspecified number of people had died after taking the drug, many with symptoms that resembled heatstroke. Anyone following the evolving debate, hoping to establish a set of irrefutable facts about Ecstasy, soon found that these were still very few indeed.

basildon, essex

"I wouldn't touch 'Ecstasy' nowadays, not unless Dr Alexander Shulgin himself appeared, clutching a vial of crystalline powder and saying: 'I've just synthesised a fresh batch, care to try some, m'boy?'" Colin Angus of The Shamen, 1995

There were no celebrations to mark 1995, the thirtieth anniversary of Alexander Shulgin's rediscovery of MDMA, but it was a watershed year for the drug culture that his backyard synthesis had enabled. Since the sixties, Shulgin had laboured to find a substance with magical effects that excelled those of Ecstasy – without success, he admitted. Now his "penicillin for the soul" finally emerged into the searching glare of public scrutiny, exposed for all to see.

Across the Atlantic, in the Essex village of Latchingdon, near Basildon, in the early hours of November 12th, a young girl was bent, retching violently, over the washbasin in her parents' bathroom. Her pupils were massively dilated. Her legs were numb. Her head throbbed with pain and her body jerked rigidly. She was sick and scared, screaming: "Please help me!" Then she collapsed into a coma from which she would never wake.

It was the kind of story that even a soap opera would have rejected as implausible. Leah Betts took the Ecstasy pill that killed her at her eighteenth birthday party, a party where her parents – her father a former police officer, her stepmother a volunteer anti-drugs worker – were in attendance. She was white, affluent, a college student, an English Rose, and lived not in the metropolitan sleaze of London or Manchester, nor the sink schemes of Scotland, but in a sleepy village in the heart of the Tory southeast: a daughter of Middle England. Anykid.

Betts remained in a coma for a week, enabling the tabloid media to crank up the momentum, dramatising the saga in bold front-page headlines, day after day, as her parents struggled to decide whether to switch the life support system off. It was, cynics pointed out, a tale so perfect in its every detail that even tabloid editors couldn't have invented it, and it fired the lengthiest and most hysterical drug panic of the decade. The tabloids produced warning posters of the comatose girl in her deathbed, launched "War on Drugs" campaigns, endorsed phone lines encouraging people to "shop a dealer". Many sent undercover reporters out to catch the "murderers" who supplied Betts, omitting to mention that, in legal terms, it was her friend who had given her the tablet and was therefore guilty of the crime.

When Leah Betts died on November 16th, the feeding frenzy didn't abate; it intensified. Her parents were determined to use her death as an anti-drugs parable, allowing a video of her funeral to be distributed to schools and her face to be used on a nationwide billboard campaign. The huge posters were a deeply strange and unsettling sight: framed in a black border like an obituary to the culture, a photograph of the teenager, smiling and carefree, shoulder-length hair swept back over her chubby cheeks, with the single word slogan writ large: "Sorted". Under her image was the grim warning: "Just one Ecstasy tablet took Leah Betts". They were plastered all over 1,500 inner-city hoardings; Leah Betts had become, in death, Ecstasy culture's first pin-up, more famous than she could ever have imagined, a symbol not of innocence defiled but of the chasm in understanding between generations.

More than anyone, Betts transformed the image of the drug-taker forever. Broadsheet press editors, who for years had been recycling "Agony of Ecstasy" headlines, realised this, and descended into a miasma of soul-searching. They had discovered that the people who took Ecstasy were their sons and daughters. "This is a nightmare for parents," agonised *The Sunday Times*. "Leah always told her mother and father she was appalled by drugs. But perhaps, like so many youngsters, she did not see Ecstasy as a drug at all."[26]

It was as if they had stumbled on an alien universe that had somehow existed for years, unknown and unseen, within their own society. They found a culture that previously had been invisible, a world where drugs were good, not bad; normal, not deviant. Journalists were dispatched to nightclubs, returning with shocked reports: educated, middle-class people – doctors, lawyers, journalists, people like themselves! – *loved* Ecstasy. The sheer volume of coverage suggested that the drug had touched something deep within the national psyche. Ultimately, many editors began to embrace harm-reduction strategies, even call for decriminalisation. *The Independent* went furthest, stating: "Young people such as Leah Betts need to be protected. The way to do that is to understand what they are consuming and control its quality. That may mean making it a substance whose use is frowned upon, but not criminalised: like smoking or parking on double yellow lines."[27] It was a new chapter in the history of moral panics over drugs, yet it was motivated by simple realism, as framed in a headline in *The Times*: "Dangers will not make us change our habit, say Ecstasy users."[28]

This was true, and confirmed by the speculation rocketing around the clubs as to why Betts died. Was it dodgy gear? Had she drunk too much booze on top of the E? Many, as usual, refused to believe that MDMA was to blame. One contributor to an Internet e-mail list even sneered that Betts was a "light-weight who couldn't handle her drugs". Although for some, doubts raised by the American scientific papers were crystallised by Betts's death, a vox pop of clubbers in *Mixmag* confirmed *The Times*'s observation: it was tragic, certainly, but it was some kind of freak accident that wouldn't put most people off swallowing another pill that Saturday. "There's been plenty of deaths," said one. "You just go out and do it the next weekend." "Alcohol rots your brain and your guts and no one stops drinking when someone dies from that," insisted another. "I know the risks, and I'm willing to keep on taking them."[29] The largest-ever survey of British Ecstasy users, conducted by Lifeline and *Mixmag* in 1996, offered yet more evidence: as the nineties progressed, more people had tried Ecstasy for the first time each year, and few anticipated giving it up in the near future.

The picture became increasingly unclear. A study in the northeast of England suggested that the "Sorted" billboard campaign had encouraged more young people to try Ecstasy. Jim Carey of *Squall* noted that the "Sorted" posters were produced by an advertising agency, Knight Leach Delaney, and a "youth consultancy", FFI, both of whom were also involved in promoting Red Bull, an "energy drink" which was, according to FFI's Mark Mathieson, "very popular at the moment because it's a substitute for taking Ecstasy".[30] Carey believed that the agencies were employing scare tactics to sell their product. Meanwhile, rumours circulated that dealers had begun selling pills named "Leahs".

Although what Leah Betts had taken was MDMA and the cause of death was given as "Ecstasy poisoning", after the coroner's inquest, Dr John Henry stated his belief that it was actually the result of water intoxication: dilutional hyponatremia. Betts had panicked when the experience turned bad, and gulped down enough liquid to kill her. Perhaps there was also something about Ecstasy that interfered with the kidneys' ability to process fluid, or perhaps it induced compulsive behaviour. It further transpired that, contradicting the seraphic image the tabloids had marketed, this wasn't the first time she had taken the drug. Ultimately, despite the fact that the furore had brought the sum of medical knowledge on MDMA into the popular domain, launching scientific terms like "serotonin" and "neurotoxicity" into the pages of youth magazines and the vocabulary of clubland, the ideological lines held: the Ecstasy evangelists argued that MDMA hadn't killed her. Their opponents pointed out that if she hadn't taken it she wouldn't be dead.

Essex police poured huge resources into tracking down the dealers who sold the drug to Leah Betts. Thirty-five officers were involved in an investigation which lasted over a year. But after a prosecution costing an estimated £300,000, the only people who were convicted of supplying Ecstasy to Betts were three teenagers – her friends, Stephen Smith, who was given a conditional discharge, Sarah Cargill and Louise Yexley, both of whom were cautioned. Each had admitted the offence; none went to prison. Another friend, Steven Packman, was acquitted after a retrial.

During Packman's trial, a very ordinary tale of drug distribution emerged, typical of the many thousands of petty deals which had taken place each weekend for almost a decade all over Britain. A nineteen-year-old student bought some pills for his girlfriend in an unremarkable provincial nightclub. The girl passed them on to her mates, who took them at a birthday party. None of them considered themselves drug dealers or criminals; they were just helping out friends. "I didn't realise I was doing anything wrong or illegal," said one, naively. Money changed hands, but no profit was sought or gained. The "evil dealer" was the clean-cut, suburban college chum. The "murderer" was the best friend.

The case did, however, expose the criminal underworld which kept Ecstasy culture and its nightlife in business. A few months after Betts' death, Detective Chief Superintendent Anthony White of the Metropolitan Police had tried to explain to Ecstasy users, through the pages of *Mixmag*, exactly who was profiting from their pleasures: "Ecstasy is a mass-produced drug, and the people who produce it and traffic it are extremely high up in the criminal hierarchy. They don't look like clubbers, they don't look like the lead singer of The Prodigy, they look like me. They're big, violent, sad old gits, they're scumballs. They have no view on drugs other than making profit out of them."[31] This came closer to the truth than many would care to admit.

Leah Betts' pill was purchased at Raquels, a Basildon dance club whose door staff were part of a gang which controlled the drug dealing in numerous venues around Essex, Suffolk and south London. In *So This is Ecstasy?*, his vicious, illuminating autobiography, gang member Bernard O'Mahoney (alias Patrick Mahoney, alias Bernie King), the head doorman at Raquels, detailed their activities. As well as selling Ecstasy, O'Mahoney alleges they stole drugs shipments from other gangs, took protection money, carried out punishment beatings and enforced debt collection with violence. Most of them carried weapons constantly – knives, machetes, ammonium sprays, handguns – and weren't averse to using them. They also enjoyed the drugs that their dealers sold.

"Nobody connected to us paid to get in anywhere. Nobody paid for drugs," stated O'Mahoney. "Huge bags of cocaine, Special K [Ketamine] and Ecstasy were made available to the firm and their associates."[32] Any rogue dealers selling drugs in "their" clubs would have their money and pills confiscated, and possibly be beaten up. Club managements turned a blind eye to the gang's business. "They knew it was the drug culture which was filling their club to capacity. They were hardly going to root out the very thing that caused this new interest. It's the same story all over the country with rave clubs: what else do people think kids do in a club for eight to ten hours where there's no alcohol on sale?" The clubs would continue to insist that they were doing everything in their power to prevent drug use: "The line was that these people took drugs while queuing up. We could search them, but we couldn't be held responsible for anything they did outside. As usual, it was bollocks."[33]

As the gang's operations became more lucrative, their drug intake accelerated: "People had turned to cocaine trying to reach the elusive high that had faded as their bodies became used to the effects of Ecstasy," recalled O'Mahoney. "Instead of one or two Ecstasy pills per evening, some were consuming between eight and twelve. They were topping that up with lines of cocaine and amphetamine sulphate." Many of them rapidly crossed the line into paranoid psychosis, and the random brutality escalated. "The violence and the excessive use of cocaine had turned the meekest of men into explosive psychopaths."[34]

O'Mahoney, who also worked as a bouncer at the Ministry of Sound on occasions, had links with many other London

gangsters, armed robbers and contract killers, including sixties
kingpins and convicted murderers, the Kray Twins. His book put
many of the beatific myths about Ecstasy culture into stark
context. Organised crime, he explained, had become synonymous with the Ecstasy trade: "Drugs had riddled every part of
the underworld like a cancer. The unlikeliest of men had become
involved. Everyone had some connection, whether it was as
enforcers for the dealers, importers or wholesale stockists. Even
car dealers were used to clean drug money. Reggie [Kray], who
epitomised the old school, began using drugs and looking at the
money that could be made in deals . . . Reggie had started using
Ecstasy, cocaine and cannabis. He was always asking what was
going on in the clubs . . . For Reggie's birthday, the firm were
going to send him in a parcel of Ecstasy and cocaine to
celebrate."[35]

The central figure within the "firm" was Tony Tucker, a
bodybuilder, steroid freak and friend of world champion boxer
Nigel Benn; Tucker used to lead Benn into the ring before his
fights. At first he was "the quietest, deepest person I ever met",
insisted O'Mahoney, but a combination of Ecstasy and steroids
turned him savage: he once forced a man who had crossed him
over a drug deal to take massive doses of cocaine and Ketamine,
injected him in the groin with yet more drugs until he was
unconscious, then dumped him in a ditch and left him to die.

Less than a month after Leah Betts' death, Tucker and two
other gang members, Pat Tate and Craig Rolfe, were themselves
found dead in Rolfe's metallic blue Range Rover on a desolate
country lane near Rettendon, Essex – an area in which some of
1989's largest raves had taken place. Each of them had been shot.
"When news of the Range Rover shooting came through, I rang
Tony Tucker's mobile number," said O'Mahoney. "It rang and
rang and rang. He wasn't going to answer. Unknown to me at
the time, his mobile phone was still in his hand. The police had
not yet removed it from the body."[36] The trio had been executed

after attempting to con another gang in a cannabis transaction that turned sour.

Although members of the Tucker firm were arrested after Leah Betts' death, none was brought to trial. On the night of Tucker's funeral, Raquels closed its doors for the last time – although it was soon to reopen, renamed Club Uropa, as part of the European Leisure chain. "The police demanded the club was shut down," commented O'Mahoney, "but within twelve months, you had magistrates saying: 'We'll give you back your licence on three conditions: water is freely available, there are chill-out areas and paramedics on site.' Everything the drug user wanted but was frightened to ask for!"

In February 1997, the Leah Betts case was closed.

The dividing line between legal and illegal drugs is largely a social construct, reliant on tradition, morality and culture as much as science and logic, making rational debate about drug use extremely difficult. Nevertheless, a range of surveys in the mid-nineties indicating that around 50 per cent of British youth had tried illegal substances offered a clear message: prohibition had failed. Where did this leave government anti-drug rhetoric – the "War on Drugs"? If Ecstasy had been incorporated into the mainstream leisure/pleasure equation, if, as an often-cited estimate suggested, half a million people were taking it each week, what did that make Britain's youth? A generation of criminals, to be arrested and incarcerated? Such a strategy could only foster further disenchantment with the law and its makers. While politicians on all sides kept up the rhetoric, terrified of breaking what they perceived to be a moral consensus, fearful of being labelled "soft on drugs", the police force had already begun to take a more pragmatic line. The upper ranks, in club argot, knew the score. "You are more likely to be offered drugs for the first time by a member of the family or a close friend than by the archetypal stranger at the school gates," noted Commander John Grieve, then head of Criminal Intelligence at the Metropolitan

Police. "When parents demand we arrest the dealers, it is their own children they are referring to."[37]

Not only was the relentlessly escalating drug phenomenon a huge drain on police resources, but many high-ranking officers had come to believe that traditional policies of strict enforcement were not only unworkable, but could never solve the problem on their own. As Ecstasy culture had demonstrated once again, prohibitionist laws nurtured and sustained the criminal economy. In line with strategies on crimes like shoplifting, the police had begun to caution, rather than prosecute, many first-time offenders for possession of small amounts of anything from cannabis to Ecstasy to cocaine. As drug seizures shot up, so did the cautioning rate, from 2 per cent to 50 per cent or higher in a decade. Officially, the police didn't see it as a let-off or a quiet form of decriminalisation – the caution went on record and could be used in future prosecutions – but its relative leniency did appear to be at odds with government thinking on drugs. As Home Secretary Michael Howard announced a fivefold increase in cannabis possession penalties and Prime Minister John Major threatened to use MI5 in the battle against traffickers, the Association of Chief Police Officers' spokesman on drugs, Keith Hellawell, suggested that "the cautioning rate will gradually rise as years go by". Furthermore, top policemen insisted that despite the fact that thousands had been prosecuted for Ecstasy possession since 1988, they never actually went out to arrest drug users at all, only dealers. "Users should be targeted," confirmed Hellawell, "but not necessarily through criminal prosecution."

But was cautioning enough? At an ACPO conference on drugs in May 1993, John Grieve stated: "We are at the crossroads . . . we have to come up with new options. We need to think the unthinkable."[38] The "unthinkable" option that Grieve cited was licensing for illegal drugs. A force insider suggested that perhaps four or five out of the forty-two Chief Constables favoured some kind of decriminalisation, as did other senior law enforcers like Raymond Kendall, Secretary General of Interpol: "Making drug abuse a crime is useless and even dangerous. I'm totally against legalising drugs, but in favour of decriminalisation for the user," he stated. "I've got to ring alarm bells and tell the politicians that, if we continue to fight drugs like we have over the past twenty years, then we will lose the battle forever. Perhaps we have already lost it."[39]

Considering the political climate, decriminalisation was an option that, as Hellawell noted, "no government in this country or in Europe would consider this century at all. It's just not going to happen." Yet Hellawell – outspoken, pragmatic and unafraid of opening up controversial debate on other taboo subjects such as the legalisation of prostitution – continued to gnaw at the drug question, his silver moustache and badger haircut becoming ubiquitous in print and on screen, his cautious statements sounding somehow radical from the mouth of a serving officer. While upholding the enforcement principle, he would come out with unprecedented soundbites, admitting that people took drugs *because they enjoyed doing it*, or that raves were "very friendly, happy atmospheres because people are under the influence of Ecstasy". And the drug war? "I don't like the term 'War on Drugs'," he offered, "because it means we're actually warring on ourselves, having a go at our own people." Hellawell seemed to be raising questions that could only be answered by government.

The government, too, sent out contradictory signals as it attempted to come to terms with mass drug culture and the failure of prohibition. When John Major announced a new policy initiative, *Tackling Drugs Together*, he hyped it as the start of the "biggest ever War on Drugs". The final document, launched a week after Leah Betts's death and five years on from Peanut Pete's debut, was not the promised crackdown, but incorporated elements of harm-reduction methods and messages, even acknowledging positive experiences of drugs. Scare tactics were out. *Tackling Drugs Together* was a shift in attitude, but it was also a delicate political balancing act, introducing a liberal tone that emphasised the role of health and education at the same time as reassuring the public that law enforcement was still the priority.

A few months later, in the run-up to the 1997 general election, a time of escalating hysteria about declining social values, the black economy and the drug trade, politicians battled to outdo each other with aggressive rhetoric about personal morality and being "tough on crime". While John Major delivered an upbeat message about the British economy, claiming that he had engendered a prosperity that had nurtured, amongst other things, the country's vibrant pop culture and its "packed" clubs, Home Secretary Michael Howard reverted to tough talk. Summoning the ghost of "a bright young girl with her whole life ahead of her" – Leah Betts – he outlined new proposals to give local authorities the power to shut down dance clubs immediately if police could provide evidence of a "serious drug problem" on the premises; taken literally, this could apply to the majority of house and techno venues. "Clubs are a magnet for drug pushers," Howard stated. "Sometimes the clubs are in on the act – the bouncers, the managers, even the owners. The police often know which clubs these are. But they can't close them because they don't have the powers they need. The law must change."[40]

The baton was passed to Barry Legg, MP for Milton Keynes South-West. Legg launched his Public Entertainments Licences (Drug Misuse) Bill at a press conference, flanked by Leah Betts' parents, and politicians on all sides offered their support. The Bill sought to give local councils powers to revoke the licences of clubs immediately if police believed that "a serious problem relative to the supply or use of controlled drugs" – drug-taking or dealing – was occurring "on or near" the premises. No convictions were required: police evidence would suffice. What constituted a "serious" problem went undefined, and the burden of proof of innocence would rest with the clubs.

"You can only wonder what happened to the 'innocent until proven guilty' part of the law," commented veteran activist Alan Lodge. "What proof will be needed? Will vague 'suspicion' be enough? Will pupil sizes be measured?"[41] "We accept that the provisions are tough, some would say draconian, but that's precisely the intention," responded Home Office spokesman, the Earl of Courtown.[42] This was, potentially, a devastating weapon, for what dance club in the late nineties was drug-free?

The four-hour debate over the second reading of the Bill in the House of Commons in January 1997 demonstrated how much knowledge about Ecstasy had entered the public domain during the nineties. One MP called for free water to be distributed in clubs and "chill-out" facilities to be provided to alleviate the problems of heatstroke; another noted how criminal gangs and club doormen controlled the drug trade in most major cities.

Nevertheless, old clichés resurfaced: some speakers confused Ecstasy with heroin, and the majority refused to accept that dealers were responding to a huge demand from clubbers. "Most young people do not actively seek drugs, but in many clubs drugs are literally pushed on to them," insisted Barry Legg. One Tory MP even advocated the death penalty for drug possession. Only Paul Flynn, the maverick Labour MP for Newport, dared to dissent: "The Bill is framed in the light of the well-intentioned but mistaken views of ten or twenty years ago. We have moved far beyond them." Flynn suggested that young people would view MPs as hypocrites who enjoyed their own drugs of choice whilst censuring others' pleasures: "There you are in your Parliament with its fifteen bars telling us not to do drugs – you standing there with a glass of whisky in one hand and a cigarette in the other, and a couple of Paracetamols in your pocket for your headache tomorrow morning."[43]

But Legg's message, blaming the rise of Ecstasy culture on the failings of the "permissive society" and the legacy of sixties liberalism, a recurring Tory refrain during the Thatcher and Major years, carried the day: "The problem in our country is that we have been too permissive about drugs. We cannot afford to give the impression that drugs can be used for recreational purposes – one pill can kill. Nightclubs feature prominently in any attempt to strike at the heart of the supply of drugs. In all too many cases, those clubs and the associated dance culture have thrived on the presumption that drugs are a necessary and harmless part of a night out. The message put round in many clubs is: 'What's wrong with joining the chemical generation?' "[44] The Bill progressed to the House of Lords, where Liberal Democrat peers secured a concession: in order for a club to be closed, drug-taking or dealing would have to occur on the premises, not merely nearby as Legg had originally intended.

The campaign against the Bill, run from Norwich under the banner Shake a Legg!, was small, underfunded and, like the opposition to Graham Bright's rave Bill in 1990, could not muster mass support amongst clubbers, most of whom remained unpoliticised hedonists, unconcerned with the implications for civil liberties of a law which would concentrate yet more power in the hands of the police. There were no mass demonstrations like those against the Criminal Justice Act in 1994; the burgeoning direct-action movement was caught up in protests against the building of motorway bypasses and airport runways. Although some club promoters opposed the Bill, fearing that it might damage their trade, and major players like Rank Leisure, the British Entertainment and Discotheque Association and the Brewers and Licensed Retailers Association lobbied Parliament in an attempt to neuter the Bill's more extreme measures, a few venues embraced it happily, seeing an opportunity to reinforce their establishment credentials. Some had even been involved in its drafting. "I helped to write the drugs bill," claimed James Palumbo, owner of the Ministry of Sound. "It gives the police fairly draconian powers to close down clubs, but we have to go a lot further."[45]

Shortly afterwards, the Public Entertainments Licences (Drug Misuse) Act became law; one of the final pieces of legislation to be passed by John Major's government, slipping under the wire, almost unnoticed, just before the 1997 general election. It was another desperate attempt to contain recreational drug use –

many years too late – and it seemed, not for the first time, that dance culture was under pressure on two fronts; from authorities who would regulate and restrict it, and from businessmen who would sanitise and commodify it.

westminster

"A new dawn has broken, has it not? And it is wonderful." Tony Blair, May 2nd, 1997

Dawn broke radiantly over the grey backwash of the River Thames. This was to be another fine spring day. Inside the Royal Festival Hall on the South Bank, a synthetic house beat pounded relentlessly as the swelling chorus drove its message home: "Things can only get better! Can only get better! Can only get better!" Bleary-eyed, ecstatic revellers danced and cheered, smiling and hugging each other, spilling out over the pavements of the Embankment in triumphant glee.

The night of May 1st had been a remarkable one. In a stunning, comprehensive victory, the largest of the century, Labour had seized power in Westminster. The party had won its highest-ever number of Parliamentary seats, while the Conservatives suffered their lowest count since 1929; they were completely wiped out in Scotland and Wales. Seven Tory cabinet ministers including Michael Portillo, the golden boy of the Tory right, whose campaign was mastermineded by former Freedom to Party backer David Hart – lost their seats. Tony Blair became the youngest prime minister since 1812. A record number of female, black and Asian MPs was returned. "I am weeping for the Conservative Party," declared Portillo. "It has been a terrible evening for us."[46]

At the Royal Festival Hall, Labour was holding its post-election party. "A political gathering of a kind I had never witnessed before in my thirty-seven years working as a reporter," said

BBC correspondent Nicholas Jones.[47] ITV's Jonathan Dimbleby agreed: "This is the face of New Labour. All ages, different nationalities, races, sexes . . ."[48] The party reached its climax at 5.30am as the new prime minister, Tony Blair, ascended to the podium – rictus grin, as ever, fixed on his face – and delivered a victory speech employing one-nation rhetoric strangely reminiscent of a utopian house anthem: "It will be a Britain renewed . . . where we build a nation united. With common purpose, shared values, with no one shut out, no one excluded, no one told that they do not matter. In that society, tolerance and respect will be the order of the day . . ." As he concluded, the crowd erupted into vociferous joy and the optimistic anthem blasted back into life: "Things can only get. . . . Can only get . . . Things can only get . . . Can only get . . ."

Under John Major's premiership, the Thatcherite project had run out of steam. After eighteen years in power, the Conservative party had become bitterly split over European unification, mired in allegations of sleaze and corruption, mocked by the public for its ineptitude and indifference to the human suffering it had caused: a discredited, spent force. Although the election turn-out was the lowest since 1935, the groundswell of popular desire for change that swept Blair to power seemed to indicate a collective wish for a more caring, less divisive country; a healing of the fissures caused by aggressive free-market economics.

The euphoria would not last. Blair's "New Labour" party, "modernised" and divested of traditional socialist ideals, attempted to blend the capitalist entrepreneurial ethos with more inclusive concepts of social justice: the same uneasy synthesis of individualistic and collective impulses which had been central to acid house over the previous decade. His populist vision of a "New Britain" – "young", "vibrant", "dynamic" – echoed John Major's attempts to claim credit for the industrious nocturnal economy of "Cool Britannia". Soon after the election, Blair invited pop stars and DJs, including Oasis songwriter Noel Gallagher, the subject of tabloid wrath over his pro-drug statements

– and whose *Wonderwall* hit had been played at Leah Betts' funeral – to a drinks party at 10 Downing Street.

As his election campaign theme, Blair had chosen to replace the socialist standard *The Red Flag* with an Ecstasy anthem, *Things Can Only Get Better*, written by an Ecstasy user, Peter Cunnah of D:Ream. Blair's closest colleague, chief spin doctor Peter Mandelson, had been loaned a chauffeur-driven car for the campaign by James Palumbo of the Ministry of Sound – who was later given a minor government consultancy role. Nevertheless, Labour government attitudes to Ecstasy culture would mirror those of the Tories.

During the campaign, at a staged photo opportunity, Blair had posed in front of a group of Aberdeen schoolchildren with a "Dennis the Menace" Ecstasy capsule and declared: "Just say no, and say it with confidence."[49] Labour press officer Atul Hatwal stated that "Britain's innovative and creative club scene is the envy of the world", then cautioned: "Drug use is harmful, even in small amounts as the death of Leah Betts shows. Labour is absolutely committed to tackling the problem." The inherent contradiction – the fact that Britain's nightlife boom, the creative motor of "Cool Britannia", was inspired by Ecstasy – appeared to have bypassed the new regime, just as it had the Conservatives.

Although Barry Legg, the architect of the Public Entertainments Licences (Drug Misuse) Act, lost his seat in the Labour landslide, his legislation was to remain: another part of the Conservative legacy, like cuts in welfare payments, that Labour declared it would uphold. Two club scene candidates, Dan Farrow of the All Night Party and Lenny Beige of Happiness Stan's Freedom to Party Party, stood at the election in protest against the Legg Act; both lost their deposits.

Ecstasy culture had provided a shadow history of the long era of Conservative rule. The Tory years were now over, but Tony Blair immediately signalled that the macho posturing of the drug war was to continue. One of his first moves was to appoint a "Drugs Czar"; a phrase sampled from America, where the regime of the US Drugs Czar, General Barry McCaffrey, had presided over an increase in drug use and the highest incarceration rate in the world.

The post, with its official title of "UK Anti-Drugs Co-Ordinator", went to the controversial, contradictory figure of West Yorkshire Chief Constable Keith Hellawell. This came as no surprise: Hellawell was ambitious and media-friendly; a moderniser like Blair himself. Earlier in the year, the teetotal, non-smoking policeman had demanded that pop songs be banned from using lyrics that glorified illicit substances, while simultaneously admitting: "I know drugs have played a part through the ages with art."[50] Now he stated that his intention was to "cut down demand and interest in illegal drugs among young people" through education, while being "tough on enforcement" – but at the same time warned: "Those who are expecting a significant cut in the demand for illegal drugs within my three-year tenure may well be disappointed."[51]

As if by way of illustration, a few weeks before Hellawell's appointment, two London police officers appeared in court charged with supplying Ecstasy and a Buckingham Palace guardsman died after taking the drug in a club – MDMA had even permeated the police force and the army – and soon afterwards, it emerged that Hellawell's new assistant in the Drugs Czar post, Michael Trace, had admitted to smoking cannabis while at college.

As 1997 drew to a close, William Straw, the seventeen-year-old son of new Home Secretary Jack Straw, whose hard-line "zero tolerance" attitude rejected any reconsideration of the drug laws, was arrested and cautioned for cannabis dealing. Straw insisted that the incident would not change his views. Despite all the signs that drugs had become inextricably entwined with British society at every level, the policies that Tony Blair's government determined to follow were the same ones that had comprehensively failed the Conservatives.

So this was not, after all, the end of the War on Drugs, but it demonstrated how much things had changed since Ecstasy helped fire the acceleration of British drug culture. Politicians, the police, health workers, the leisure industry, all had been forced to rethink their attitudes and actions as recreational drugs became commonplace, ordinary. In one short decade, Ecstasy, it seemed, had transformed whole areas of the social landscape of Britain – but into what, exactly, was still unclear.

The eighties were a long way away now, almost innocent in hindsight. For the children of Ecstasy, gulping down their first pill in the pleasuredomes of the late nineties, the euphoric frontiersmanship of acid house must have seemed like ancient history, its roots in black gay culture all but forgotten. Many weren't even ten years old during 1988's Summer of Love. But for all that had changed, old uncertainties and contradictions remained – between a commodified culture and the illicit drugs that fuelled it, between big money investors and criminal entrepreneurs, between rhetoric and reality, between knowledge and ignorance. And underpinning it all, still, was the restless search for bliss. Although the past ten years had been a long, strange journey, in some ways it felt that the story was only just beginning.

notes

prologue

1. Hakim Bey, *The Temporary Autonomous Zone, Ontological Anarchy, Poetic Terrorism*, Autonomedia, Brooklyn, 1991

chapter one

1. Ian Young, *The Stonewall Experiment*, Cassell, London, 1995
2. Albert Goldman, *Disco*, Hawthorn Books, New York, 1978
3. Albert Goldman, *Disco*, Hawthorn Books, New York, 1978
4. David Toop, *The Rap Attack*, Pluto Press, London, 1984
5. Albert Goldman, *Disco*, Hawthorn Books, New York, 1978
6. *Streetsound*, 1992
7. *Vibe*, 1993
8. *Collusion*, unknown date
9. *Vibe*, 1993
10. *Vibe*, 1993
11. *Muzik*, 4/96
12. From an unpublished interview by Calvin Bush
13. Paul Gilroy, *There Ain't No Black in the Union Jack*, Hutchinson, London, 1987
14. *The Face*, 5/88
15. Ann and Alexander Shulgin, *PIHKAL*, Transform Press, Berkeley, 1991
16. Ann and Alexander Shulgin, *PIHKAL*, Transform Press, Berkeley, 1991
17. Bruce Eisner, *Ecstasy – The MDMA Story*, Ronin Publishing, Berkeley, 1989
18. Ann and Alexander Shulgin, *PIHKAL*, Transform Press, Berkeley, 1991
19. Jay Stevens, *Storming Heaven*, Paladin, London, 1989
20. *Chic*, 7/85
21. Bruce Eisner, *Ecstasy – The MDMA Story*, Ronin Publishing, Berkeley, 1989
22. Jerome Beck and Marsha Rosenbaum, *Pursuit of Ecstasy*, State University of New York Press, Albany, 1994
23. Jerome Beck and Marsha Rosenbaum, *Pursuit of Ecstasy*, State University of New York Press, Albany, 1994
24. *Life*, 5/8/85
25. *Tampa Tribune*, 11/6/85
26. Drug Enforcement Administration press release, 31/5/85
27. Hugh Milne, *Bhagwan – The God That Failed*, Caliban Books, London, 1986
28. Arno Adelaars, *Ecstasy*, In de Knipscheer, Amsterdam, 1991 (translation: Rina Vergano)
29. Soft Cell, *Memorabilia*, 1982
30. Boy George with Spencer Bright, *Take it Like a Man*, Sidgwick & Jackson, London, 1995
31. Boy George with Spencer Bright, *Take it Like a Man*, Sidgwick & Jackson, London, 1995
32. George Michael and Tony Parsons, *Bare*, Michael Joseph, London, 1990
33. *The Face*, 10/86

chapter 2

1. Paul Richardson, *Not Part of the Package*, Pan, London, 1993
2. Jon Savage, *Time Travel*, Chatto & Windus, London, 1996
3. *Boy's Own*, 1988
4. *i-D*, 6/88
5. *i-D*, 6/88
6. *The Sun*, 17/8/88
7. *The Sun*, 12/10/88
8. *The Sun*, 19/10/88
9. *Daily Telegraph*, 4/11/88
10. Jerome Beck and Marsha Rosenbaum, *Pursuit of Ecstasy*, State University of New York Press, Albany, 1994
11. Nicholas Saunders, *Ecstasy Reconsidered*, Nicholas Saunders, London, 1997

chapter 3

1. *Time Out*, 19/10/88
2. *Daily Mirror*, 7/11/88
3. *Daily Mail*, 26/6/89
4. *The Sun*, 26/6/89
5. *Daily Mail*, 26/6/89
6. *Daily Mail*, 27/6/89
7. Seumas Milne, *The Enemy Within*, Verso, London, 1994
8. Seumas Milne, *The Enemy Within*, Verso, London, 1994
9. *The Sun*, 14/8/89
10. *The Sun*, 14/8/89
11. *Politics of Dancing*, article by Kirk Field, unknown source
12. *The Guardian*, 30/7/94
13. *The Guardian*, 14/7/93
14. *Hansard*, 9/3/90
15. *Hansard*, 9/3/90
16. *The Sun*, 2/1/90
17. *Time Out*, 20/12/89
18. *Daily Telegraph*, 26/1/90
19. *Time Out*, 7/2/90

chapter 4

1. Colin Ward, *Steaming In*, Simon & Schuster, London, 1988
2. *The Times*, 11/5/88
3. Richard Giulianotti, Norman Bonney and Mike Hepworth (eds), *Football, Violence and Social Identity*, Routledge, London, 1994
4. *The Independent*, 5/5/90
5. *Digest of Football Statistics 1992–1993*, The Football Trust, Leicester, 1994
6. Tony Thompson, *Gangland Britain*, Hodder & Stoughton, London, 1995

chapter 5

1. *The Face*, 1/90
2. *NME*, 21/4/90
3. Sarah Champion, *And God Created Manchester*, Wordsmith, Manchester, 1990
4. *The Face*, 1/90
5. *The Face*, 1990
6. *Melody Maker*, 10/11/90
7. *Manchester Evening News*, 8/12/89
8. *The Face*, 8/91
9. *Spin*, 1992
10. *Hansard*, 9/3/90
11. *Hansard*, 9/3/90
12. *Melody Maker*, 13/5/95
13. *Manchester Evening News*, 13/12/90
14. *The Guardian*, 31/1/91
15. *Manchester Evening News*, 1/2/91
16. *Vox*, 6/91
17. *The Face*, 1/90
18. *NME*, 16/11/91
19. *Select*, 9/92
20. *Melody Maker*, 13/5/95
21. *Vox*, 7/95
22. *Spice*, 1990
23. *Select*, 3/92
24. *i-D*, 5/95

chapter 6

1. *A Series of Shock Slogans and Mindless Token Tantrums*, Exitstencil Press, London, 1982
2. *The Guardian*, 31/5/95
3. *Stonehenge*, National Council for Civil Liberties, London, 1986
4. George McKay, *Senseless Acts of Beauty*, Verso, London, 1996
5. Albert Goldman, *Disco*, Hawthorn Books, New York, 1978
6. *i-D*, 11/94
7. *Wired*, 5/94
8. *Mixmag*, 10/95
9. *NME*, 8/6/91
10. Martin A Lee and Bruce Shlain, *Acid Dreams*, Grove Weidenfeld, New York, 1985
11. *Eternity*, 8/95
12. Richard Lowe and William Shaw, *Travellers*, Fourth Estate, London, 1993
13. *i-D*, 4/92
14. Terence McKenna, *The Archaic Revival*, Harper San Francisco, New York, 1991
15. *i-D*, 8/92
16. Rudy Rucker, RU Sirius and Queen Mu (editors), *A User's Guide to the New Edge*, Thames & Hudson, London, 1993
17. Rudy Rucker, RU Sirius and Queen Mu (editors), *A User's Guide to the New Edge*, Thames & Hudson, London, 1993
18. Timothy Leary, *Chaos and Cyber Culture*, Ronin Publishing, Berkeley, 1994
19. Spiral Tribe press release, 4/92
20. *NME*, 10/4/92
21. Richard Lowe and William Shaw, *Travellers*, Fourth Estate, London, 1993
22. Press release issued by Spiral Tribe solicitor Peter Silver, 2/2/94
23. *Festival Eye*, 1992
24. Richard Lowe and William Shaw, *Travellers*, Fourth Estate, London, 1993
25. Richard Lowe and William Shaw, *Travellers*, Fourth Estate, London, 1993

26. *The Independent*, 27/5/92
27. *The Independent*, 12/6/92
28. *The Guardian*, 20/6/92
29. *The Independent*, 13/2/96
30. Andy Brown, *Rave – The Spiritual Dimension*, 1994
31. *i-D*, 8/93
32. *Pod*, 1994
33. Richard Lowe and William Shaw, *Travellers*, Fourth Estate, London, 1993
34. *The Guardian*, 19/10/94
35. Press release issued by Spiral Tribe solicitor Peter Silver, 16/2/94
36. *Exodus: Movement of Jah People*, Channel 4, 11/11/95
37. *The Guardian*, 7/10/94
38. *The Guardian*, 8/10/94
39. *The Guardian*, 10/10/94
40. *The Guardian*, 4/11/94
41. United Systems International Free Party Network bulletin, Spring 1995
42. *Mixmag*, 8/95
43. *Mixmag*, 6/97
44. Reclaim the Streets web site, 1997
45. *Mixmag*, 6/97

chapter 7

1. *i-D*, 7/92
2. *i-D*, 4/90
3. *Time Out*, 19/12/90
4. *Mixmag*, 6/93
5. *Mixmag*, 7/94
6. *The Wire*, 1992
7. *The Wire*, 1992
8. Pete McKenna, *Nightshift*, ST Publishing, Dunoon, 1996
9. Gwen and Josh Lawford (editors), *Ravescene Yearbook*, Yage Corporation, London, 1992
10. *Ravescene*, 12/92
11. *Mixmag*, 11/92
12. *i-D*, 7/92
13. *Mixmag*, 3/96
14. Two Fingers and James T Kirk, *Junglist*, Boxtree, London, 1995
15. *Mixmag*, 6/93
16. *Ravescene*, 4/93
17. Two Fingers and James T Kirk, *Junglist*, Boxtree, London, 1995

18. *DJ*, 11/95
19. *i-D*, 5/94

chapter 8

1. *Mixmag*, 4/95
2. *The Guardian*, 14/4/97
3. *The Star*, 4/11/94
4. *The Guardian*, 6/11/97
5. *Highflyers*, Booth-Clibborn Editions, London, 1995
6. *The Big Issue*, 3/11/97
7. Nigel Fountain, *Underground*, Routledge, London, 1988
8. *The Independent*, 17/8/92
9. *The Sunday Times*, 8/5/94
10. *Squall*, 1996
11. *Squall*, 1996
12. *The Face*, 11/95
13. *i-D*, 6/96
14. *The Face*, 11/91
15. *E by Gum!*, Lifeline, Manchester, 1990
16. *The Sun*, 13/6/91
17. *The Star*, 29/1/92
18. *Hansard*, 20/2/92
19. *British Medical Journal*, 4/7/92
20. *The Lancet*, 15/8/92
21. *The Star*, 2/1/92
22. *Mixmag*, 2/93
23. *Time Out*, 27/10/93
24. *Time Out*, 27/10/93
25. Karl Jansen, *Adverse Psychological Effects Associated with the Use of Ecstasy (MDMA), and Their Treatment*, in Nicholas Saunders, *Ecstasy Reconsidered*, Nicholas Saunders, London, 1997
26. *The Sunday Times*, 19/11/95
27. *The Independent*, 14/11/95
28. *The Times*, 17/11/95
29. *Mixmag*, 1/96
30. Jim Carey, *Recreational Drug Wars, Alcohol Versus Ecstasy*, in Nicholas Saunders, *Ecstasy Reconsidered*, Nicholas Saunders, London, 1997
31. *Mixmag*, 7/96
32. *The People*, 6/4/97
33. Bernard O'Mahoney, *So This is Ecstasy?*, Mainstream, Edinburgh, 1997
34. Bernard O'Mahoney, *So This is Ecstasy?*, Mainstream, Edinburgh, 1997
35. Bernard O'Mahoney, *So This is Ecstasy?*, Mainstream, Edinburgh, 1997
36. *The People*, 6/4/97
37. *The Independent*, 19/3/94
38. *The Guardian*, 14/5/93
39. *Europa Times*, 6/94
40. Conservative Party press release, 8/10/96
41. The Right to Party newsletter, 2/97
42. PA News, 6/2/97
43. *Hansard*, 17/1/97
44. *Hansard*, 17/1/97
45. *The Times*, 15/5/97
46. Nicholas Jones, *Campaign 1997*, Indigo, London, 1997
47. Nicholas Jones, *Campaign 1997*, Indigo, London, 1997
48. Brian Cathcart, *Were You Still Up For Portillo?*, Penguin, London, 1997
49. *Daily Telegraph*, 26/3/97
50. *The Independent*, 7/7/97
51. *The Guardian*, 25/10/97

index

acknowledgements

Without the advice and encouragement of Steve Beard and Jim McClellan, this book would never have reached completion. Special thanks are also due to Mandi James, Rav Singh, Kodwo Eshun and Bethan Cole for invaluable help with research; to our agent, Lisa Eveleigh, and our editor at Serpent's Tail, Laurence O'Toole.

Thanks to the many people who offered research material, resources and assistance: James Baillie, Richard Benson, Bill Brewster, the British Library, Frank Broughton, Calvin Bush, Rowan Chernin, Audrey Collin, Richard Collin, Will Collin, David Davies, Bruce Dessau, DiY, Steve Dixon, Tony Elliott, Ekow Eshun, Tracey Ewart, Terry Farley, the Football Trust, Sheryl Garratt, Sven Harding, Lee Harpin, Mark Harrison, Nicky Harwood, Alan Haughton, Jayne Houghton, Institute for the Study of Drug Dependence, Chris Jones, Nick Knight, Simon Lee, Lifeline, Avril Mair, Jon Marsh, Peter McDermott, Jimmy McKenzie, Hannah McLennan, Multidisciplinary Association for Psychedelic Studies, Peter Nasmyth, National Newspaper Library, Richard Norris, John Oakey, Frank Owen, Dom Phillips, Dave Piccioni, Michael Pilgrim, Denis Ramadan, Mark Ratcliff, Simon Reynolds, Jonathan Richardson, Ian St Paul, Harry Shapiro, Kellie Sherlock, Pam Smith, Paul Staines, Jay Strongman, Peter Stuart, Dave Swindells, Jag Takhar, Sonny Takhar, Ken Tappenden, Tracy Thompson, Wolfgang Tillmans, Alan Tribe, Rina Vergano, Ian Wardle, Irvine Welsh and Tony Wilson.

Thanks to the hundreds of people who gave up their time to

be interviewed. All interviews by Matthew Collin and John Godfrey except: Frankie Knuckles, Cedric Neal (Frank Broughton); Fabio, Grooverider, Kemistry, Storm (Bethan Cole); Tony Colston-Hayter, Dave Roberts (Kodwo Eshun); Eric Barker, Paul Cons, Stephen Cresser, Anthony and Chris Donnelly, Graham Massey, Chris Nelson, Leroy Richardson, Justin Robertson, Derek Ryder, Tommy Smith (Mandi James).